CALIFORNIA NATURAL HISTORY GUIDES

INTRODUCTION TO ENERGY IN CALIFORNIA

California Natural History Guides

Phyllis M. Faber and Bruce Pavlik, General Editors

Introduction to

ENERGY IN CALIFORNIA

Peter Asmus

UNIVERSITY OF CALIFORNIA PRESS

Berkeley   Los Angeles   London

This book is dedicated to my father, the late
Hans Werner Asmus

California Natural History Guides No. 97

University of California Press, one of the most distinguished university presses
in the United States, enriches lives around the world by advancing scholarship in
the humanities, social sciences, and natural sciences. Its activities are supported
by the UC Press Foundation and by philanthropic contributions from individuals
and institutions. For more information, visit www.ucpress.edu.

University of California Press
Berkeley and Los Angeles, California

University of California Press, Ltd.
London, England

© 2009 by the Regents of the University of California

Library of Congress Cataloging-in-Publication Data

Asmus, Peter.
    Introduction to energy in California / Peter Asmus.
        p. cm.—(California natural history guides : v. 97)
    Includes bibliographical references and index.
    ISBN 978-0-520-25752-8 (cloth : alk. paper)—ISBN 978-0-520-25751-1 (pbk. :
alk. paper)
    1. Power resources—California.   2. Energy conservation—California.
3. Economic development—Environmental aspects—California.   4. Energy
policy—California.   I. Title.

TJ163.25.C2A856 2009

333.7909794—dc22   2009006141

Manufactured in China
15   14   13   12   11   10   09
10   9   8   7   6   5   4   3   2   1

Cover: Finavera pilot project featuring solar, wind, and wave power generation
technologies, deployed near Newport, Oregon. Photo courtesy of Finavera
Renewables.

The publisher gratefully acknowledges
the generous contributions
to this book provided by

Chevron
and
Moore Family Foundation

CONTENTS

LESS IS MORE
California's Energy Legacy
Art Rosenfeld

One late Friday night in 1973 I conducted a small experiment that changed my life forever and that would have wide-ranging implications for California and, ultimately, the rest of the world.

Since I knew I would have to wait a half-hour in line to fill up my car with gasoline because of the oil embargo imposed by the Organization of Petroleum Exporting Countries (OPEC), I decided to go through the 20-office floor where I was working on the University of California campus and turn off all the lights I could get my hands on, and then calculate the energy savings.

A back-of-the-envelope calculation revealed that turning off the lights in my office alone—representing one kilowatt of electricity demand—saved the equivalent of 5 gallons of natural gas over the weekend that would have otherwise been burned in a power plant. It took me 20 minutes to find all of the light switches on my floor, many of which were hidden behind bookshelves and other obstructions, but this one-time act saved 100 gallons of fossil fuel in this single office floor over just one weekend!

Shortly thereafter, I teamed up with researchers in California, Princeton, and other U.S. universities and began to better understand why we Americans consumed such enormous quantities of energy when compared to our European and Japanese counterparts. The main reason was that energy was too cheap! Even today, in the twenty-first century, gasoline costs less than milk. Within just a week, my fellow researchers and I had discovered (some might say blundered into) a massive oil and gas field buried in our buildings, factories, and cars that could be extracted at costs far below what we were paying at the pump or at our electricity meters.

Thus began a revolution in thinking on energy. Given the mounting evidence regarding global climate change and its link to our fossil fuel addictions, it is a good time to take stock of how California has led the nation in doing more with less energy. Lessons learned here have helped wean the country from inefficient and polluting energy practices.

The United States has made impressive gains in reducing its wasteful habits, significantly improving its "energy intensity" (energy use per unit of gross domestic product). It is interesting to note that the "energy intensity" of the nation as a whole has dropped at five times the historical rate prior to the first oil embargo in 1973. This reduction compared to business-as-usual consumption levels equates to $700 billion in annual savings. The corresponding reductions in the greenhouse gases linked to climate change represent the equivalent of taking one billion cars off the road. (To put that figure in perspective, consider the fact that there are roughly 600 million cars on the roads throughout the world right now.)

Since about two-thirds of these energy savings can be attributed to smart and extremely cost-effective public policies, the United States is saving roughly $500 billion per year due to energy efficiency, about the same amount of taxpayer dollars invested in the Iraq war as of the end of 2006.

The vast majority of these savings and associated reduction in pollution are attributable to energy efficiency, a power supply choice pioneered and refined in California. California's leadership on energy matters has been followed by the United States as a whole as well as by other states and countries. Its appliance energy efficiency standards were ultimately copied by the federal government in 1987. The state's building standards have recently been copied by Russia and China. Nonetheless, California will need to do more—much more, in fact—to deal with global warming. California is looking to accelerate and expand its trend-setting work on energy efficiency, renewable energy, cleaner forms of fossil fuel generation, the development of a "smart" electricity grid, and other technologies, practices, and behaviors.

To put the challenge facing California in perspective, consider that roughly $100 billion is spent every year to power up the Golden State. The population of California has doubled since 1965, a rate of growth that exceeds all other comparable developed regions of the world. And the state Department of Finance projects that California's population will swell to almost 60 million by 2050.

California's enormous energy appetite translates into the unfortunate reality that we put a lot of stuff in the air that contributes to global climate change. No doubt California has served as a model in cutting pollution and in developing new alternative sources of energy. California adopted stringent tailpipe emission standards for motor vehicles as early as 1966. Before the oil crisis of the 1970s, over half of the electricity supplied in the state came from burning petroleum, a legacy of the state's geologic history and enthusiastic exploitation. Today, clean-burning natural gas provides over 40 percent of the fuel for power plants, while the state's portfolio of renewable sources is expanding to meet a state policy goal of 20 percent of total electricity supply by 2010.

Despite such notable strides—and the aforementioned aggressive energy efficiency program that led the nation—California ranks second among the United States (behind Texas) in terms of greenhouse gas emissions, with approximately 500 million metric tons (MMT). The passage of

AB 32, the Global Warming Solutions Act of 2006, requires California to cut greenhouse gas emissions by 29 percent by 2020. Since 81 percent of California's contribution to climate change comes from the combustion of fossil fuels, it's no secret where the state and the world need to go in the future.

But how to get there? That's the real question, and there is still considerable debate on this weighty topic, given past investments in infrastructure, current costs of alternative energy sources, and a host of interconnected and complex challenges.

This book by journalist and consultant Peter Asmus, who has been covering state, national, and global energy developments for two decades, represents a primer on all energy sources, including controversial ones, such as nuclear reactors and liquefied natural gas, that have made recent headlines. It also reveals the rich human history of California's earliest energy developments with oil and hydroelectricity, as well as the natural history underpinnings of this state's cornucopia of energy sources. By combining history with an up-to-date assessment of potential energy answers, this book is invaluable as a resource for those wanting to become part of the solution to our present day energy challenges. Free of jargon and political posturing, this book provides a frank and sobering view of the conundrum of energy. It also is filled with scientific facts that will allow the reader to make up their own minds about which resources can help fuel a more sustainable energy future.

Among the prime messages of this book is that we can do more with less. Solar, wind, and the other renewable supply options are all vitally important, as are other advances in fossil fuels and perhaps other traditional forms of energy production. Yet energy efficiency is the cheapest and cleanest form of energy. California and the rest of the nation, as well as the entire world, should reduce wasteful consumption first and foremost, and then turn to the supply choices that have dominated debates about the age-old question of energy, the primordial essence of modern society. The timing for such a book could not be better. It is my hope that readers come away with a profound appreciation of the role California has played in energy trends, and the critical work that lies ahead for all of us.

INTRODUCTION
Energy Makes California Go Around

Energy, in all of its grand manifestations, is fundamental to *all* existence. The science of energy is so all-encompassing that few of us can really grasp it, even though it is the stuff that literally makes the world go around.

Without energy, all life would cease. Our entire bodies are wired for electric impulses originating in the brain that regulate our most fundamental functions. Whether talking about the processing of internal organs, thoughts racing through your mind, or the simple act of walking, flows of energy are at the core of the activity. However, that is just the beginning. There is then the great, big, wild world outside of your human body. Energy is constantly being generated, expended, and recovered among animals and plant life. Inanimate objects, such as rocks and stones, are also subjected to the power of energy flows in dramatic ways (earthquakes) as well as more subtle changes (the erosion of a hillside over time).

Everywhere you look, energy is at play. However, energy is often a phantom force. Here is how author Richard Heinberg describes this enchanting enigma:

> Physicists have no more insight into energy's ultimate essence than do poets and philosophers. They therefore define energy not in terms of what it is, but by what it does: as "the ability to do work" or "the capacity to move or change matter. . ." Though we are considering something inherently

elusive (we cannot, after all, hold a jar of pure energy in our hands or describe its shape or color), energy is nevertheless a demonstrable reality. Without energy, nothing happens.

—Heinberg 2003:10

Like the other topics covered in the California Natural History Guide series—water, air, and fire—energy is a basic building block of our world. Energy, however, seems to be something bigger than water, air, or fire. Energy flows serve as the very foundation of California's natural history. This natural history, in turn, sets the stage for a remarkable story full of innovation, greed, and, in the end, an ecological quagmire: global climate change. Energy manufactured by humans has pushed modern civilization to the brink.

Physicists may have the most precise definition of energy—*overcoming resistance*—but those two words hardly do justice to what happens during everyday expenditures of energy whizzing around us. Energy is everywhere. Yet we can never just reach out and touch energy. Rarely do we directly see it (only its consequences), and we feel it only through diverse transactions too numerous to mention.

The sun, a star nearly 100 million miles away, is the most important energy source for Earth. Sunlight provides energy flows that feed photosynthesis, which is the conversion of solar radiation into biomass that ranges from tiny microscopic sea phytoplankton to towering redwood trees, the tallest living creatures on Earth. These plants and other living creatures serve as the foundation of all life, including human civilizations. Here is how the author John M. Fowler described the situation:

> For most of life, animal and plant, energy means food; and most of life turns to the Sun as ultimate source. The linked-life patterns—the ecosystems—that have been established between plants and animals are very complex; the paths of energy wind and twist and double back, but ultimately they all begin at that star that holds us in our endless circle.
>
> —Fowler 1975

Produced by intense thermonuclear processes, solar radiation not only helps spur the stockpiling of chemical energy in all things that grow, but it is also the genesis of the kinetic energy of water and wind power. The sun also provides us with heat, and its energy is preserved in fossil fuels.

With the stored energy of fossil fuels, whose origins date back to the days of dinosaurs, there was no need to ever interrupt a person's routine or habits when wood was wet or scarce, the sun went down, the wind stopped, or the stream dried up in late summer. These fossil fuels, after all, were solar energy stored in biomass that then decayed and became transformed into solids (coal), liquids (petroleum), and gas (natural gas). Tapping into these primordial energy sources propelled a new lifestyle that allowed citizens more time to engage in activities that went beyond the mundane tasks linked to daily survival. These energy sources also greatly multiplied the energy amounts that each human had at his or her disposal.

Humanity's need to find food and to stay warm introduced and revolutionized the concept of manufactured energy. Wood fuel became the first external energy source employed to solve both the need for heat and to make food more digestible (and thus energy conversion more efficient). In fact, wood fuel has remained a key energy source throughout the world for millennia. We ultimately harnessed the power of coal, petroleum, and natural gas as well as other sources found in nature: direct sunlight itself, the wind blowing across land and water alike, and the water gushing down through alpine streams. Modern science also spawned highly complex technologies such as nuclear reactors, which rely upon nuclear fission—whereby atoms are literally split in half—to create energy. More details on the evolution of each major current energy technology can be found in the Mainstays and Alternatives parts of this book.

It was not until the invention of the steam engine that the industrial revolution could take place. Losing 99 percent

THE LAWS OF NATURAL ENERGY

Two key laws of physics govern energy. The first law of thermodynamics states that the total sum of energy is fixed. Despite the myriad of energy transfers populating the universe, the total quantity of energy is always constant. On earth, energy inventories are kept in rough balance through ageless natural processes. What comes from the sun as radiant energy is equal to what dissipates into outer space as heat. Because the sum total amount of naturally occurring energy cannot be created or destroyed, the management of energy flows has preoccupied scientists for centuries.

It is the second law of thermodynamics—sometimes described as "time's arrow" or "entropy"—that poses challenges to society today. This law can be summed up in the following sentence: energy spontaneously tends to flow only in one way, from being concentrated in one place to becoming diffused or dispersed in another. The concept of "entropy" refers to the disorder in a system that ultimately diminishes energy available for the human invention of work through loss of heat. Pollution represents society's tampering with the underpinnings of this second law.

of their available energy from wood or fossil fuels through entropy, the first steam engines still provided the equivalent energy of 200 humans. By 1900, improved efficiencies allowed steam engines to provide the equivalent energy of 6,000 humans.

The twentieth century shattered previous notions of what was possible in terms of harnessing energy for individual use. Society has deployed and employed more energy since 1900 than all of human history before 1900. If measured on a per-capita basis, each human being on the planet is now responsible for 4 to 5 times as much energy as was the case in ancient times. If we relied solely on human power, each of us would need 20 individuals working 24 hours a day for 365 days of each year to accommodate our energy appetite.

Nevertheless, fossil fuels are finite, hence society's conundrum with the manufactured energy supplies that have historically propelled the world economy. A siren was sounded over a half century ago in a report to U.S. President Dwight Eisenhower:

> If the growing populations in the United States and throughout the free world are to make ever greater demands for the output of energy, while avoiding the further serious increases in unit costs, then alternative low-cost sources of energy should be made ready to pick up some of the load by 1975.
>
> We must look to solar energy. Efforts made to date to harness solar energy economically are infinitesimal. It is time for aggressive research in the whole field of solar energy—an effort in which the United States could make an immense contribution to the welfare of the free world.
>
> —President's Materials Policy Commission 1952:1

At present, relying directly upon solar energy still provides less than 1 percent of California's total electricity supply, and California has more solar power online than any other U.S. state. Society, obviously, still has a long way to go when it comes to creating a sustainable energy economy. Today's questions about energy seem to keep tracing back to that star we call the sun. An overreliance upon finite fossil fuels is clearly a dead end. The warning signs are all around us as to why society needs to transition to renewable resources that replenish themselves naturally. In the big picture, the ultimate solution to the question of energy is to manufacture technology to harness fuels abundant and free—solar, wind, geothermal, biomass, or water—while simultaneously shrinking our collective energy appetite.

This book focuses on humanity's efforts to harness sources of energy to power industrial efforts, light up homes, and fuel our desires to travel. It is also designed to serve as a key reference guide for the array of energy technologies clamoring for our attention in the twenty-first century. Whether in the form of electricity—once considered divine magic—or in the liquid transportation fuels we depend upon to support our mobile and global lifestyle, energy makes our modern society work.

This modular book is structured in the following way. It begins with a chronological Overview of energy development in California, documenting the state's pioneering spirit in pushing nearly all new forms of energy. Whether recollecting about the early hydroelectric innovation that followed the gold rush or the wild race to drill for oil right on southern California beaches, this state's energy history speaks to the wonders of human ingenuity. None of these inventions would have been possible, though, without the natural resources that underpin this colossal state. For example, the lack of coal—and abundance of sunshine—will forever shape California's approach to energy development.

The next two parts of this book are a compendium of all of the energy sources found in California, first the Mainstays of the traditional electrical grid and fossil fuels, then the Alternatives of renewable and nuclear energy (pl. 1) and hydrogen. These two parts constitute a reference guide that can be read carefully or quickly scanned before moving on. For each major energy source that could be used by Californians, this guide provides a brief history, the status quo, its pros and cons, and what types of contributions it can provide in the foreseeable future.

The next part describes several key Challenges facing California today. It brings the state's energy history up to date, picking up where the first part left off with the energy crisis at the turn of the last century. The following part delves into several hot-button Innovation issues facing California,

Plate 1. The Diablo Canyon Nuclear Reactor near Morro Bay in San Luis Obispo County.

the nation, and the rest of the world today. The last section of the book offers some examples of Progress: experimental solutions to the just-described challenges, chronicling stories of pioneering technology and systems thinking here in the Golden State.

From global climate change to the terrorist threat, Californians are once again breaking new ground, taking risks, and plowing boldly forward. My hope is that this book serves as a foundation for you to better understand the world of energy and make more informed choices when you vote, when you eat, when you drive, and when you buy. Energy is indeed everywhere. Yet the lack of affordable, reliable, and clean energy might just be the world's most daunting challenge, deeply interwoven with issues such as global poverty, the lack of adequate drinking water, and the ever-present search for a better quality of life.

OVERVIEW

From Indigenous
Stewardship to Millennial Crisis

OVER 400 MILLION years ago, tectonic plates that shaped the earth's crust started to rock and roll in California. In some areas, earthquakes caused a dramatic reshuffling in land formations, carving mountains, valleys, rivers, and lakes. Shifting rock and sands left their marks on a landscape we can now only imagine, but whose history is captured in the geological record. Various organic materials, including early forms of life, would get trapped. Volcanoes erupted and then sat still, only to explode again when there was no other way to release the pressure.

The San Andreas Fault (pl. 2), which creates the earthquakes that still keep some people from settling in California, is only 30 million years old, and it runs nearby my Marin County home. This earthquake fault, whose most visible mark to an observer high up in an airplane is the slender Tomales Bay in the Point Reyes National Seashore, is responsible for the Coastal Range as well as the mighty Sierra Nevada approximately 200 miles to the east. There was no place to go but up as the North American Plate collided with the Pacific Plate, and the San Andreas Fault system was formed. This fundamental geological framework continues to shape today's search for energy by Californians, who would ultimately learn how to tap a bounty of diverse and abundant energy sources.

California's indigenous peoples were relatively good energy stewards. They were, by and large, sedentary and could survive by relying upon local resources. Because of the kindness of the weather and the ridiculously fertile land, the state's Native Americans could afford to be frugal when it came to energy. The moderate winters and long growing seasons limited their demand for energy too. Hunting and gathering activities were sufficient to provide the food—also energy—for survival. There was sufficient wood readily available for light, heat, and cooking. They tapped renewable resources when they dried salmon with the sun. In the Central Valley, where temperatures can soar to over 100 degrees F

Plate 2. Aerial view of the San Andreas Fault near Carrizo Plain in south-central California.

in the dog days of August, Native American tribes constructed homes dug deep into the earth in efforts to provide passive cooling systems. These cave lodgings also provided protection from winter cold, when chilling fog descended upon the valley floor.

Geothermal hot springs were used for cooking and as sacred pools where warring tribes could put down their weapons, bathe, and then relax in peace. Ironically enough, when John C. Fremont's survey party happened upon this steam rising up from the ground in Napa County's Calistoga region (pl. 3), they thought they had entered the gates of hell.

Plate 3. Calistoga's "Old Faithful" Geyser in Napa County.

California Native American tribes, such as the Yokuts and Maidu, used petroleum not as a source of mechanical energy, but for ritual fires and recreation. Other uses of these fossil fuels by tribes included paving, roofing, and waterproofing of dwellings, for which they used the very thick oil, now called "asphaultum," found oozing from surface natural tar seeps. These oil-based materials held their canoes together too.

The Spanish who began to settle California in the 1760s, first settling in San Diego and then Monterrey, introduced new energy technologies that slowly increased energy use patterns. It was Father Junipero Serra, a Franciscan missionary, who helped pave the way for early immigrant settlements that reached as far north as the city of Sonoma. These missionaries employed Native Americans as manual laborers as they tried to convert them to Christianity. With the help of modern metal tools, wood fuel-gathering operations expanded dramatically during this time. In the process, these early energy development efforts left their mark on California's ecosystems. As was common in Europe, the Spanish introduced domestic horses and donkeys to the land, employing these animals in tasks ranging from simple transportation to cattle management and other agricultural chores. Manipulating streams, ponds, and lakes for crop irrigation also expanded energy capture and corresponding consumption.

California remained at the edge of civilization until the mid-nineteenth century, when Russian fur traders settled in Fort Ross on the Sonoma coast. John Sutter, hailing from Switzerland, founded "New Helvetia" in what is now Sacramento, one of California's first large human settlements, a haven for weary immigrants who survived the treacherous climb over the great Sierra Nevada. It was no accident that early settlers would declare this wonderful valley spot their home, as it sat at the confluence of the American and Sacramento Rivers in the middle of an enormously fertile valley.

At this point in time, California's total population was less than 100,000 people. Within 10 years, that number grew fourfold before surpassing the one-million-resident mark by 1890. To support these increases in population, California's early residents would begin to investigate ways to tap fresh sources of energy to fuel agricultural enterprises and other activities deemed necessary for human progress.

Gold Miners Shape Early Energy Development

Perhaps the largest impact on California's growth in population and early economic development was the discovery of gold in 1848—the same year that California joined the United States. It was the famed '49ers, who descended upon the golden hills of California in search of instant riches, who shaped California's first large-scale energy developments. Ironically enough, the hydraulic knowledge and technologies employed to provide power for gold mining set the stage for widespread hydroelectric development.

The Sierra Nevada—an enormous mountain range composed of granite that straddles the eastern border of the state, running north and south for a distance of 360 miles—initially served as an obstacle to the state's economic health. However, it would soon prove to also be the basis for wealth and, later, energy innovations. With mountain peaks exceeding 14,000 feet, numerous deep river canyons cut through from east to west. These rivers—the Yuba, American, Pit, and others—are relatively short in length. Still, the steep grades allowed for multiple sites for productive dams and powerhouses. The Feather River (pl. 4) is only 70 miles in length, for example, yet this river ended up hosting so many electricity generators that it has been referred to as a "Stairway of Power."

If you drive along Hwy. 49, which traverses the western side of the Sierra Nevada foothills, you are in the midst of the most notorious hydroelectric facilities in the world. Small northern California towns, such as Nevada City and Folsom, are sites of early breakthroughs when it comes to channeling the power of water for human use. Whereas the '49ers imposed deep scars into the formerly pristine Sierra Nevada through giant hydraulic guns that literally scraped away entire hillsides (pl. 5), they also inadvertently left behind infrastructure that would serve as the underpinnings of California's early hydropower development. Indeed, some of the same ditches, flumes, and dams once used to extract gold from the land were converted directly into hydroelectric power plants. As a result of knowledge

Plate 4. A train follows the contour of the Feather River.

gained from the '49ers, engineers soon transformed water cannons into nozzles used to direct high-pressure water onto waterwheels, which then generated electricity. Techniques used to drill and drive tunnels into the hard rock that composed much of the Sierra Nevada also played a key role in hydroelectric power.

Early reports implied that California would have adequate coal supplies to fuel traditional forms of industry and other forms of economic development, including the extraction and processing of gold. There were actually a few significant discoveries of coal within the state's borders, many of them made by despondent former gold miners seeking other forms of wealth when the majority

Plate 5. Hydraulic gold miner working during the 1860s at Grizzly Flat in El Dorado County.

of gold had already been washed out of mountain streams. Contra Costa County reported decent coal deposits as early as 1860, and there was a brief moment in time when ill-informed Californians bragged of substantial coal deposits that rivaled those of other states.

By 1900, the so-called Diablo mines located in Contra Costa County had provided 4.7 million tons of coal, which represented roughly 80 percent of the state's total coal mining yield. However, the quality of this coal was below that of most other sources, including coal deposits in the Pacific Northwest, which began to be shipped to San Francisco. As costs of shipping declined, California's in-state coal industry could no longer compete. The downhill slide in coal production was already underway as early as 1883. California also relied upon coal imports from places as far away as England and Australia, as trade vessels loaded with other goods also brought coal to isolated California. In this case, California reaped the benefits of early globalization of the economy.

Plate 6. The Tesla Coal Mine on eastern slope of Altamont Pass in Contra Costa County.

The last California coal mine was located in the Altamont Pass, just southeast of Oakland in Alameda and Contra Costa counties. Named after the great inventor Nikola Tesla, this mine (pl. 6) pioneered a coal briquetting process that relied upon the crushing of local coal deposits and then mixing this local lignite with superior coal imports brought in from San Francisco's ports. The nation's first commercial coal briquetting plant was established at Tesla, but it was short-lived. By 1900, Californians used 35 percent less coal than the rest of the country and paid 40 percent more for it.

In the absence of a robust, regional supply of quality coal, California proceeded to tap firewood to meet the majority of its needs before hydropower matured into a fully commercial enterprise. Rampant deforestation fed the state's appetite for energy, but it also caused early contamination of its air quality, as smoke often filled the skies. As much as 90 percent of initial wood harvesting went to residences, but the railroads here were also wood-fired. Then the gold rush came, which spurred on a massive and even more frenetic hunt for fuel wood. By 1870, it was estimated that as much as a third of the state's entire inventory of forests had been harvested, hardly a sustainable approach to energy management. The strands of nonnative eucalyptus scattered throughout California are remnants from this period of our collective energy past. These eucalyptus groves now stand as reminders of the rampant reforestation that forever changed California. They were planted to reforest lands because of their ability to grow so rapidly and then be quickly harvested to feed the state's expanding appetite for energy.

California's wood consumption (fig. 1) peaked in 1880, and, as was the case in the rest of the country, wood thereafter became a frill for all except those residing on farms or in rural areas. At about this time, small lumber towns, such

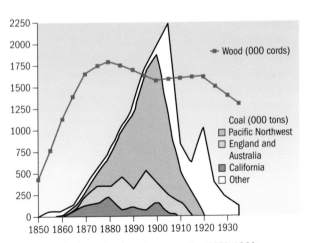

Figure 1. California coal and wood consumption, 1850–1930.

as Scotia in Del Norte County near the Oregon border, were completely powered by wood-fired plants that also provided steam and mechanical power to lumber mills. The nation's first stand-alone biomass power plant, for example, was built in the small town of Burney in Shasta County. Yet, for the great masses of people flocking to growing cities such as Sacramento, San Francisco, and then Los Angeles, dependence solely upon wood for energy was clearly not viable over the long term.

It is then easy to see why California looked to alternative fuels to meet its growing energy appetite, and water power—often considered a green, renewable resource—would rush in to fill in the gaps.

Making Hydro History

California's hydroelectric system would evolve into something substantially different than any other part of the country. The brutally rugged topography of California's Sierra Nevada, coupled with its unique seasonal rainfall patterns, required a sophisticated engineering approach that was quite different from anything used elsewhere. Instead of the typical combination of immense horizontal volumes of water dropping down relatively low elevations, California's hydroelectric systems would feature smaller water volumes but steeper drops in elevation.

Another distinguishing feature of California's elaborate approach to managing its hydro resources was the fact that virtually all of the state's annual rainfall occurs in winter and spring. Because of this unique, yet consistent, weather pattern, the state's humanly engineered hydropower system also irrigated agricultural operations throughout the entire Central Valley. Farmers in the eastern United States did not have to worry about such matters, since precipitation was scattered throughout the entire year. In California, this was not the case. The Sierra Nevada's seasonally immense snow pack soon became recognized as a key fuel source. As temperatures increased every spring, this snow would melt, providing a continuous flow of water during spring and summer.

Because of all of these factors, California's hydroelectric plants evolved into some of the most advanced of the time. Only one of the Sierra Nevada's western slope rivers, the Cosumnes, was not damned for power generation, a fact that underscores how thoroughly California looked to water and snow to fuel its growing economy. While many rivers would help fuel the growth of electricity consumption throughout California, it would be the Yuba River—flowing through the heart of gold mining country—that would become the setting for some of the state's most pivotal advances in hydroelectricity.

The Pelton water wheel (pl. 7)—invented by Lester Allan Pelton in 1878 in the Yuba County town of Camptonville—introduced a more efficient method of extracting energy out of moving water, thereby accelerating hydroelectric development in California and throughout the world. This new twist on technology was particularly suited to the gushing streams of the Sierra Nevada. The smaller, lighter, and more compact wheel design split the water into two streams, taking advantage of the energy in rushing water without having the water fight itself. By changing the angle of the water's impact against two cups instead of just one, power and efficiency were greatly enhanced. It was also certainly convenient that this new power generation technology was also first manufactured in Nevada City at Allan's Foundry, now known as the Miner's Foundry and a preserved historical site.

In August 1887, the first Pelton wheel was employed to generate electricity in Nevada County, among the very first successful hydroelectric demonstrations. Two months later (October 1887), the Highgrove Plant was put in service to deliver direct current (DC) power for arc lights in Riverside

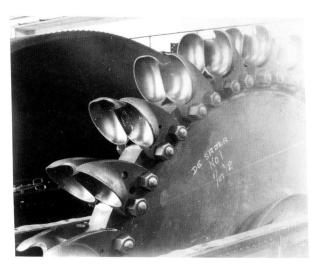

Plate 7. Close-up of the Pelton water wheel, which featured separated cups that achieved higher efficiency at higher water speeds than existing hydroelectric generation technologies.

and Colton, utilizing a 50-foot drop in a canal. These early, small demonstrations generated DC. The hydroelectric business would not seriously develop until alternating current (AC) systems were developed.

The pioneering AC work in California took place in the Pomona–Riverside–San Bernardino area—first with a single-phase AC plant on San Antonio Creek in November 1892 and then the first three-phase AC plant in the west, Mill Creek No. 1, in September 1893. These plants demonstrated the most significant technical concept that would launch the hydroelectric business on a large scale in California. This concept was done by using step-up transformers to allow power transmission at high voltage and then stepping down the voltage at delivery points.

Because of the previously noted rampant deforestation and corresponding wood shortages, water power quickly became the most cost-effective source of power in the Sierra Nevada region and ultimately the rest of California. While California's water power sources were extraordinary, they were far from the urban clusters of humanity such as San Francisco, which clung to California's coastline approximately 150 miles to the west. Accessing these water power sources was not always easy and often required workers to drill through remnants of California's natural history (pl. 8).

This distance between fuel sources and end-use customers ultimately spawned major innovations in the development of technologies to transport electricity over long distances, yet another example of Californian ingenuity. To expand this source of water power to other regions of

Plate 8. Workers boring into rock to help build an early hydroelectric power plant in the Sierra Nevada.

the state would require major innovations in transmission of power. Sacramento would be the first major municipality to receive long-distance transmission of hydroelectricity on July 13, 1895, when a hydro facility located on the American River at Folsom transmitted AC electricity at 11,000 volts over a 22-mile transmission line. Approximately 30,000 people gathered later that year at the State Capitol to witness the miracle of electric lamps lighting up the rotunda and a lavish parade heralding the wonders of electric lighting.

Because of a drought in 1897 and 1898, however, the Folsom Powerhouse could not deliver enough electricity to power Sacramento's electric trolley system, the dominant mode of public transit at that time. It just so happened, however, that entrepreneurs already in the hydro business in the Nevada County region, located approximately 60 miles to the east of Sacramento, would soon come to the rescue.

The Birth of Pacific Gas & Electric

Eugene J. de Sabla (pl. 9) was born in Panama to a family whose French ancestors were considered nobility because of their valiant defense of the king's Parisian palace. The de Sabla family was deeply involved with the development of the Panama Canal and, later, with copper mines in the southwest. De Sabla, with a few partners who included Alfonso A. Tregidgo, had already begun developing small hydroelectric projects in the region as early as 1895. However, the situation in Sacramento would prompt them to think about new ways to grow their business.

De Sabla compatriots included John Martin, an agent for all kinds of hardware, including iron pipes and electricity-generating dynamos. Despite the fact that Martin knew

Plate 9. Eugene De Sabla.

virtually nothing about electricity or engineering, he had secured the rights to sell the new generators to be used in the first power generation facilities developed by de Sabla and his other cohorts. The geographical origins of Pacific Gas & Electric (PG&E) can be traced back to a Nevada City bar, but the first tangible results of partnerships that would slowly put into place the building blocks of PG&E were found in the so-called "Rome" powerhouse. The facility derived its name "Rome" as an oblique reference to Romulus Riggs Colgate, considered by some to be the rich uncle of the small pioneer firms that would eventually merge and become PG&E. A descendent of the same Colgate family that gave us soap and toothpaste, Romulus would serve as the deep pocket of several early hydrogeneration plants, typically taking a majority stake in each of these power generation facilities.

The next power plant developed by the Martin–de Sabla–Colgate team was the Yuba Powerhouse in 1898. However, the most important of these early hydroelectric plants—if viewed from the perspective of the evolution of PG&E—was the Colgate Powerhouse (pl. 10), which was prompted by the power shortage in Sacramento.

Construction on Colgate began in March 1899 at a river crossing once cluttered with gold seekers. The facility ultimately was capable of generating 15.5 megawatts of electricity and began delivering power to Sacramento in September of the same year, just four days after Martin had promised his power-hungry Sacramento clients that it would be delivered. This power plant's greatest claim to fame, however, was when it transmitted electricity 142 miles to the west, across the Carquinez Straits all the way to the City of Oakland, an unprecedented feat fraught with unknown risks and fears. Many farmers, for example, worried that the super-charged, high-voltage transmission lines might fall and crush their

Plate 10. The Colgate Powerhouse was pivotal in the evolution of PG&E. This photo was taken in 1941.

The first step in creating this pioneering hydroelectric plant was to construct a crib-style wooden dam three-and-a-half miles upstream. Next, flumes (long wooden channels) over six feet wide and four-and-a-half feet deep were placed in an old mining ditch. The flume helped contour the water along a horizontal plane some three-and-a-half miles long in order to hold its grade until intersecting with the penstock, a steep tube that then dropped the water down 200 feet to the Pelton wheel generators housed in the powerhouse along the banks of the river. (This drop length is referred to as "the head" in the hydro business.) The original facility generated roughly 300 kilowatts of electricity, the rough equivalent to a 400-horsepower engine.

The wooden flumes of this and other early hydro plants were regularly monitored by ditch tenders, who would walk along small platforms located on top of these long wooden pipes to repair and patch problems. Because they were made of wood, these flumes would need replacement roughly every decade. To fully appreciate the task at hand, consider that there were no roads in this region at this point in time (pl. 11). The heavy generator equipment, as well as all other components of the powerhouse, had to be lowered with ropes down the steep canyon walls. Roughly 110 people worked for approximately four months to build the flume portion of this initial powerhouse.

Looking to boost power production, a second penstock was installed from an 800-foot head water source, feeding its water power into a second powerhouse located right next to the original powerhouse. This boosted the total capacity of the facility to 1,260 kilowatts.

The Rome Powerhouse (pl. 12) operated for 15 years.

Plate 11. The logistics and transportation challenges for early hydroelectric projects were immense. This photo shows how many horses were necessary to haul a dynamo to an installation site.

Plate 12. The historic Rome Powerhouse on the south Yuba River near Nevada City.

precious cattle. However, like other California energy entrepreneurs, de Sabla and Martin pushed forward. It was this successful long-distance transmission of electricity that set the stage for a series of mergers that would piece together the now substantial service territory of what is now PG&E.

The most difficult chore facing these energy pioneers turned out to be finding investors for these new power generation facilities. California's financing of power generation was hardly a mature business at this point in time. Unlike the industrialized eastern United States and Great Lakes regions, where coal, oil, and steam plants had been developed in densely populated urban clusters, California was rural and decentralized, making it difficult for power companies to grow and prosper. Without a track record of dependable revenues from existing customers, folks such as de Sabla had to forge new ground on the power plant financing front, especially before Colgate came along. Most power plant entrepreneurs traveled all the way to New York City to sit down with Wall Street types. However, de Sabla turned to novel local sources of cash to supplement Colgate's steady financial support.

After all, he was operating smack dab in the middle of a part of California that had obtained tremendous wealth from gold that was found in the very same streams he now sought to tap for electricity. The risk-taking culture was emerging in California as a result of the gold rush, which encouraged investors to engage in this new potential gold mine.

While de Sabla and other investors worried about customers for their risky investments in this new form of energy, California's population growth kept boosting the need for more power. By the time each of his power plants came online, demand for electricity exceeded its capacity (fig. 2). By 1900, some 25 hydroelectric plants had been constructed in California, stretching from Eureka in the north down to the previously mentioned Mill Creek facility in the south (map 1).

As a result of hydropower being transmitted from the Sierra Nevada to coastal cities in the north and south, the

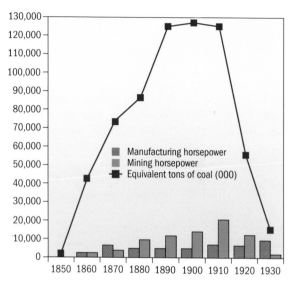

Figure 2. California water power, 1850–1930.

rural communities of the Central Valley became convenient customers to utilities seeking to run its power plants around the clock to boost revenues. By the mid-1920s, almost a quarter of California's farmers had electricity, which was the highest percentage in the nation, while only 3 in 100 farms nationally were connected to the grid.

One of the first widespread methods of generating electricity in the United States, hydropower supplied 40 percent of the nation's electricity in the early part of the twentieth century. In California, and throughout the west, hydropower provided roughly three-quarters of the total electricity supply as late as World War II. In PG&E's service territory, 98.5 percent of farms had electricity by 1950, underscoring the growing relationship between water, power, and farming as California's economy expanded in response to this widespread reliance upon falling water for power generation.

Map 1. By 1900, spotty transmission systems linked hydropower Power Houses (PH) but left the vast majority of the state without electricity.

Author James C. Williams, author of the book *Energy and the Making of Modern California*, summed up the growing appeal of hydro-dependent electric utilities such as PG&E in this way:

> As people discovered that they could save time by expending energy, they increasingly sought energy technologies and systems that demanded little expenditure of their individual time and required little personal ingenuity. They also sought reliability in technology, a concept closely related to the idea of saving time, and this led them to embrace energy resources, technologies and systems that appeared to be inherently more reliable and resilient than others. Therefore, with the intention of saving time and effort, as well as gaining convenience, people gradually gave up localized energy production based on technology such as windmills (pl. 13) in favor of centralized production and distribution systems that promised affordable and reliable energy and service, such as electric utilities.
>
> —Williams 1997:4

Who Says Water and Oil Do Not Mix?

It was not just water that fueled California's emergence into a national leader on energy technologies. Oil put California on the map in an even bigger way, stimulating yet another rush to strike it rich on the western fringes of the civilized world.

Like the gold rush, California's oil rush would forever change the face of California—not only in the form of highways, filling stations, see-sawing pumpjacks, and towering refineries but in the design of our cities, our urban sprawl, and virtually all land use patterns. No other fuel can challenge oil's magnanimity in underwriting our modern lifestyle as well as shocking our land, air, and water. California mixed water with oil, and the result was an economy that

Plate 13. Water-pumping windmills such as this one were an early form of renewable energy development in California and throughout the nation.

transformed this state into a cutting-edge global super power.

After the gold rush came and went, California turned increasingly to nonrenewable energy sources such as oil and natural gas. By the beginning of the twentieth century, roughly half of the energy consumed in California came from renewable sources such as water, wind, and the sun. Nevertheless, fossil fuels, especially oil, would soon surpass these renewable energy sources as the prime movers behind the state's expanding economy.

As early as 1850, Californian settlers relied upon fossil fuels for energy, initially digging pits by hand in the Los Angeles area to produce fuel for primeval oil lamps at the San Fernando

Plate 14. Crude oil blowout at McNee #6 Tower in Taft in 1912, just 21 years after the state produced its first gusher at Adams Canyon.

Mission. In 1854, the first oil well was drilled manually way up in Humboldt County, but these efforts came up dry. One year after the end of the Civil War, crude oil was successfully tapped in Ventura County at Rancho Ojai in 1866 at a depth of 550 feet. Known as "Ojai 6," this Ventura County oil well produced 15 to 20 barrels of oil per day, a significant sum in those days.

In 1891, the state's first gusher in Adams Canyon near Santa Paula spewed 1,500 barrels of oil per day, most of it washing out to sea because of the lack of storage technologies (pl. 14). Five years later, the first steel-hulled oil tanker, dubbed *George Loomis,* began transporting as much as 6,500 barrels of oil from Ventura north to San Francisco, the dominant urban center of California because of its location as an attractive West Coast port. In 1909, the famed "Midway

The first commercially successful oil well in the western U.S. was a gusher on September 26, 1876, in Pico Canyon, California, just north of Los Angeles. The oil suddenly shot up to the top of a 65-foot oil derrick known as "Pico Number 4" (pl. 15).

Pico Canyon derived its name from General Andres Pico, who led Mexican forces in the Mexican–American War of 1846. He made this canyon home once the war was over. After Pico passed away, Demetrius G. Scofield arrived here to take over several of Pico's disputed oil claims. Luckily, he found the perfect partner in Charles Alexander Mentry. Hailing from Titusville, Pennsylvania—the city credited with the birth of the nation's oil industry—Mentry knew his stuff.

After successfully drilling three productive wells in the canyon and exploiting what locals called the "Pico Oil Springs," Mentry sold each of them off and was ready

Plate 15. California Star Oil Works in Pico Canyon in the San Fernando Valley in the 1880s.

to move on to further adventures elsewhere. However, Scofield urged Mentry to stay on and keep drilling, applying his legendary striking skills to advance their mutual financial interests. Using one of California's first steam-powered oil rigs, Mentry drilled down 300 feet and hit the big time on his fourth Pico Canyon well. Averaging 30 barrels of oil per day, this now famous well helped Scofield and Mentry become very rich men indeed.

However, getting the oil to the market proved to be difficult. At first, Mentry relied upon a recent extension of the Southern Pacific Railroad line at the eastern end of the Santa Clarita Valley to transport his crude to refineries. Mentry was not too happy, nonetheless, about the fees the railroad began charging, taking advantage of a monopoly on transportation options. In 1879, Mentry's ingenuity paid off again. He constructed California's first oil pipeline. It was only two inches in diameter and five miles in length, connecting his precious well in Pico Canyon to the state's first oil refinery in Newhall.

Oddly enough, the pipeline never transported a drop of oil, because Southern Pacific responded to this creative end-around by dramatically lowering its shipping rates.

With a salary of $300 per month, a rather large sum at the time, Mentry built an extravagant Victorian mansion that can still be seen near the entrance of a public park. In October 1900, Mentry passed away unexpectedly. Once the oil wells ran dry, Scofield was long gone, and the migrant workers packed up their makeshift dwellings, leaving nothing but their footprints and stories behind.

The site of the Pico Number 4 strike has, unusually for an oil development site, been transformed into a public park, chronicling the story of how oil prospectors came and went in a tale of luck, skill, fortune, and death. Small oil springs can still be found in mountain streams that trickle through Pico Canyon to this very day.

Gusher" blew out near the town of Fellows in Kern County, foreshadowing development of the billion-barrel Midway–Sunset oil field, the largest producing field in the entire continental United States.

Ultimately, California's primary oil extraction regions would extend to the western edges of San Joaquin Valley in the north, where California's oldest and best-traveled roads passed along a series of oil seeps, though exploration activities also occurred in Colusa, Santa Clara, San Mateo, Mendocino, Marin, and Contra Costa counties. Kern County, Los Angeles basin, and the Santa Barbara coast were the dominant oil-producing regions in the south and would serve as the primary sources behind California's increased reliance upon fossil fuels.

Legal Wars over Energy Resources Begin

Conflicting claims over the ownership rights to this precious black goop lying beneath the ground prompted the federal government to develop policies to shape the future development of oil throughout the nation. Because of California's culture of embracing free enterprise, private industry gained the upper hand here. Westerners had little sentiment for nationalizing this precious commodity, as was the instincts of many lawmakers from the east.

During the early days of California's oil rush, intense debate revolved around ownership issues. Who should reap the benefits of God's gifts of nature? Laws on the books dating back to the nineteenth century sided with a "rule of capture" model, which implied that the owner of any subdivision or real estate lot had rights to whatever resources, including oil, that lay beneath the ground of their private property. As one can imagine, this dynamic set off a race to drill for oil to protect each landowner's fair share of the bounty seeping below the surface. Why? Since this "gold" was a liquid, the more straws that went into these underground basins, the faster this finite resource would be depleted. Wealth could literally slip out of your hands if you did not strike quickly.

During the nineteenth century, economic development was the top concern of most governments, an understandable priority given the levels of poverty common at the time. Therefore, laws and regulations reflected the belief that the United States was awash with "free" resources that just had to be harnessed and put to work for the good of individuals, and this free market would inevitably serve the higher purpose of generating economic well-being for anyone willing to work for their dream. Federal, state, and local governments were literally giving away natural resources for free (and, in many cases, still do). Land owned by the public sector served as the underwriter of services performed by government, as sales of public lands (and the resources located on these public lands) often funded the government. From that perspective, the whole system seemed to be working.

In the first few decades of the twentieth century, however, geologists and conservationists working for the government began to espouse a different political view. The nation's environmental movement was birthed on the watch of President Theodore Roosevelt, and his chief forester Gifford Pinchot played a key role in advancing notions of conservation and a new environmental ethic. In 1907, Roosevelt advocated that the federal government should retain its title to fuel sources, and one year later, federal government geologists argued that petroleum lands, particularly in California, should also follow this new model of government ownership and management to reduce competition that was driving development in the Wild West in ways that encouraged fraud and other unsavory manipulations.

Disputes between private firms and the federal government over the rights to oil located under California's crust continued for years to come. Then the now legendary Teapot Dome scandal came along, which revealed bribes for oil leases in California. The controversy boiled over and culminated with the passage of the federal Mineral Leasing Act in 1920. It was in that same year that oil was discovered under Signal Hill, a plot of land zoned for residential use near Long Beach. Speculation drove land parcel prices through the roof, and wooden oil derricks (pl. 16) popped up everywhere on the hill, creating a human-made forest . . . and an enormous potential fire hazard!

Plate 16. Early Midway field rig construction. The workers inside the rig provide a sense of scale.

Despite this free-for-all, the nation looked to California for leadership at this point in history on how to update ownership and royalty rules governing oil and other mineral wealth. Lobbying by a number of former California state legislators and other state government representatives in Washington, DC, resulted in the passage of compromise federal legislation, setting the stage for the modern-day oil business. This law would govern mineral development on public domain property for years to come. Oil companies were now required to pay royalties under a new lease arrangement, but the royalties were sufficiently low to enable handsome profits.

Ironically enough, the royalties included in these oil leases channeled significant funds to pay for dams, roads, and other essential services, casting the oil companies into a new role as bankroller of essential goods and services for the general public. The measure was designed to bring a halt to speedy development of California's oil resources. Yet it actually included incentives to drill for oil even more aggressively.

Paul Sabin, in his book *Crude Politics: The California Oil Market, 1900–1940*, summed up California's conflicted relationship with the oil industry in the following way:

> When oil operators began rushing to the coast of Santa Barbara and Ventura in 1927, post–World War I prosperity had already attracted residential and commercial interests to the area's beautiful coastline. Two competing economies in the state clashed over the use of coastal resources. Was the Pacific coastline a site for extraction of raw materials and harbor shipping or a serene place of relaxation, recreation and realty? This simple polarity breaks down, to be sure, since oil development itself enabled the beachfront economy by fueling the sprawling automobile-dependent settlements of the Los Angeles Basin and the

state's increasing auto tourism. But on the coast itself, the two sets of interests clashed.

—Sabin 2005:56

Those in favor of oil resource development gained the upper hand in early skirmishes, as oil derricks popped up right alongside beachfront residences in not only Long Beach but also Venice. It was not uncommon for people to sunbathe beneath the oil derricks in Huntington Beach (pl. 17). In 1932, however, a ballot measure put forth by oil industry heavyweights to expand exploitation to offshore reserves was rejected by voters, as a majority instead declared that beaches should be preserved for recreation. Supporters of the ballot measure were quick to highlight the tax revenues that would be generated, but California voters went with their eyes and hearts instead of their pocketbooks. A "Save the Beaches" movement began to grow in popularity. As a result of low prices, some oil companies with inland holdings also opposed offshore development, as they worried about maintaining higher margins in times of oversupply.

A deal was cut in 1938 by the state legislature that would forever cement an odd relationship between coastal

Plate 17. Oil derricks at Huntington Beach.

protection and oil development in California. When signed into law, the State Lands Act dedicated 30 percent of the state's oil royalties to parks, a nod to the fact that conservationists (often working with smaller, independent, and inland oil industry factions) had frustrated development of coastal oil resources since the late 1920s. These groups gave up thwarting all off-shore oil development in exchange for a secure future funding source for a state park system with few rivals. A State Parks Commission had been in existence since 1927, but state parks had expanded rapidly over the ensuing years, despite the fact that stable funding for expansion and ongoing management had been lacking. That changed with the 1938 State Lands Act, which provided a steady stream of revenue to expand and improve California's state parks.

Emergence of Electricity as a Prime Power Source

The first company to generate and then sell electricity in California formed in 1878 and was located in downtown San Francisco at 4th and Market streets. Billing itself as the "California Electric Light Company," the firm's supply portfolio boasted two tiny brush dynamos that could supply power for 21 arc lights. A chief sales pitch was the promise of providing light from sundown until midnight for $10 per lamp per week, excluding Sundays and holidays, of course.

The pitch darkness of night spurred on early electricity ventures in the twilight of the nineteenth century. San Francisco soon boasted the first comprehensive electric street lighting system in the country. Nevertheless, it was not until municipal trolley systems started springing up just before the turn of the century that the business of generating and distributing electricity started to make some decent profits for the state's privately operated utilities. Before these systems were in place, transmission and distribution lines remained idle during much of the day. Once these trolleys and lighting systems started relying upon the existing hardware employed to provide electrical power round the clock, demand for power increased dramatically and so did the profits of purveyors of this invisible and seemingly magical form of energy. Los Angeles proceeded to develop the country's largest municipal electric streetcar system, known as the "Big Red Trolleys."

After the great earthquake in San Francisco in 1906, the appeal of Los Angeles grew among the immigrants making the trek out west to California, and it soon surpassed its northern rival port in population. In the case of both of these large cities, impressive electric cable car and railway energy systems encouraged development on previously inaccessible land (map 2). Electric vehicles that could travel 100 miles between recharges had already been put on the market in 1900, but the lack of charging stations rendered them impractical for most of California. Gasoline was also about half the cost of electricity, which meant that many residents could not yet afford the convenience of electric vehicles, let alone electricity in their homes.

The state's oil industry, working hand-in-hand with Detroit's auto industry, would deliver a stinging defeat to the state's electric utilities. Car, tire, and oil companies

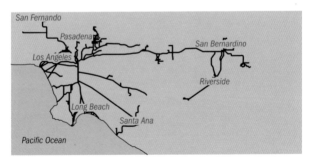

Map 2. Map depicting the rail lines of Pacific Electric Railway Company throughout the Los Angeles area.

collaborated to buy up and dismantle electric trolley systems in Los Angeles as more modern roads were constructed, thereby increasing the demand for petroleum transportation fuels to staggering heights. Gas-powered motor vehicles, free to roam the open road, captured the imagination of almost everyone, especially in southern California.

As time would wear on, this would prove to be a rare victory for oil over electricity in California. As transmission and distribution technologies improved, electricity would soon become the most popular purveyor of energy for a society increasingly plugged into new ways to add convenience and entertainment to their lives.

In the early twentieth century, competing electricity providers each established their own transmission and distribution lines. The end result of this entrepreneurial free-for-all was poles and wires strung about major cities like a maze of metal spaghetti. Not only was this unsightly, but competing firms found it difficult to survive. A protégé of Edison, Samuel Insull, came up with a nifty solution to this dilemma. Claiming that the capital-intensive electricity business was too risky to leave to the forces of free enterprise, Insull—with the backing of Edison—proposed that exclusive franchises for the provision of electricity made far more sense and were in the best interests of consumers. Instead of local governments regulating the business of electricity, he proposed state regulation. Once this basic business structure was approved by federal lawmakers, it paved the way for the creation of state-regulated utility monopolies that still carve up the country with exclusive franchises today.

At the core of this transformation of the energy business was Thomas Edison's conviction that electricity was not some mystical force that should be given away—as was the view of the eccentric and utopian inventor Nikola Tesla (pl. 18). No, instead, electricity was just another commodity like wheat or lumber. The best way to make money off of this invisible force field, which apparently was everywhere, was to

Plate 18. Nikola Tesla, the so-called "New Wizard of the West."

calibrate it and sell it in units, hence terms such as "kilowatt hours" that serve as the basis of your monthly electric bill.

In 1911, the state's new Public Utilities Commission began to regulate electric utilities at the state level in California. These newly ordained geographic monopolies—entities that would become PG&E, Southern California Edison (SCE), and San Diego Gas & Electric (SDG&E)—developed business strategies to boost demand for their product. Armed with Edison's patents on a variety of gadgets that ran on electricity, SCE was particularly adept at expanding each customer's consumption of kilowatt hours of electricity through aggressive sales of vacuum cleaners, electric stoves, and other home appliances. While now under state regulation, critics of this new monopoly system emerged over time, claiming these now large and formidable business entities could charge virtually whatever they wanted to captive customers. In many parts of the country, they saw little profit in serving sparsely populated rural regions, though this was not the case in California.

Southern California's Energy History

Northern California dominated the state's early industrialization and corresponding path of energy development. Yet it would be southern California that would, over time, become the destination of choice for the majority of people migrating to the state, spurring new efforts to satisfy the state's growing appetite for energy. Between 1880 and 1930, for example, southern California, with an increasingly cutting-edge Los Angeles serving as a migrant magnet, went from less than 10 percent to well over half of California's population (fig. 3).

Not only was oil developed on a massive scale in southern California, but natural gas and electric utility companies based here would rise into national prominence.

Did you know that early advances in lighting technology here trace back to concerns about the large number of gamblers, villains, and assorted kooks that roamed the small town of Los Angeles in the mid-1800s (pl. 19)? Consider that the total population of Los Angeles at this point in time was only 5,000 people. Approximately 40 gas lamps were installed along Main Street in 1867 by the Los Angeles Gas Company to make the streets safer at night for upstanding citizens. Initially deriving their gas from asphalt-like tars,

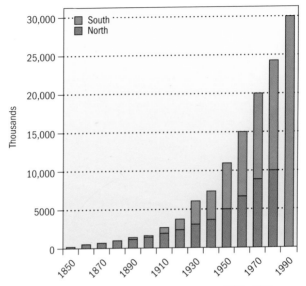

Figure 3. California Populations, North versus South, 1850–1990.

these early gas providers soon turned to crude oil as their feedstock. Ironically enough, Thomas Edison's light bulb put a major dent into this seemingly up-and-coming business here and elsewhere, forcing the gas companies to seek out new applications, introducing gas-fired stoves and heaters to the local populace as a way to build demand for their fuel products.

A San Francisco–based firm eventually purchased the Los Angles Gas Company, and a familiar scenario of consolidation and mergers entailed. Though natural gas is often found in conjunction with crude oil, its beneficial properties as an energy source were not fully appreciated until 1909. That is when a phenomenal natural gas field was uncovered near Taft in Kern County. Because colorless, odorlessly burning natural gas has twice the heating value as the gaseous fuels derived from coal or oil, the company expanded its service

Plate 19. Chinatown gamblers roaming Los Angeles at night.

territory by building pipelines to deliver this fuel throughout southern California. In 1941, the company introduced new storage techniques utilizing natural underground traps up to two miles beneath the earth's surface. These sorts of innovations—and a surging population—allowed what soon became the Southern California Gas Company to grow into the largest supplier of natural gas in the country. Today, the Southern California Gas Company's natural gas transportation and distribution pipelines cover 49,000 miles and serve 19.8 million customers.

On the electric side of the energy equation, teeny-weeny firms with names like Ventura Land & Power and Visalia Electric Light & Gas Company began providing electric arc lighting to southern Californians about the same time oil was discovered in the state. The Civil War had just ended, and the nation turned its attention to rebuilding the economy. Crafty San Francisco financiers obtained a license from Thomas Edison—the president of General Electric (GE) Company—to use his name and patents to organize the Los Angeles Edison Electric Company (pl. 20). Hydroelectricity

Plate 20.
Thomas
Edison with
dynamo.

came to the rescue in the southern part of the state too. Perhaps the most celebrated of these hydroelectric facilities was the Mill Creek Plant, located near Redlands (pl. 21), which began delivering power in 1892. Its outstanding feature was a three-phase form of AC that GE was pushing. This configuration became a model for subsequent hydro plants, creating an instant market for GE's electricity transmission technology.

By 1896, the population of Los Angeles had increased to 100,000 people, with most of the electricity being provided by primitive steam engines located downtown. That same year, the Southern California Power Company began to build a power plant to tap hydropower on the upper Santa Ana River. When the hydro facility came online, electric current at approximately 33,000 volts traveled 83 miles to downtown Los Angeles, a feat recognized as the longest high-voltage transmission in the country at this point in

Plate 21. The interior of the historic Mill Creek hydroelectric plant.

time (pl. 22). Shortly thereafter, the Los Angeles Edison Electric Company and the Southern California Power Company merged.

Five years later, eastern banks invested $10 million into a major expansion of this utility throughout southern California. Again, a California utility would tap hydropower, this time from the Big and Pitman Creeks as well as the larger Kern River (pl. 23) to help meet the growing demand for more electricity. To celebrate the achievement of growing from a small Los Angeles–based utility to a vast regional network of electricity service now spanning five counties, this utility company changed its name to Southern California Edison (SCE) in 1909. The end result of approximately 200 mergers and acquisitions of locally based electric utilities, SCE also emerged as one of the largest electric utilities in operation today. It currently serves 13 million people in over 400 cities with a service territory spanning 50,000 miles.

Plate 22. Modern transmission towers juxtaposed against the broken remnants of a farm cart.

Meanwhile, further south, other smaller utilities also begin to link up to better compete with their larger northern rivals. The San Diego Gas Company, for example, traces its history back to 1881. Instead of hydro, its start-up fuel was gas derived directly from petroleum. With only 89 customers and an investment of $30,000, this firm also grew exponentially over time. Unfortunately, its first fuel of choice—"oil gas"—clogged up the main generator with tar. The company then made the switch to coal gas.

The population of San Diego was a mere 4,000 in 1885, but a boom in real estate increased those numbers to 30,000 in just three years. It was electric lights and trolley

Plate 23. This hydroelectric facility, serving Southern California Edison, is located on the Kern River.

systems that drove demand for electricity up. After the turn of the century, demand picked up more steadily, and the company improved technology to switch back from coal to oil (as California's supplies of oil were far greater than those of coal). Meanwhile, the San Francisco–based Pacific Lighting Company, looking for markets for their newly invented Siemens gas lamp, looked south and saw promising markets in the Los Angeles area. In 1889, three different gas and electric firms in the region were purchased for $1 million and merged into the Los Angeles Lighting Company.

By 1930, Los Angeles led the nation in natural gas consumption, and Pacific Lighting, which purchased Southern California Gas Company in 1929, was the largest natural gas utility in the country. A series of mergers and nonenergy business transactions involving firms such as Thrifty drugstores, then a bankruptcy in the early 1990s, and a radical reorganization are all a part of the history of a company that then merged with SDG&E to constitute Sempra Energy.

This corporation also now owns Southern California Gas Company.

The Public Power Alternative

Among the critics of private utility monopolies that kept growing in size was New York Governor Franklin D. Roosevelt. Outraged that he had to pay ten times the price for electricity in his upstate resort as he did in the state capital of Albany, he pondered how to address this perceived inequity. At that point in time, only 10 percent of rural America had electric service. In contrast, European countries, such as Denmark, had extended electric service to 90 percent of its rural regions. (Of course, Denmark is a small peninsula, whereas the United States is a huge expanse of various types of real estate.) He ultimately came up with the idea that the state's St. Lawrence River should be harnessed to generate hydroelectricity by a public agency, and the price would be the yardstick against which the prudence of state-regulated utility rates could be judged. As president of the United States, his response to the Great Depression of 1929, and the subsequent outbreak of World War II, would be to apply this state public power model to newly created federal agencies to construct some of the largest power generation facilities in the world and then reserve this low-cost supply to a new cadre of locally owned utility providers.

California's municipal utilities (table 1) date back to 1887, when the cities of Alameda and Ukiah created municipal lighting districts under the California Constitution's municipal affairs doctrine. Until Roosevelt pushed hydropower development by federal agencies, however, these typically small utilities had limited capacity to develop their own cost-effective power supplies to adequately compete against the larger and more sophisticated privately owned electric utilities.

TABLE 1 California's Municipal Utilities

Member	Population	Established
Alameda	74,259	1887
Anaheim	336,000	1895
Azusa	45,000	1898
Banning	26,000	1895
Biggs	1,400	1904
Burbank	100,300	1913
Colton	17,631	1897
Corona	142,000	2003
Glendale	200,000	1913
Gridley	4,000	1910
Healdsburg	10,017	1909
Hercules		2002
Imperial Irrigation District	22,000	1936
Industry		2003
Lassen MUD	25,000	1987
Lodi	58,850	1910
Lompoc	43,284	1923
Los Angeles DWP	3,800,000	1925
Merced Irrigation District	120,000	1996
Modesto Irrigation District	200,000	1923
Moreno Valley		2003
Needles	5,930	1983
Palo Alto	61,500	1898
Pasadena	134,800	1906
Redding	80,000	1921
Riverside	262,300	1911
Roseville	83,200	1912
SMUD	1,202,100	1947
Santa Clara	102,985	1896
Shasta Lake	4,000	1948
Trinity PUD	15,000	1982
Truckee Donner PUD	25,000	1948
Turlock Irrigation District	185,839	1923
City of Ukiah	15,000	1887

continued ➤

TABLE 1 (Continued)

Member	Population	Established
Victorville	69,077	2003
City of Vernon	89	1933
Co-ops:		
Anza		
Plumas–Sierra Co-op	11,000	1937
Surprise Valley		
Joint Power Agencies:		
Northern California Power Agency		
Southern California Power Agency		
TANC		
Total	7,483,561	36

The first large Californian municipality to successfully abandon the service territory of a private utility was Los Angeles, but it was not easy. Public power advocates took their first steps toward creating their own publicly owned utility way back in 1898, but did not purchase the infrastructure assets of SCE located within its municipal boundaries until 1922. The Los Angeles Department of Water and Power is the largest "muni" in the United States, serving a population of 3.8 million people in a densely populated urban service territory of just 456 square miles.

Interestingly enough, San Francisco, which began receiving federally subsidized water from the Hetch Hetchy reservoir around this same time period—and was mandated to create a public power agency—is still served by PG&E. A public power agency was created for San Francisco, but it only serves its municipal facilities. Repeated efforts to extend municipal electricity service to San Francisco residents and businesses have consistently failed, often after expensive referenda political campaigns. A recent vote occurred in 2001, when a $2 million opposition campaign organized by PG&E

and its business allies barely defeated two different ballot measures in an election marred by bizarre voting irregularities.

Sacramento petitioned to follow in the footsteps of Los Angeles and become a municipal utility in 1923. PG&E, however, refused to sell its distribution system even after Sacramento raised the bond money in the 1930s. Finally, after 12 years of litigation, PG&E sold its electric distribution system to the Sacramento Municipal Utility District (SMUD) for $13 million in 1946. Today, SMUD is the sixth largest municipal in the nation in terms of customer base, serving a population of 578,000 in a service territory encompassing 900 square miles. An effort to extend its municipal utility service to bordering Yolo County was also defeated after an even larger opposition campaign sponsored by PG&E in 2006. All told, roughly 25 percent of Californians receive their electric service from a public power entity, including other public power utility structures, such as public utility districts, irrigation districts, and rural cooperatives (map 3).

For a detailed history of Sacramento's history as a municipal utility—as well as additional background on the public power movement—please see the book I coauthored with former SMUD board member Ed Smeloff, titled *Reinventing Electric Utilities: Competition, Citizen Action and Clean Power* (Smeloff and Asmus 1997). The focus of this book details the story of how SMUD is the only utility in the United States to close a nuclear reactor in response to a public referendum vote, but the book also discusses other utility experiences—both public and private—with nuclear power.

California's current electricity supply is still dependent upon the federally subsidized hydropower. The Bonneville Power Administration (BPA)—a federal power marketer based in Portland, Oregon—began delivering electricity from the Bonneville Dam on the great Columbia River in 1938. Shortly thereafter, the Grand Coulee Dam was completed in 1941. Roosevelt did approve federal funding for what would become the backbone of the California irrigation system, the

Map 3. California's current electric service areas. Map shows utilities with retail sales.

Central Valley Project, which also developed a series of hydro-electric dams on the upper portion of the Sacramento River.

California also receives federally subsidized hydropower from the Western Area Power Administration (WAPA), which broke away from the federal Bureau of Reclamation in 1977 to become the nation's fourth federal power marketer. The U.S. Department of Interior also markets federally subsidized hydropower from humongous dams such as the Hoover Dam on the lower Colorado River in Arizona, considered the world's largest hydroelectric facility between 1939 and 1949.

Public power comes in many permutations. Beyond a municipal utility district, business structures available to deliver electricity include rural cooperatives as well as public utility districts and irrigation districts. All three of these utility structures are an outgrowth of efforts to provide services to parts of the country that were not attractive to profit-seeking private utilities. Whereas rural cooperatives were authorized by federal laws passed in 1935, public utility districts and irrigation districts were created by the California Legislature. A public utility district is akin to a municipal utility district, except it can include more than one county and is typically created in rural regions. Likewise, irrigation districts are authorized by state government to provide water for farming communities. They are also authorized to generate electricity to power their irrigation systems.

A rural cooperative is just like any other cooperative. It is a private business, but it is owned by its customers instead of shareholders.

The Colorful History of the Plumas–Sierra Rural Cooperative

Perhaps one of the most interesting rural cooperatives in California is the one established in 1937 in Plumas and Sierra Counties (pl. 24). (That same year, the Surprise Valley rural

Plate 24. Some unidentified pioneers of the Plumas–Sierra Rural Electric Cooperative.

cooperative was established in the far northeastern corner of the state.) PG&E tried to buy out the Plumas–Sierra Rural Cooperative (PSREC) in 1939, but the ruggedly independent folks in this mountain region turned them down defiantly.

Cooperatives took hold traditionally in fringe regions of the state. PSREC, for example, is located between the service territories of PG&E and Sierra Pacific Power, a private utility based in Nevada that was an offshoot of an old lumber company. Because of its isolation, PSREC became a pioneer in electricity transmission, constructing what would become the longest distribution line in the country at 75 miles in length. The federal Rural Electrification Administration—predecessor to today's Rural Utilities Service—was a pioneer in developing long-distance transmission technologies, which was critical to establishing electricity service in sparsely populated areas throughout the country. The key to reducing transmission line costs was the ability to take advantage of higher-strength wire that reduced the number of necessary poles per mile and to develop systems-wide planning rather than pole-by-pole additions. According to Bob Marshall, general manager of PSREC, "the Rural Electrification Administration was one of the best government programs in history." Despite this endorsement, Marshall's acknowledged reliability was spotty. Word has it that in Plumas and Sierra counties, locals would say, "Hold up a candle to see if the light is on." The morning meeting place for line workers was a local bar, and the struggling cooperative took 20 years to break even.

Marshall also freely admitted that his cooperative, as well as many others, had its fair share of skullduggery. "Our first manager was found guilty of embezzling," he pointed out with a chuckle. One of the more amusing episodes involved a subsequent buyout effort by PG&E prompted by the fact that, as Marshall put it, "our reliability was garbage." In his words, the attitude of PG&E was something like "thank you for much, it's now time for the professionals to take over."

Legend has it that the cooperative accounting clerk that was double-checking the votes on whether locals wanted to abandon the cooperative in lieu of PG&E kept stuffing the "sell" ballots into his shirt sleeves. "Rumor has it he had so many of the ballots hidden in his clothes, that he crinkled when he walked over to the bathroom," claimed Marshall. Yet another challenge to the cooperative movement came in the 1950s and 1960s during the Red scare, when some Americans viewed rural cooperatives as part of a Communist conspiracy. In fact, a proposed rural cooperative in Twentynine Palms in southern California was defeated on those grounds, as the sentiment of a nearby Marine base shaped local opinion to reject that move.

Things began looking up for the cooperative when it was able to obtain low-cost hydroelectricity from the Central Valley Project up from the dam at Shasta, though

PG&E fought these deliveries to the small cooperative for a decade. For a time, the cooperative could go back and forth between PG&E and Sierra Pacific for backup power, a situation the savvy cooperative took advantage of, admits Marshall.

After Marshall arrived in 1986, the cooperative plugged into new business ventures, including satellite TV and Internet service. "Where is our membership being underserved? That's where our business opportunities lie," said Marshall. Building upon the legacy of rural cooperatives and innovation in the wires side of the electricity business, the cooperative won an award from the Cooperative Research Network in 2007 for utilizing state-of-the-art telecommunications to synchronize and optimize its interconnections with PG&E and Sierra Pacific.

Among the other success stories at this cooperative is its geothermal heat pump program, the most successful program in the entire country. More than 30 percent of new homes in its service territories rely upon this renewable energy source of heating and cooling. Because renewable energy supply is cheaper in Nevada than in California, PSREC is looking to build 11 miles of new transmission lines to access a 22.5 megawatt wind farm. When completed, PSREC will become the smallest transmission utility in the nation, another feather in its big cap.

Populations Boom, Driving Energy Use Up and Up

We can blame World War II for the state's ascent into a technological wonderland when it comes to energy, driven by rapid increases in demand, setting up a clash in values between energy and environment. That is when California's population exploded (fig. 4), and an enormous influx of humanity continued unabated through the 1980s. Between

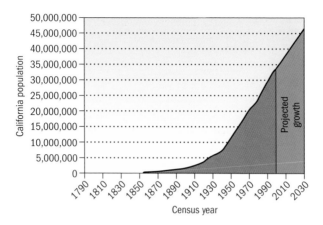

Figure 4. Past and projected California population growth.

1940 and 1950, the state's population surged from 6.9 million to 10.5 million residents. By 1960, the popularity of the Golden State attracted more than 5 million more people to this Promised Land. By 1970, the state's total population hovered near 20 million people, with no sign of any abatement in immigration to a state that had clearly captured the imagination of not only much of the United States, but the entire world.

Decentralized urban clusters in the south were linked by freeways modeled after Hitler's Autobahns, steeply subsidizing fossil fuels and our supreme attachment to our cars. It was the undeniable appeal and power of the fossil fuel industry working in tandem with the nation's auto industry back in Detroit that helped glamorize cars to the rest of the country. Because of clever advertising, the automobile came to represent a new form of freedom in the public's collective consciousness, and nowhere was this more evident than in sunny southern California. In 1940, before the United States entered World War II, roughly one in 13 Americans owned

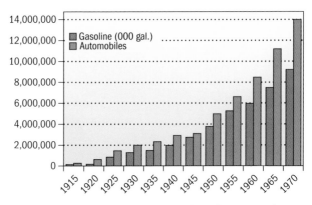

Figure 5. California automobile purchase and gasoline consumption trends, 1915–1970.

their own car. In southern California, where oil was still king, almost one in three owned a car (fig. 5).

It was the Santa Barbara well blowout of 1969, which contaminated 30 miles of Santa Barbara's prized shore (pl. 25), that rallied California citizens to place a moratorium on future offshore oil development altogether. This incident was perhaps a defining moment and a cultural turning point in the state's energy history, signaling a fundamental shift away from the precious oil supplies that had previously dominated much of the federal government's interest in the state's energy affairs. The majority of state citizens no longer wanted to see the direct results of their addictions to fossil fuels being displayed off of California's gorgeous coastlines, except in those few places in which the industry had already prevailed. The wealthy citizens who resided in Santa Barbara, as well as tourist and real estate industries, joined forces with environmentalists to deal California's once dominant oil industry a major blow. In a sense, state citizens turned their back on the oil industry that California's wildcatting culture had nurtured so well

Plate 25. The Santa Barbara oil spill of 1969 turned public opinion against California's oil industry.

in earlier times and that had helped feed the state's rapid economic fortunes.

The offshore oil derricks near Santa Barbara are stark reminders that ecological and recreational concerns did not always win in California's schizophrenic relationship to energy. Drive around on California's maze of freeways in southern California, and you can find ample evidence of our collective energy past, with oil wells still pumping away among the cotton fields near Bakersfield or along Hwy. 101 near San Ardo in southern Monterey County. In fact, these freeways themselves are products of the state's early oil development. Hollywood helped glamorize these cars, which quickly came to represent freedom, independence, and seemingly endless upward mobility.

A state in a constant state of reinvention and hype, California has many identities: the magical sheen of Hollywood; the gadgetry of Silicon Valley; and the bohemian ways of that Baghdad by the Bay, San Francisco. Californians do not think of themselves as coming from a petroleum state. Even agriculture trumps oil when it comes to self-identity in California. Petro-politics, nevertheless, forever changed the map of California in the twentieth century and left a lasting imprint on the state's housing, employment, and recreation trends.

And then came nuclear power.

Chic Nuclear Power

SCE was the first private utility in the United States to generate electricity from a nuclear reactor not earmarked for military purposes. This momentous event occurred in 1956 at the Santa Susana Experimental Station in Ventura County. Relying upon a sodium coolant, the most power this research and development (R&D) project ever produced was 7.5 megawatts, less than 1/100th the size of today's typical utility-scale reactors. On November 12, 1957, nearby Moorpark became the first small town in the world to be completely powered by nuclear energy from this experimental nuclear reactor. The utility trumpeted this accomplishment as the launching of the "Age of Atomic Energy," when electricity, it was widely predicted by nuclear engineers, would literally "be too cheap to meter."

Not to be outdone by its southern competitor, PG&E unveiled the Vallecitos Nuclear Power Plant near Pleasanton in 1957. Operated jointly by GE and PG&E, and financed entirely with private capital, this 30-megawatt reactor boiled water to run its turbine. In 1963, the 63-megawatt Humboldt Bay Nuclear Plant, located just south of Eureka, came online. Also developed by PG&E, this reactor continued to operate until 1976, when a previously unknown earthquake fault was discovered just off the coast, and this plant too is closed down. (By the way, on July 26, 1959, the Santa Susana mini-reactor suffered a partial core meltdown, releasing radioactivity and requiring closure in February 1964.)

California's first large-scale nuclear reactor to operate commercially (pl. 26) came online in northern San Diego County near the Camp Pendleton U.S. Marine Corps Base in 1967. Known as "Unit One" of the San Onofre Nuclear

Plate 26. The San Onofre Nuclear Generating Station, located next to Camp Pendleton near the border of Orange and San Diego Counties, at night.

Generating Station (SONGS), the project was a joint venture between SCE (75.05 percent) and SDG&E (20 percent). Two tiny municipal utilities—Anaheim (3.16 percent) and Riverside (1.79 percent)—also bought into the first fully commercial reactor to supply long-term electricity to California's grid.

This exuberant initial embrace of nuclear power underscores how California jumped into developing fad energy technologies with gusto. California was again on the cutting edge of new energy technologies; this time it was nuclear power, an energy source that dazzled the imagination of utility engineers and executives alike.

From the state's utilities perspective, they had no choice but nuclear power, the latest and greatest technology dreamed up by the nation's premier utility engineers. Uranium fuel could be harvested in the Rocky Mountains and the southwest, so there were domestic fuel supplies readily available. This was the technology that could transform the nation's nuclear weapon legacy with Japan and World War II into a story with a happy ending with the so-called "Atoms for Peace" movement. Among the biggest proponents of nuclear power as part of a mass electrification policy was Chauncey Starr, who founded the Palo Alto–based Electric Power Research Institute in 1973, a utility-financed think tank that pooled utility investments in R&D.

This was the heyday for California's and the nation's electric utilities, as their plans for finding the resources to keep the lights on were typically rubber-stamped by state regulators. The business of electricity was managed by a small fraternity akin to a secret cult. Terms such as "capacity factors" or "load-building" or "spinning reserves" befuddled most ordinary citizens. The electricity business was not only dense, but it was full of confusing acronyms. Decisions that carried incredible economic and environmental consequences were made—more often than not—without little fanfare or public debate.

Beginning in the 1970s and continuing through the 1980s, California's population growth shifted again, this time away from the pricey coast and into the more affordable inland valleys. In the south, suburban sprawl, supported by freeway infrastructure, fanned out to Riverside and San Bernardino, placing people farther and farther into the desert and heat. Further north, it was the Central Valley, and cities such as Sacramento, that would boom as residents sought relief from some of the highest real estate prices in the land, especially along the coast. This push inward, however, exacerbated energy shortages, as air conditioning demand skyrocketed, increasing the chance of power shortages during late summer, when hydro capacity was at its lowest point, and temperatures running through California's interior often surpassed the century mark.

As more and more people filed into California, the state's electric utilities—whether privately or publicly owned—continually sought new supplies. Concerns over fish populations and other environmental concerns, nonetheless, limited large-scale hydro projects beyond those already constructed. California banned oil as a fuel for electricity generation, despite the fact there were ample local supplies. California also halted construction of any future in-state, coal-fired power plants because of concerns about air pollution.

At one point, things got so bad that plans were on the drawing boards for a fleet of nuclear reactors up and down the Central Valley and scattered along California's beloved coastline (map 4). All told, the state's utilities reported that California would require 60 nuclear power plants by the year 2000 to boost the state's total electrical capacity to over 100,000 megawatts. (California's peak demand capacity in 2006 was approximately 67,000 megawatts.)

While electric utilities were gung ho on the virtues and prospects of nuclear power, opposition to nuclear power was growing among the ranks of a budding environmental movement gaining critical traction in California.

Anti-Nuclear Movement Finds a Champion in State Legislature

Charles Warren was elected to California's State Assembly in 1963 to represent downtown Los Angeles. He soon found himself serving on the legislative committees overseeing California's land use policies. At that time, utilities seeking to construct new nuclear power plants needed to get a green light from local governments. Complex and new technologies such as nuclear power were quite a challenge for these local governments, so decision making was slow. Utilities were worried that they would never be able to build the number of necessary nuclear reactors in time if they could not speed up and streamline the power plant approval process.

In 1970, the state's private utilities came to the California Legislature seeking to preempt local land use decisions on power plants with a "one-stop" state government siting

Legend:
- ■ Existing nuclear plants
- ▲ Nuclear plants under construction
- ● Most likely sites for nuclear plants

Map labels:
- ■ Humboldt Bay
- ● Tehama South
- ● Buttes
- ● Yuba City
- ■ Rancho Seco
- ● Modesto/Waterford
- ● Merced
- ● Madera
- ● Los Banos
- ● Kettleman City
- ▲ Diablo Canyon
- ●● / ●● Wasco
- ■▲ San Onofre
- ● Vidal
- ● Sundesert

0 — 100 mi
0 — 150 km

Map 4. Projections of California nuclear supply scenarios developed in 1979 for the year 2000.

agency. Senator Alquist agreed to carry a bill on behalf of the utilities. When the bill came before Warren's land use committee, he sent the proposed legislation to "interim study." In many cases, the interim study status is akin to killing a bill. In this case, however, the RAND Corporation—a Santa Monica think tank best known for its national defense expertise, but which was diversifying into domestic issues—was hired with outside funding to prepare an independent analysis of nuclear power prospects for California.

When the RAND Corporation released its report to the newly created Subcommittee on Energy Reform in 1972, the first state legislative body devoted to energy matters, "my life changed," recalled Warren, the committee's new chairman. "The fundamental conclusions of the report were that current utility practices could be described as 'demand accommodation,' with energy consumption increasing 6 to 7 percent annually. At that rate, the report noted, utilities had to double their electricity generation every 10 to 11 years," Warren said. The same report also highlighted major concerns about nuclear power, including the potential for meltdowns and the challenges of waste disposal.

"At that point in time, the downsides of nuclear power were not well-known," recalled Warren. "With the RAND report in hand, our Subcommittee concluded that the utility business-as-usual demand accommodation would have to be abandoned, and that California should investigate conservation savings." Warren introduced legislation that would create a new state agency—the California Energy Commission—with equal power to the California Public Utilities Commission (CPUC), but with a focus on ways to save energy and to encourage public participation in all of its proceedings. As a compromise, the Alquist one-stop siting idea was incorporated into the same bill. Then, Governor Ronald Reagan vetoed the bill as "dangerous social engineering"! That same year, a ballot measure proposing a moratorium on nuclear power in the state brought the same issue to a public vote,

Plate 27. Long lines of cars at service stations were the norm in 1973.

but it too failed, as grassroots activists could not overcome the clout of state utilities.

Then came the Yom Kippur War, the oil embargo, and the energy crisis of 1973 (pl. 27). "Suddenly, energy was the topic of the day." Warren then became chairman of the Energy and Diminishing Resources Committee, and he reintroduced his same piece of legislation. This time, Reagan convened negotiations with utilities, and to Warren's surprise, they only suggested minimal changes to the legislation that had been previously vetoed. The bill passed by a single vote in both the Assembly and Senate, and Reagan signed it into law in 1974.

During this approximate time period, SDG&E, the smallest of California's three private utilities, had quietly begun planning to construct the Sundesert Nuclear Power Plant, which was to feature two 950-megawatt reactors. The utility purchased land in 1975 near the small city of Blythe near the eastern border of California, just 10 miles from the Colorado River. This was the first power "thermal" plant to come before the newly created California Energy Commission's one-step licensing approval process. (The term "thermal" refers to any electricity generator that relies upon heat to create steam to drive a turbine.) The Los Angeles Department of Water and Power and three small southern California municipal utilities (Glendale, Pasadena, and Riverside) were the proposed partners in the project, but SDG&E was the biggest player, proposing to consume half of the total output.

The California Energy Commission gave the project a green light, but only after reducing the project's size in half and saddling it with numerous conditions. A series of legal battles ensued, but ultimately the project was rejected by the State Assembly on the basis of lingering concerns about nuclear waste storage. It did not help that the proposed project was located near an earthquake fault line.

Nuclear Victories—and Defeats

This battle over regulatory authority over nuclear power continued for years, with the utilities arguing that any state moratorium on nuclear power violated federal jurisdiction over nuclear energy with the recently created U.S. Nuclear Regulatory Commission. Surprisingly, the U.S. Supreme Court sided with the State of California, rejecting the arguments of California private utilities *and* the federal government. The rationale for this momentous decision did not rest with safety issues, as the courts agreed these sorts of issues fell under the purview of the federal regulation. The U.S. Supreme Court instead focused on the ability of state government officials to reject nuclear power plants on the basis of economics and land use concerns. As was the case with oil, California was once again defining who had jurisdiction over energy sources—oil and now nuclear—that have transformed world history.

Proposition 15, yet another antinuclear ballot measure, failed again in 1976. Yet the key provision of this ballot measure—prohibiting any future licenses for nuclear reactors until there was proof of an effective radioactive waste disposal system—would become official state policy despite the loss at the polls. Just before Proposition 15 failed at the polls, new Governor Jerry Brown signed a law that Warren wrote and pushed through the State Legislature that did essentially the same thing as the ballot measure, setting in place a de facto moratorium on nuclear power in California, which remains in place today.

Despite this major setback for the nuclear power industry, California would witness additions to the state's nuclear energy portfolio, as nuclear reactors that had already been in the utility resource plan cue were allowed to proceed. In southern California, Units 2 (1,070 megawatts) and 3 (1,080 megawatts) of SONGS came online in 1983 and 1984, respectively, and continue to operate today. The SONGS Unit 1 was closed in 1992 when its owners declined to invest $125 million in necessary repairs. PG&E added to the state's nuclear capacity in 1985 and 1986 with Unit 1 (1,073 megawatts) and Unit 2 (1,087 megawatts) of the Diablo Canyon nuclear reactor, located near San Luis Obispo on California's central coast (pl. 28).

The only other nuclear reactor to come online in California was the 913-megawatt Rancho Seco nuclear reactor, which came online in 1975 and was the only nuclear reactor in California to be completely owned by a municipal utility serving Sacramento. In contrast to SONGS and Diablo Canyon, however, Rancho Seco's performance was less than stellar. A near meltdown, and rate increase after rate increase, took its toll on SMUD's ratepayers' patience. After a long and controversial battle between local activists and the national nuclear reactor lobby, Rancho Seco became the only nuclear power plant in the entire country to be closed by a public vote in 1989.

California's energy history consists of many high and low moments for nuclear advocates. This was the first state to

Plate 28. The control board of the Diablo Canyon nuclear power plant.

embrace the bright potential of nuclear energy, and it was the first state to specifically ban further development. It is important to note that as the state's current nuclear capacity was coming online in the face of growing antinuclear sentiment across the country, California once again struck out on its own with other new power generation technologies, including the radical notion of saving—rather than producing—more energy.

Ironically enough, PG&E's Diablo Canyon nuclear reactor—the object of some of the most strident antinuclear protests in the state—is currently one of the top performing nuclear power plants in the entire country.

Negawatts Displace Megawatts

The de facto nuclear ban in California, and the creation of a new high-powered state agency in charge of energy conservation, catapulted California into a role model on "green" energy policy in the 1970s. Young scientists and activists such as David Goldstein, inspired by older physicists such as Art Rosenfeld, began to challenge the supply plans presented to the state's utilities own resource plans.

Rosenfeld helped convene a meeting at Princeton in 1974 that brought the best and brightest minds in physics to think creatively about the energy conundrum facing the United States. "By the end of our first week of discussions, we realized we had blundered into one of the world's largest oil and gas fields. The energy was buried, in effect, in the buildings of our cities, the vehicles on the roads, and the machines in our factories," recalled Rosenfeld. At a hearing before Warren's energy committee in 1975, PG&E was so shocked by testimony by Rosenfeld that California's energy consumption could be cut from 5 to 1.2 percent that they called the University of California at Berkeley and asked that he be fired immediately. That never happened, of course, but PG&E's outrage ultimately turned to respect, as actual energy growth did slow down to 2.2 percent, less than half of what the utility had projected.

Portrayed in the best possible light in the 1984 book *Dynamos and Virgins,* authored by David Roe with the Environmental Defense Fund (now Environmental Defense), these bright and persuasive academics built a credible case for building "conservation power plants" by simply making buildings and appliances that consumed less energy, defraying the need for constructing traditional power plants. Roe also became enamored by the idea of energy conservation, questioning utilities such as PG&E over their assumptions about future energy consumption trends. Here is a telling quote from Roe's book:

> My parents did not doubt the truth of any single fact that I was telling them. But the implication of what I was saying was that Pacific Gas & Electric was being grossly mismanaged, to its own detriment, by the eminently respectable and worldly businessmen who were peers of my parents' friends.

My parents didn't know any PG&E officers personally, except for the chairman of the board—he and my father were members of the same club, and infrequently saw each other at lunch—but the men downtown who had risen to the top of such an established institution must have known their business. Details might slip from time to time, but improvements on the scale I was expounding were inherently improbable. Could we really claim to know more about the utility business than thirty-two floors worth of well-paid utility executives?

"If what you saw is right," my father said, "why isn't PG&E already doing it?"

It was exactly the right question.

—Roe 1984:66–67

Among the more noteworthy early findings of Rosenfeld, Goldstein, Roe, and other conservation and efficiency advocates was that the most energy-efficient refrigerators on the market cost about the same as the least energy-efficient. If California implemented an efficiency standard that eliminated half of the wasteful fridges, the state could displace one-and-a-half nuclear reactors (i.e., 1,500 megawatts). This was one among many state efficiency standards that helped eliminate the need for the army of nuclear reactors that the state's utilities had projected coming online in California over the next several decades. Generally speaking, refrigerators are the largest single electricity consumer in a typical residence, so making better refrigerators was a logical early step in the war against wasteful energy practices. National refrigerator standards alone have offset the need to construct 130,000 megawatts of new power plant capacity nationwide (fig. 6), a figure that represents two and half Californias' worth of total electricity consumption.

Soon, new software programs were developed that made it easy for residents or businesses in different climate zones to calculate energy savings from a growing list of energy-saving devices and practices. Thus, a whole cottage industry sprung

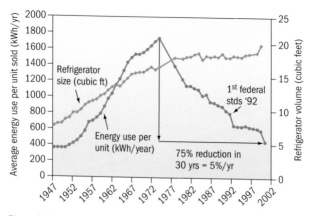

Figure 6. Refrigerator energy use in the United States over time, highlighting the role of California appliance standards.

up, with growing numbers of entrepreneurs inventing new ways to do more with less.

Just how much progress has California made through its energy efficiency efforts in the electricity sector, such as the appliance and building standards put into place in 1976 and 1978, respectively? If California had followed the path of the rest of the country, the state would have required 50 additional medium-sized, 500-megawatt power plants. Roughly half of these energy savings can be attributed to the state's aggressive energy efficiency programs (fig. 7).

Luckily, California's leadership on energy matters often is imported by other states and even nations. Its appliance energy efficiency standards were ultimately copied by the federal government in 1987. The state's building standards have recently been copied by Russia and China. A new code governing building construction in Russia modeled after California's pioneering standards is dropping energy consumption by 40 percent, and similar, if not more aggressive, savings are expected in China. It is important to note that

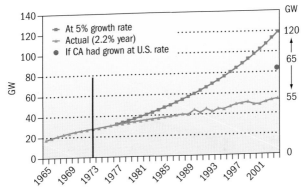

Figure 7. California's peak electricity demand, 1965–2004.

California continually updates and upgrades these standards. For example, a 2005 update for buildings and appliances will avoid the need to build five 500-megawatt fossil fuel power plants over the next decade.

Another innovation on efficiency in California was the novel idea of decoupling utility profits from electricity sales. Without such mechanisms, electric utilities still have financial incentives to sell us more, rather than less, electricity. Five other states (Oregon, Utah, North Carolina, Ohio, and Maryland) have now followed suit on decoupling and several others (Idaho, Washington, Wisconsin, New York, New Jersey, and New Mexico) are considering proposals to put into place this important incentive to foster greater efficiency when it comes to energy supplies.

Although critics of California's energy policies often malign this state for its high retail electricity rates, the actual bills that residents and businesses pay have, in fact, declined over time. Since 1973, energy bills in California have averaged $100 less than those of the nation as a whole. All told, California's economy receives a boost of between $7 and

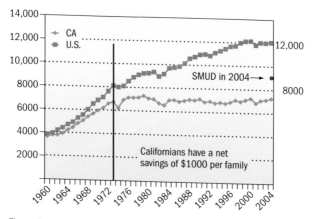

Figure 8. California's per capita electricity consumption has remained flat, while the national average has climbed over time.

$10 billion per year as a result of the state's pioneering efforts on energy efficiency.

In essence, California has cut its projected power supply needs in half. This savings is the equivalent of taking 12 million cars off our congested freeways. Imagine, one out of every three motor vehicles on the road just disappearing. That is the magnitude of the savings generated by this achievement of replacing megawatts with negawatts. The net gain can also be measured in financial terms: $1,000 for every California family (fig. 8).

The Renewable Rush

Without coal, oil, or nuclear, California once again set out on its own path, mining California's rich geology and native natural resources to construct one of the most diverse and sophisticated energy systems that can be found anywhere in the world. In the course of just five years, a combination of tax credits, long-term power purchase contracts, and state technical assistance jump-started the wind, solar, geothermal, and biomass power industries.

The passage of the federal Public Utility Regulatory Policy Act (PURPA) in 1978 allowed private companies to build new power plants relying upon renewable fuels. California was the most aggressive state when it came to implementing PURPA. This law jump-started the entire renewable energy industry in the United States, especially California, because it required electric utilities to purchase power from these independent power producers at "avoided cost" rates. Among the incentives offered for wind power developers were generous state investment tax credits (which augmented federal tax credits), standard long-term utility power purchase contracts that featured fixed prices during the first 5 to 10 years of operation, and a state-funded wind resource assessment that identified California's best wind energy opportunities.

California promoted solar, wind, geothermal, and biomass energy sources like no other state in the country, with its own tax credits and attractive, stable long-term power prices for private generators to build these new power plants (pl. 29). These incentives were put forward because the costs of utility-owned nuclear reactors, such as PG&E's Diablo Canyon, had greatly exceeded original estimates. Ratepayers were required to cover $5 billion in cost overruns for this single nuclear reactor, a fact that led to a unique performance-based cost recovery scheme. Opening up the power generation sector to competition spawned an entire domestic renewable energy industry in California, accelerating the deregulation of wholesale electricity generation throughout the country.

At this point in time, introducing competition into the power plant building business was seen as a way to let ratepayers off the hook when something went wrong at an electricity

Plate 29. This 100 kW wind turbine was the mainstay of U.S. Windpower, which later changed its name to Kenetech.

generating station. On the watch of Governor Jerry Brown, California embarked upon a series of wild experiments with new cleaner and smaller power sources that stunned utilities nationwide. Wall Street shysters and environmentalists were suddenly working together as California lurched forward into an untested energy future.

For example, approximately $1 billion was diverted from federal and state taxes into wind farms between 1981 and 1985 to jump-start the world's wind power industry in California, currently the world's most successful renewable energy business. The end result of this effort was the addition of 1,700 megawatts of new wind power capacity to the state's power plant portfolio, which represented over 90 percent of the world's total wind power capacity. Both federal and state investment tax credits were terminated in 1986, however, because of publicity surrounding the abuse of this investment tax shelter, perhaps the last of the great tax scams in recent U.S. history. Congressman Pete Stark of Hayward led the fight to terminate the investment tax credits by proclaiming, "These aren't wind farms; they're tax farms."

Once again, California's effervescence over new technologies would engender a backlash. Yet California's public policies created a global market for wind as well as other renewable energy technologies. A valid claim can be made that California's policies to promote renewable energy technologies was the most successful commercialization effort in the history of the United States.

California also offered attractive utility power purchase contracts and other public support for other renewable energy technologies that yielded these significant developments:

- California pushed new solar thermal electric systems known as "parabolic troughs" into commercial operation. At present, nine distinct solar thermal trough systems generate 354 megawatts of peak power in smoggy southern California. A total of 650,000 parabolic mirrors stretch over 1,000 acres of the desolate Mojave Desert. At this site, originally developed by a joint Israeli–U.S. venture beginning in 1983, expansion plans have been delayed for years despite the fact that the performance of solar thermal parabolic troughs has been excellent, even after more than 10 years of operation.
- Geothermal power was also pioneered here (pl. 30), though in this case, the world's largest geothermal facility had been originally constructed back in 1960 up in

Plate 30. This is the 240 MW Coso geothermal complex, located near the China Lake Weapons Reserve, just south of Owens Valley on Highway 395.

the Geysers region. However, this type of geothermal fuel—flash steam—was rare, so the technology developed here did not work well as the state's other primary geothermal steam resources, such as those in Imperial County in southern California. In 1979, Magma Power Company generated electricity from a water-dominated geothermal fuel. A year later, it was federal R&D investments that helped ORMAT demonstrate a "binary" power generation technology, which then paved the way for utility-scale development. This new form of geothermal power generation is so efficient that ORMAT paid off its federal government loan in just one year.

- California quickly became the nation's top producer of electricity from biomass power plants, and we are still the leader. Today, roughly 625 megawatts of capacity currently is online. Of the 62 biomass power plants built in the 1980s, approximately 35 are still operable today. At the industry's peak, 45 power plants were online generating electricity, thereby diverting 9.7 million tons of solid urban wood waste from California's crowded landfills.

In each major renewable energy category—solar, wind, geothermal, and biomass—California quickly jumped into the category of global pioneer. It was not always pretty, as anyone who drives to the wind farms near Palm Springs on Hwy. 10 can attest to. However, it was remarkable that a single state—albeit a giant one with a plethora of renewable energy in the northern, southern, eastern, and western parts of the state—could spawn an entire industry in less than a decade. Grants, financing, and expertise from the world over were involved with these pioneering efforts, harshly criticized by the state's utilities as well as industry skeptics all across the country.

Remarkably, California's natural history and the corresponding energy streams that flowed from the sun, wind, biomass wastes, and volcanic activity below the surface all provided the basis for a slow transformation of electricity infrastructure that attracted attention all over the world, both for its boldness and its seeming naïveté (fig. 9).

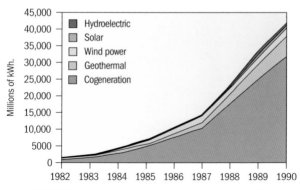

Figure 9. PURPA gave a large boost to the production of electricity from alternative sources in California.

California's Free-Fall into Chaos

In the 1990s, things started to unravel, and California—the shining light for many looking to alternatives to business-as-usual—began to lose quite a bit of its sheen. Leading renewable energy companies such as Kenetech of Livermore, California (pl. 31)—the world's largest wind power company—went belly-up, attributed, in large part, to California's unstable power market conditions. A planning process for new power plants that was supposed to be "biennial" dragged out for eight years and then was overturned by federal regulators. Some 1,458 megawatts of planned new supply, including approximately 500 megawatts of new wind and geothermal capacity, was never put into the ground.

Heeding the signs of the times, California began to investigate how to best deregulate electricity services. Having built up one of the most sophisticated systems of planning for new

Plate 31. Experimental blades from Kenetech's wind farm fleet.

resources, California was now turning from this comma....
and-control resource planning model to an alleged "free
market" for electricity. Building on the state's historical
legacy of relying upon independent power producers, the
state was again poised to push the envelope. However, this
time, it would heed a growing chorus of experts predicting that electricity was ready to move beyond the monopoly
structure in place for almost a century. Economists boldly
endorsed competition to allow new ideas to flourish in a
state that had become synonymous with cutting-edge
energy experimentation.

Marathon legislative negotiation sessions led by former State Senator Steve Peace (D-Chula Vista), who was
once producer of the underground film classic *Attack of
the Killer Tomatoes*, had shaped state legislation that would
revamp the nation's largest electricity market. Typically,
such bills are drafted behind closed doors, with competing lobbyists shaking hands over cocktails or cigars. In
this case, Peace—acting a bit like Phil Donahue—would
bring all of the special interests into one room, get them
to sit at one table in legislative chambers, and would go
around with a microphone, quizzing and putting people
on the spot with his tough questioning. While Peace was a
brilliant politician and managed to craft a bill that sailed
through the California Legislature (pl. 32) without a single dissenting vote, he unknowingly set the state up for a
major wake-up call.

"We take the risk if our costs go up," acknowledged Gordon
Smith, PG&E chief executive in 1997, referring to AB 1890,
the law that Peace pushed and that restructured California's
$23 billion electricity market. More than any other special
interests, the state's large private utilities helped shape AB
1890, a 100-page-long law that restructured California's
electricity market. Though large energy consumers initially
pushed for the restructuring of California's power market,
AB 1890's most generous financial provisions delighted

Plate 32. Late-night sessions at the State Capitol set the stage for passage of the nation's most comprehensive restructuring of power markets.

investor-owned utilities. PG&E and Edison International (the parent company of SCE) each reaped $10 billion in profits between 1998 and April 2000 as a result of provisions that allowed the utilities to charge ratepayers for all of their past debts under a compressed schedule.

While the state's restructuring law of 1996 promised lower rates and the opportunity for citizens to vote for clean energy with their ratepayer dollars, the compromise legislation set the stage for one of California's darkest hours. First came rolling blackouts in 2000, which continued through 2001. Then, astronomical wholesale prices were charged by the likes of Enron. PG&E and SCE sank billions of dollars of debt, with PG&E ultimately declaring bankruptcy. Still later, the stock market crash and terrorist attacks dramatically slowed the economy, spawning low-cost power surpluses. And then came the climb in price for virtually all energy sources, including natural gas (our current dominant electricity fuel) and oil (our dominant transportation fuel).

To solve the California energy crisis, California Governor Davis ultimately thrust the state Department of Water Resources (DWR) into the role of becoming the sole purchasing agent of electricity for most Californians. This agonizing decision required the largest public bond issuance in state history. More than 30 contracts with wholesalers worth $40 billion were signed with the DWR. Roughly 70 percent of those contracts sell power from facilities that had not yet been built, investments in facilities that will operate for 30 years or more. All but 2.5 percent—120 megawatts—of these electricity generators are fueled by natural gas, a fuel subject to extreme price fluctuation.

When natural gas prices go up, the cost of electricity from these power plants increases dramatically. Experience has shown us that it is never good to depend primarily on a single fuel to generate electricity. As in an investment portfolio, diversity is necessary to hedge against risks. While California has since emerged from this debacle, ratepayers will be paying off debts for this $40 billion investment well into the next decade.

At this point, California seemed to be teetering between two worlds, neither of which served the public interest. Free markets? Why, wasn't that the cause of skyrocketing prices and rolling blackouts? Big government? A state takeover of electricity purchasing ran up huge state budget deficits to be borne by state taxpayers locked into large blocks of "dirty" electricity at high prices. California's ongoing experiment with governance of power markets seemed to deliver more of the same to state consumers: high prices and long-term debts for sources of polluting power.

Managing the ebbs and flows of energy supplies offers a unique set of challenges to policymakers. California's roller coaster ride during 2000–2001 was a result of an untested power market that was heralded as a "free" market when in reality, it was a political plan based in blind faith in markets with just enough progressive elements (such as support for renewable energy and efficiency) to get every legislator's vote. Though it allowed wholesale prices to fluctuate, retail prices were frozen, a feature intended to protect residential ratepayers. This is why the PG&E and SCE seemed powerless as the crisis persisted. When wholesale prices that utilities paid skyrocketed (largely because of an untested power market structure that proved to be a disaster), prices paid by retail consumers still stayed the same. Apparently, no one had envisioned prices going up under the new regulatory framework. The assumption all along was that the wonders of a market would drive costs down. It was the difference between wholesale and retail rates that created a crisis.

California is not the only state disappointed by the promise of deregulation in delivering a better electricity system. The large industrial consumers who originally pushed for these sorts of radical reforms were also extremely disappointed. Here are some of the reasons why markets have not delivered a cheaper and cleaner energy product:

- Most markets, including California's, were designed to pay all producers the same highest price in auctions.
- Producers discovered that it is relatively easy to withhold power to create artificial shortages, thereby increasing prices.
- This market proved easy to manipulate in a way that approached collusion but skirted just within the confines of the law.
- In other markets, customers always have the opportunity to walk away. This is not the case with electricity, which has become a vital aspect of everyday life.
- In the stock market, vast numbers of buyers and sellers tend to keep prices in balance. In California's power

Plate 33. Surreal transmission towers.

markets, just six firms that generate electricity can essentially set prices for all state consumers.

- Whereas stock trades are transparent, much of the prices and purchase details of electricity trades are shrouded in secrecy.
- Since electricity needs to be produced, transmitted, and consumed instantaneously (pl. 33), there are few avenues for inventory.

A study at Carnegie Mellon University found that buyers and sellers of electricity could learn how to game power markets after roughly 100 rounds of bidding. These increasingly clever bidders were able to capture up to 90 percent of the prices an unregulated monopoly could have charged. In other words, prices went through the roof. Sarosh N. Talukdar, the professor who published this study, summed up her findings in this way: "My studies show that it is easy to learn from the signals given by others how to get the benefits of colluding without breaking the law."

Stanford University professor Frank A. Wolak, who supports the notion of competitive markets, adds that the

Jeffrey Skilling, former Enron CEO, once bragged Enron would evolve into the world's top corporation, period. Instead of being "vertically integrated" like its asset-heavy compatriots, Enron would be "virtually integrated." Deregulation would break up traditional firms into thousands of tiny niche players. Enron's strategy was to "wire those thousands of firms back together cheaply and temporarily," relying upon its unregulated Internet-based trading platforms to squeeze out profits from other people's assets.

The quick disintegration of Enron—a firm once ranked as the seventh largest in the world based on annual revenues—virtually had no effect on maintaining the reliability of power supplies in California or the rest of the country.

Enron did not generate electricity; it merely traded the juice. Enron operated, more or less, like a publicly held huge hedge fund. What Enron failed to do was inform its shareholders that it had evolved into a high-risk investment firm carrying huge debts that accounting gimmicks glossed over. Though demonized by activists and politicians dismissing electricity deregulation, Enron did not reap anywhere near the profits its fellow energy marketers and generators made, firms such as Calpine of San Jose. The very competition Enron championed as its golden opportunity started cutting into already-thin profit margins as the economy slowed and wholesale electricity prices plummeted. Since it owned no power plants, all Enron did was repackage electricity and then resell it. As wholesale prices fell, Enron's profit margins kept getting thinner and thinner.

Ironically, one of the few assets the company maintained was its wind turbine manufacturing subsidiary, which it had been trying to sell for over a year. Given that wind power has been the fastest-growing power supply source over the past decade, Enron seemed to get lost in a virtual world of online real-time trades and Internet connections, and they forgot about fostering real innovations in supplying electricity from actual hardware that can offer lasting solutions. To its credit, Enron was a proponent of curbing emissions to global climate change. Yet the firm failed to recognize the value of the one hard asset it owned: Enron Wind Corporation, which showed tremendous profit potential as a result of global climate change concerns.

current hodgepodge of regulated and unregulated markets that currently exist throughout the country sends too many mixed signals and therefore cannot reduce costs. "Even small flaws in the design of markets can cause enormous harm to consumers in very little time," he observed.

Two bright spots emerged from California's energy crisis of 2000–2001: first, a record number of distributed renewable energy systems, particularly solar photovoltaic (PV) panels, were installed, many by corporations and local governments seeking clean, reliable electricity supplies (pl. 34); and second, the voluntary conservation savings state consumers supplied over the summer of 2001 far exceeded expectations and dwarfed energy demand reductions encouraged by energy-efficiency programs managed by utility monopolies.

The energy crisis also happened to bolster the case for demand-side management (DSM) programs, a close relative of energy efficiency. In the case of DSM, as it is called within industry circles, energy savings are time-dependent and often require active participation on the part of the consumer. For example, the state's "Flex Your Power" campaign launched

Plate 34. Large solar PV array near Lake Oroville at dusk.

during the summer of 2001 offered financial incentives for residents and businesses to not use electricity during peak demand periods in the late afternoons and early evenings. A massive installation of compact fluorescent light bulbs and high-efficiency motors helped California save 5,000 megawatts, the equivalent electricity to power a city the size of Los Angeles. Unfortunately, roughly half of these efficiency gains disappeared in 2002, when the crisis ended and the sense of urgency and camaraderie waned.

These two success stories point the way to the future. They are the direct result of California's experiment with opening up markets to new players, some of which gouged state consumers, others of which helped push forward the next generation of clean power technologies.

None of this human drama, interestingly enough, would have been possible if not for natural processes that evolved over millions of years and that never knew the difference between a "blue" or a "red" state or a private or public utility. The next two sections of this book provide an overview of all of the energy sources you depend upon to support your current lifestyle, with particular emphasis on electricity, fossil fuels, and renewable energy. For each energy source examined, particular attention is placed on the role California played in their maturation as a viable option in today's carbon-constrained world.

MAINSTAYS
Electricity and Fossil Fuels

AS IS NOW CLEAR, energy can be garnered from a cluster of fuels in a variety of mediums and formats to serve society. From the liquid fuels you put in your vehicle's gas tank to the flipping of the light switch in your bedroom or kitchen, you are constantly plugged into a maze of energy transactions in your daily life.

At present, the largest source of your energy portfolio is petroleum (pl. 35), which provided roughly half (46 percent) of all of the primary energy consumed by Californians in 2006. Natural gas was the second largest source during that same calendar year, providing just under a third (29.5 percent) of the remaining primary energy use. Although California generated the majority of electricity consumed in the state (78 percent), just under half of the crude oil (45 percent) consumed here is imported from foreign sources. Whereas California produced 39 percent of the crude oil consumed here, only 13.5 percent of the natural gas came from sources located within California's borders.

The sector of the economy that is responsible for the greatest energy consumption is transportation, comprising 41 percent of the total energy use in California. (This should come as no surprise, given the statistic above about petroleum, which so clearly dominates our transportation options.) Industrial activities are the second largest category of energy use, representing just under a quarter of the remaining consumption (22 percent). The remainder of the energy is consumed by the commercial enterprises that line Main Street and nearby malls (19 percent) as well as by you and your neighbors (18 percent).

Electricity is considered a secondary energy medium because a primary energy source such as natural gas, uranium, or solar energy must be used to generate it. The disadvantage of electricity is that there is also a dramatic energy loss during the conversion process. Yet, because electricity can be generated from so many different fuels, it has become increasingly popular as an energy medium. Theoretically, the medium of

Plate 35. Oil usually does not flow spontaneously out of wells but must be raised by pumpers like these near Bakersfield, with their characteristic walking beams and horseheads.

electricity can allow society to shift over to a completely renewable energy system. Hydrogen is yet another secondary energy medium that can be created by way of a variety of fuels, and you will learn about this much-hyped solution to our energy woes in the following Alternatives part of this book.

Bringing Energy into Your Own Life

Have you ever thought about how electricity has changed your life?

I am a Baby Boomer, born in 1956, so I have witnessed quite a dramatic change in my own electricity use, fueled, in large part, by the technologies I use on a daily basis as a writer. When I started my career as a professional journalist in 1984, I sometimes still used an old-fashioned manual typewriter. Living in Sacramento at the time, in an old apartment downtown that lacked air conditioning, I still recall sweating so badly under deadline that the ink I used to make corrections on the page began to smear and run all over the page. I had to start typing the page all over again, a very frustrating experience indeed when you think about how easy it now is to modify documents through computer word processing programs.

Today, I work on a portable laptop computer that can be plugged into the wall socket but can also operate remotely on batteries. Although I do not rely upon wireless telecommunications at my home office, I do take advantage of this electricity-based form of communications when on the road. All of my work is submitted via e-mail over the Internet. I spend far more time communicating via e-mail and searching websites than I do speaking with people face to face, in libraries looking up reference books, or doing phone interviews.

Yet, I do not text-message or use any of the fancy video features on my cell phone—still other technologies that boost electricity consumption, albeit from new kinds of microbatteries. However, think about all of the latest gizmos and gadgets that allegedly keep making our lives better, more convenient, and more satisfying. Even our motor vehicles are beginning to run—at least in part—on electricity in the case of the ever-popular hybrids manufactured by Toyota and Honda, and soon the rest of the world's auto industry.

Now, more than ever, electricity has emerged as the energy medium of choice. Society's growing addiction to electricity shows no signs of abating anytime soon. Of course, the one bright spot in this evolution of energy transfers is that a diversity of fuels can be used to create electricity. The somber and darker reality is that fossil fuels will need to be displaced over time with larger and larger amounts of renewable energy. This transition will require new and more intelligent systems to manage, store, and then deliver power to each one of us individually and society as a whole. Hydrogen could play a similar role, but progress, to date, in moving us closer to a hydrogen-based economy has been halting.

Of course, each of our respective energy impacts upon the world still go beyond electricity. Are you one of those people who endure a California commute (pl. 36) to your job every day? It is not uncommon for state citizens to drive one or even two hours back and forth on our congested

Plate 36. Traffic congestion on the Golden Gate Bridge, and throughout California, is endemic.

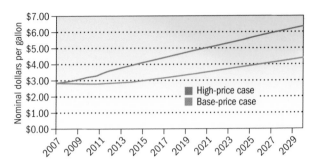

Figure 10. Gasoline price projections in 2007 failed to predict $4 per gallon prices in 2008.

freeway systems during the work week. When it comes to global climate change, it is our fossil-fuel-dependent transportation system in California—largely consisting of single-occupancy cars and trucks—that is the biggest problem.

While we might complain about high prices at the pump (fig. 10), most of us just keep driving. The United States as a whole has practiced less and less conservation. Gasoline consumption has inched up 1 or 2 percent points annually since the 1990s, though this pattern was disrupted somewhat in 2008 as gasoline hit record-high prices. According to Lisa Margonelli, an Irvine Fellow at the New America Foundation, Californians increased gasoline consumption by 1.37 billion gallons a year between 2000 and 2006. Few of us realize the role we play in a web of transactions connected to every tiny oil spill. Margonelli's research shows that leaks from our cars, trucks, and boats add up to 19 million gallons flowing into our waterways every year. Reducing our consumption by even 1 percent will free up pipeline space and keep several super-tankers the size of the *Exxon Valdez* away from our shores every year. Did you know that 33 million gallons of crude oil slip under the landmark Golden Gate Bridge in ships every single day?

Since this book is part of a Natural History Guide Series, we will soon discover how California's natural history served as a backdrop to the human history depicted in the preceding Overview. Fossil fuels dominate California's energy consumption, both in electricity and transportation fuels; therefore, these fuels will be described next. The next part, Alternatives, will then describe renewable energy fuels and technologies primarily employed to generate electricity, as well as nuclear and hydrogen alternatives.

An Overview of the Wonders of Electricity

What exactly happens when you flip the light switch on in your home? What are we really buying when most of us pay our monthly electricity bill?

Electricity is a secondary medium for energy derived from a diversity of fossil, renewable, and other types of primary fuels. Because electricity is so pervasive and the appropriateness of application so dependent upon fuel sources, this section provides a broad overview of the energy medium likely to enable California to address climate change in a strategic program. However, before we delve into the human history of electricity, we will get a quick science lesson.

Many of us have come to visualize electricity as a steady flow of tiny, tiny objects known as electrons. These specks, of which it would take about a hundred billion billion billion to weigh an ounce, are just part of the picture. In reality, electricity is composed of both electrons, which carry a negative charge, and protons, which are positively charged. (Electricity is also involved with other bantam particles with names like "antiprotons," "positrons," or "quarks," but for the sake of illustration, we will stick with the two entities that populate the most common grade of electricity flowing through your wall socket.)

Electricity is only electricity when both of these kinds of subatomic particles are present, negative and positive charges, keeping this invisible force field in balance. More often than not, negative and positive particles balance each other out. However, when conditions are dry, and you shuffle your feet on a carpet, you pick up a very, very slight excess of negatively charged electrons, which jump away as soon as you are close enough to a path back to the ground (such as a doorknob), creating the static electricity shocks we have all experienced at one time or another.

Electrons seem to get the most attention because of, well, their name. We do not call this stuff Protonicity, do we? Of course, another reason is that in the solid metals commonly used to transmit electricity, the protons are static; only the electrons move. When an electric current is created within a solid copper wire, for example, a sea of electrons moves forward, but the protons do not. However, this phenomenon is not pervasive. In fact, inside most batteries, electricity moves in both directions at once, with electrons going one way and protons going the other way, engaged in a dance that we human beings could not begin to emulate.

These bipolar displays of electric charge are all around us. In fact, they exist not only in our own human bodies but in all living organisms and in the ocean, the sky, the Earth, and virtually all realms in between.

If you are not confused yet, there is still more. During the typical electricity transaction, not only do the protons stay in one place, but the electrons barely travel as well. Electrons move along a transmission or distribution line at about the same pace as a human walking. Electricity is really more like a weightless, vibrating force field. Tiny bits of charged matter jostle back and forth, incredibly fast, nearly instantaneously, in this field instead of traversing a linear path, but it is the

Plate 37. Transmission towers in Central Valley, resembling soldiers on the march.

field itself that carries the energy at the speed of light. Hence, the immediate response when you flip the switch, even though the power might be coming from a power plant in San Diego all the way up to Crescent City (pl. 37).

Then there is electricity's close relationship to magnetism. A moving electric charge creates a magnetic field that causes a magnetized object to move, while a moving magnet, or even a magnet that stays in one place while its strength changes, produces a field that propels electric charges. In essence, each electrically charged minim in the universe dances within a huge combined electric and magnetic force field, like an aura.

Once called "an entertainment for angels rather than men," electricity has always been a substance that, like the broader notion of energy, has escaped adequate comprehension. In fact, electricity prompted philosophers and political leaders to reexamine some of their deepest beliefs about life and even God. Many praised its seeming miraculous abilities, believing electricity could cure a variety of diseases; others scorned electricity, claiming that this invisible force was a dark intrusion into the very soul of society, reducing the divinity of life to a bleak materialism

NOTABLE INVENTORS OF ELECTRIC DEVICES

There is a long list of inventors who made incremental advances in the science of electricity. Here are just a few, with their most celebrated discoveries or inventions:

1786: Luigi Galvani, an Italian professor of medicine, noticed a dead frog twitch furiously when touched by a metal knife (pl. 38), deducting (erroneously) that the muscles of the frog itself must contain electricity.

1800: Alessandro Voltra, who earlier disproved Galvani's conclusions on the frog, invented "the voltaic pile," the world's first electric battery, and discovered a new kind of electricity, one that flowed like a river instead of jumping like a lone spark.

1831: Michael Faraday, great grandfather of the modern power plant, proved that magnets could also produce

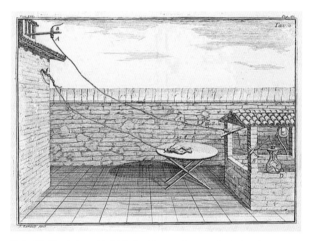

Plate 38. Depiction of Luigi Galvani's experiment stimulating the nerves of a dead frog with an electrical device.

electricity. His discoveries revealed that instead of being restricted to wire funnels, electricity was a force field. The first practical application of Faraday's discoveries was the electromagnetic telegraph.

1844: Samuel Morse, a Puritan artist who had become interested in the possibilities of electricity for instantaneous long-distance communication (in part because he was afraid Catholics were plotting to take over America) and had constructed several prototype telegraph machines, opened the first commercial telegraph line between Baltimore and Washington, DC. This invention set the stage for globalization.

1875: Alexander Graham Bell, always concerned about ways to improve the ability of people to communicate (he also developed a method to teach deaf people to talk), invented the telephone, and the Bell telephone company was born.

1887: Heinrich Hertz witnessed a spark jumping across a small, open break in a wire loop placed nearby a more powerful spark generator. This initial spark was only a hundredth of a millimeter long and lasted only a millionth of a second, yet to Hertz it proved vast, invisible electromagnetic force fields existed that could perhaps be channeled over great distances without need of solid conductors.

1879: Thomas Edison invented the incandescent light bulb.

that rendered humans as mere machines at the service of industrialism.

As is usually the case, the truth falls somewhere in between these extreme views.

Recognition of electricity as a force of nature traces back to the Greeks. Around 600 BC, the Greek philosopher Thales made the first documented observations of static electricity. By rubbing amber (a hard fossilized resin) against a fur cloth, he noticed that particles of straw were drawn to the fur. This odd effect remained a mystery until approximately 2,000 years later. It was Dr. William Gilbert (1544–1603) who first used the word "electric," from the Greek word for amber (*elektron*), as he tinkered with the reactions of amber to magnets. (The Greeks also used the word *elektron* for a natural alloy of gold and silver.)

Perhaps the most enduring legend revolving around electricity is owned by Benjamin Franklin and his infamous kite struck by lightning in 1752. Franklin fastened an iron spike to a silk kite, hoisted it into the air during a thunderstorm, and held the end of the kite string in the same hand that he also held an iron key. When lightning flashed, a tiny spark jumped from the key to his wrist. While Franklin could easily have been killed by this dangerous experiment, it proved that lightning and the sparks of static that Thales and Gilbert observed were one and the same.

We take the incandescent light bulb for granted, but it took decades of research and experimentation to bring this seemingly simple device into commercial reality.

Up until this point in time, artificial lights relied upon natural gas or oil. In fact, one of the prime reasons for whaling in the early 1800s was to obtain oil for these lights. Among the hazards from these early lights was smoke, soot, and, in some cases, even fire.

Developing the light bulb was not an easy task for Edison. Apparently, he was not only hard of hearing, but a high school dropout. While he worked in the telegraph business, he longed to prove himself. In response to a shortcoming discovered in Bell's first-generation phone systems, Edison improved upon the design, enabling voice transmissions to travel further with the help of a dedicated battery. Edison's greatest contribution to the evolution of electricity would lie, nonetheless, not as an inventor of new technology but in defining the business structure to supply this elixir of the metropolis to the masses, who would soon become addicted to its mesmerizing promises of convenience and freedom.

Development of Electricity in California

California's contribution to the development of new electricity technologies and innovations was already chronicled in depth in the preceding Overview. Additional historical as well as contemporary contributions can be found in my two Island Press books: *Reinventing Electric Utilities: Competition, Citizen Action and Clean Power* (Asmus 1997) and *Reaping The Wind: How Mechanical Wizards, Visionaries and Profiteers Helped Shape Our Energy Future* (Asmus 2001).

Electricity Today

The growth in electricity production and consumption represents the pinnacle of human ingenuity and achievements, and it remains the most prevalent form of energy utilization. Why? Electricity is so convenient. It can be transported over both large and small wires from nearly anywhere to precise points of consumption all over the world. (Portable forms of electricity are also churning current everywhere via batteries in flashlights, cell phones, and some alarm clocks.) Electricity can be turned into mechanical work, light, heat, radiant energy, and so on. It has become the most versatile medium of energy transfer, the lifeblood of today's digital society. Virtually any fuel can be used to create electricity, and end-users seem to be insulated from many of the risks that have plagued other energy sources.

Since the story of electricity is so diffuse and so different for each of the fuels and technologies deployed to create this form of energy, the remainder of this section is largely devoted to answering generic questions about the current

Plate 39. A full moon peeks through a maze of wires and latticework at a transmission substation.

status of electricity sources. (The pros and cons of each electricity fuel are discussed in this part and in the following part, Alternatives.) Like hydrogen, electricity is really a carrier of energy that can be created from a plethora of fossil and renewable energy sources. (In contrast, fossil fuels such as petroleum, described next in this section, are considered primary sources of energy since they can be put to work directly.) As is the case with all other energy sources, the medium of electricity has pros and cons, as summarized below.

The Pros and Cons of Electricity

+ Can be derived from a variety of fuels found all over the world

- + Very versatile energy carrier; available through utility distribution networks, but can also be stored in batteries and other devices
- + Because of the electricity grid, can be consumed and used far from where power is generated
- + Can be used for the widest variety of applications ranging from light and heat to industrial machinery and transportation
- + Can be used in developing nations that lack modern infrastructure via off-grid renewable energy generation
- − Generation of electricity can have a variety of environmental impacts depending upon the fuel and technology employed
- − Development of infrastructure to carry electricity—transmission towers and distribution lines—can have major impacts on landscapes (pl. 39)
- − Fears regarding public health impacts of electromagnetic fields (EMFs) flowing from transmission lines and appliances continue to remain inadequately resolved
- − Ubiquitous expansion of electric gadgets may have longstanding social impacts as consumers rely increasingly on isolated and individualized entertainment at the expense of broader social interaction

It should be noted that EMF issues involve items such as cell phones, microwave ovens, personal computers, and electric blankets. A growing body of evidence about the negative health consequences of EMF has yet to damp the enthusiasm most environmentalists have for electricity as the energy medium of choice to combat climate change. Nevertheless, greater education about how to protect public health from the EMF flowing throughout our homes, work places, and perhaps motor vehicles will be necessary before electricity can be declared society's preferred mode of energy delivery.

The Future of Electricity

The U.S. Energy Information Administration projects that the world's electricity consumption will double from 2003 levels by 2030, with the vast majority of that growth—71 percent—occurring in developing countries. In contrast, growth in electricity for the so-called "industrialized" world is projected to be 29 percent. The two countries expected to be the leaders in consumption of electricity is China and then the United States. Among the reasons for growth here in the United States are increasing reliance upon telecommunications and other office equipment, which, in effect, nullify some of the expected efficiency gains from newer, smarter, and cleaner power generation technologies. The most rapid growth in electricity, nonetheless, will be in Mexico, where politics has, up until now, stunted development of a modernized electricity grid.

Our Fossil Fuel Natural History

The origins of California's indigenous oil and natural gas in California trace back as far as 70 million years ago; however, on a geologic scale, California is but a teenager. Not as young as the Gulf of Mexico—another major hot spot for fossil fuels—but in the grand, great scheme of things, California's geology is a short story rather than a long novel. How can we know about this relative youth? The theory of "plate tectonics" has developed from a concept put forward by German geophysicist Alfred Wegener in 1920. According to Wegener, all of the continents were joined at one time. This "supercontinent," which Wegener called "Pangea," meaning "all Earth," was pulled apart largely by forces of heat emanating from the inner core of the Earth. These movements expressed themselves by pushing outward through the outer core, the mantle, and finally the Earth's crust. The forces associated with continental drift began to reshape our present-day continents' masses through several periods of time: Permian (ending 250 million years ago), Triassic (ending 200 million years ago), Jurassic (ending 145 million years ago), and Cretaceous (ending 65 million years ago).

What is now California was once a big island that collided with the rest of the continental United States eons ago. The force of this collision, and its lingering aftermath, is reflected by the region's world-famous earthquakes. This series of earthquake fault lines created ideal conditions for the slow evolution of fossil fuels, which ultimately migrate to the surface and occasionally expose themselves in dramatic fashion via oil seeps on a grand scale (pl. 40). This is the case with the La Brea Tar Pits, where fossils dating back as far as 40,000 years ago remain on display at the Page Museum in Rancho La Brea in the greater Los Angeles area.

Plate 40.
Ventura County
oil seep.

Popularized by fossils of saber-toothed tigers and mammoths—as well as dire wolves and other extinct species of animals and birds—the La Brea Tar Pits demonstrate how endemic petroleum is in California. These tar pits capture California's natural history during the last of four great Ice Ages at the end of the Pleistocene Epoch. This natural bed of sticky asphalt trapped unsuspecting creatures and plants over thousands of years. Roughly one million fossils have been found and collected here. Even today, asphalt still oozes and bubbles to the surface, still entrapping birds and small animals.

Millions of years ago, of course, the entire Los Angeles basin was under water. Marine sedimentary layers formed slowly but surely. The passage of geologic time created ideal conditions for the cultivation of crude oil and other forms of fossil fuel. Mountains in the southern third of the state sat on the coastline, bombarded by ocean waves and rivers. Erosion altered the topography; washed away armies of sand, silt, and clay sediments; and slowly exposed the fossil fuels that had been festering down below.

According to the fossil record trapped here, the weather and landscape of Los Angeles during this time period was cooler and more moist than today, though rainfall was still seasonal, with little precipitation during the summer. Some of today's trees and plants, such as coastal sage scrub and cypress, were evident. However, redwood trees also grew in sheltered canyons. The present-day environment of the Monterey Peninsula comes closest to representing what Los Angeles was like during the waning days of the last Ice Age.

Though few California residents are aware of it, the Los Angeles basin is among the most prolific crude oil basins. Known as the Wilmington field, which rests beneath the Long Beach and Los Angles harbors, it is not only one of the four largest oil fields in the entire United States but perhaps the biggest oil basin in the world. Yet a majority of this crude oil will never be tapped, as human populations that now reside in the Los Angeles basin preclude much further development, though new horizontal drilling techniques could enable some fringe crude extraction. The hills surrounding the Los Angeles basin remain barren today as a result of past oil claims and development. Most of these hills are expressions of subsurface faults. In other words, they are essentially domes pumped up to the surface because of bulging crude oil deposits. A majority of the oil yanked out of the Los Angeles basin was extracted from these hilltops (pl. 41). As you move toward the coast, the folds of land caused by the shattering of so many fault lines go deeper. That is why oil can be found off of California's coast at quite shallow drilling depths.

Plate 41. Unocal workers who drilled what was then the deepest oil well, Gardena #1, in the Dominguez oil field in southern California on July 17, 1924.

The Family of Fossil Fuels

Fossil fuels are ubiquitous in modern life. From fueling the vast majority of our automobiles to serving as the feedstock for plastics and a long list of consumer products that include our clothes and our homes, petroleum and its by-products can be found virtually everywhere you look.

Once considered a waste product, natural gas—another form of fossil fuel—has increasingly been called upon as a fuel for electricity and to power our buses and other transport vehicles (pl. 42). It has emerged as the fossil fuel of choice, since it is the lightest and cleanest of fossil fuels when combusted. Although solid forms of fossil fuels—coal—are hard to find within California's borders, consumption of coal has increased dramatically by Californians over the last decade.

All three of these basic forms of fossil fuels, also known as hydrocarbons, trace their origins to aquatic plants and animals that lived millions of years ago. These creatures ranged from tiny single-cell organisms to colossal dinosaurs and virtually everything in between. As these organisms died, they often sank to the bottom of oceans as well as inland seas and lakes. Mixing with sand and mud, this organic material eventually hardened into sandstone, shale, or limestone rock. (Granite, marble, and lava rock formations involve different processes and therefore lack fossil fuels.) This process was then repeated over and over again, creating layer after layer of organic deposits that were continually being squeezed from above by gravity and heated up from below from the Earth's molten core. Often, there was not enough oxygen to complete the decomposition process. Various strains of bacteria infiltrated these trapped pockets, as did fungi and naturally occurring chemicals, cooking up residues rich in molecules of hydrogen and carbon. Breakdown of these molecules by high temperatures and pressure slowly transformed these substances into the hydrocarbons we call crude oil and natural gas.

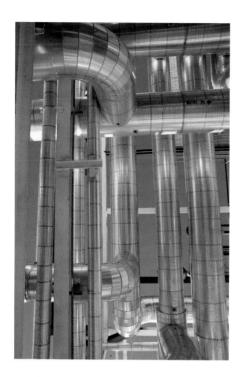

Plate 42.
Natural gas
pipelines
as art.

The hydrocarbon compounds migrate from their source rocks to permeable rocks or sediments, such as sandstone, that serve as reservoirs, where the hydrocarbons concentrate in "pools." Similar to a water aquifer, these reservoirs are not actual lakes beneath the Earth's surface. Instead, the oil or natural gas saturates the pores of these rocks. More than 90 percent of all petroleum actually escapes into the atmosphere or water, so society can only access a very small portion of the total energy stored in crude oil.

The process of creating coal seams is similar to pools of petroleum, only the organic materials gather on the surface in peat bogs where a lack of oxygen and high water tables arrested the decaying process. Bacteria, fungi, and other transformative agents also did their thing. Found sand-wiched in shale rock, coal seams can extend for hundreds of miles in uniform thickness, like a layered cake.

California's geologic history provided the ideal combination of rock types and geologic structures necessary for creating petroleum fields also rich with natural gas deposits, but coal deposits are few and far between. The "Great Valley Sequence" is what geologists call the exposed rock formations, which are described as the Santa Ynez, San Raphael, and Santa Susana Mountains on any map. The Channel Islands near Santa Barbara are part of this same system, as are the rock formations found in deep wells in the Sacramento and San Joaquin basins. Petroleum seepages can be found as far north as Humboldt County. All of these basins of petroleum (and natural gas) can be linked to fault systems and geologic shifts in geology that reshaped geography, making California what it is today and shaping our energy future.

Taken as a group, all three of these fundamental fossil fuels still dominate the world's energy picture. They have fostered tremendous strides in industrial development and accelerated and expanded human capacity to travel the globe over. Each of these broad categories of fossil fuels is described below, within the context of California's natural history, and how our energy future has been shaped by our dependence upon these energy sources.

Crude Oil

Like many other energy sources, crude oil was once thought to contain miraculous properties. The term "snake oil," for instance, refers to early efforts to peddle petroleum as a miracle cure for just about any known malady. Of course, the term "snake oil" carries a negative connotation today. Petroleum ended up being far more effective as an energy source than as a medicinal cure.

Some of the first recorded uses of petroleum include bonding the bricks in the ancient temples of Mesopotamia.

The first recorded use of crude oil in California dates back to 1769, when Gaspur de Portola's expedition came upon Chumash Indians caulking their canoes with tar collected from a nearby pool. This spot was named Carpinteria and lies on the Ventura coast. Other early southern California settlers found natural seeps of oil and tar not just in Los Angeles, but also in Santa Barbara and Orange and Kern counties, and they applied the handy lubricant to wagon wheels and farm machinery.

A great number of different types of hydrocarbons make up the substance we call petroleum. Nature is not always neat. The carbon atoms in hydrocarbon molecules can be arranged in rings or chains or other less easily defined configurations, and there may be many or a few. A molecule in asphalt may hold hundreds of carbon atoms, whereas a molecule in natural gas may have only one or two. Different boiling temperatures allow crude oil refiners to separate different products from the same raw resource. For example, gases are the lightest, and they can boil at temperatures below atmospheric conditions, while diesel fuels require temperatures of 700 degrees F to start to bubble and boil.

The first large-scale use of petroleum as an energy source in urban areas dates back to kerosene lamps in the mid-nineteenth century. Though early forms of kerosene were derived from coal, over time petroleum became the preferred feedstock. Ironically enough, gasoline—one part of crude oil—was burned off, and the heavier parts of crude oil such as asphalt were simply thrown away. Crude oil's ascent into the world's dominant source of energy began in the 1920s, as former waste products such as gasoline began to fuel our modern civilization's dependence upon the internal combustion engine for day-to-day transport (pl. 43).

California's petroleum deposits are top-notch. Good source rock for petroleum typically measures at 1 percent total organic carbon (TOC) content. Along California's coast, source rocks can measure as high as 20 percent TOC,

Plate 43. By 1917, workers at the Midway Field used both cars and mules for transportation and equipment hauling.

though 4 to 6 percent is far more common. There are more hydrocarbons per cubic inch in the Los Angeles area than in virtually any other place in the world.

While most of us may associate crude oil with the color black, it comes in a surprisingly large number of hues—yellow, green, and brown—as well as consistencies: waxy, thick, or slight and fluid. Oil found in the Gulf of Mexico and Pennsylvania is pale in color and referred to as "light, sweet crude," whereas the oil found in all of California's major basins is "heavy" crude, since it features lots of carbon atoms in its molecules; hence, it is dark, a dark near-black color. The carbon in any hydrocarbon merely serves as a carrier for hydrogen. It is also the carbon emitted into the atmosphere when petroleum is combusted that serves as the basis for concern over global climate change.

Development of Oil in California

The history of California oil development was detailed in the preceding section.

To sum up, more than a thousand oil companies were scouring California and producing roughly 12,000 barrels of oil per day by 1900. By the 1920s, California's oil production peaked at 850,000 barrels per day. The key to the rapid expansion of oil exploration activity became available when state geologists made the link between surface faults and folds above the ground and corresponding oil deposits down below.

California emerged as the world's top oil producer in the early twentieth century, if only briefly. Today, California ranks fourth in the country in terms of total oil production, behind Alaska, Texas, and Louisiana. The major technology advances for which California can claim credit are as follows:

- OFF-SHORE OIL DEVELOPMENT. California developed the first off-shore oil rigs in the world, literally building small islands off shore from Long Beach to access oil. These facilities continue to operate today, albeit at reduced levels of production.
- HYDRO-PROCESSING. Because California's crude oil is so heavy and loaded with carbon, a technology breakthrough also known as "hydro-cracking" allowed oil companies to add hydrogen in the exact right places to make hydrocarbon molecules with more energy content, creating higher-quality and cleaner fuels.
- ENHANCED THERMAL RECOVERY. The only way to access the super-thick crude oil of San Joaquin Valley was to flood oil deposits with hot steam. Three-dimensional, fiber-optic sensors can now target this steam in underground caverns to free up heavier oils that would otherwise remain inaccessible.

Though California's crude oil is "heavy" and therefore requires sophisticated cutting-edge techniques and technologies to bring it to market, the end product gasoline delivered to consumers in California is the cleanest available around the globe.

Oil Today

Oil extraction technologies continue to evolve in sophistication, reducing environmental impacts while accessing previously unrecoverable oil deposits. For example, some of the tallest structures in the world are compliant towers that dig deep down into offshore reserves. New floating production, storage, and offloading vessels are also state-of-the-art. Computer technologies are also creating "digital" oil fields where real-time sensors, monitoring, and optimization tools help increase efficiency. In the good old days, each oil well had to be inspected by humans driving around and checking to see whether everything was up to snuff. The oil fields of the future will be able to be managed by fewer people from a central computerized command center.

Despite these technological fixes, the current status of the long-term availability of oil is a topic of heated debate. Marion King Hubbert, perhaps the best-known petroleum geologist in the world, made the disturbing prediction that the world's fossil fuel period would be brief many decades ago. This was hardly a new notion, as geologists have been warning since the 1920s that the United States would run out of oil, but these dire warnings were dismissed as large oil fields were uncovered in the Persian Gulf and east Texas just a decade later.

Armed with better information over time, Hubbert went on to conclude that U.S. oil production peaked in 1970 based on a sophisticated analysis that recognized some fundamental facts: production from any oil field or province always seemed to follow a bell curve. The initial exploratory wells capture only a small amount of oil until the source is mapped out, upon which time, more and more wells are drilled and production goes up and up. Then, in the final stages, the gradual but certain drop comes in production as the wells run dry.

From Hubbert's vantage point, the fact that more oil has been found in the 1930s than any decade before or after also

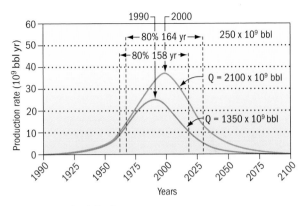

Figure 11. Hubbert's Peak.

implied that discovery of oil also formed a bell-shaped curve. His graphical presentation of our fossil fuel era is commonly referred to as "Hubbert's Peak" (fig. 11). His last prediction before he died in 1989 was that global oil production would reach its peak in 2000, but that date proved to be wrong. Yet those who have followed in Hubbert's footsteps point out that Hubbert was not far from the truth.

Though several industry experts have criticized Hubbert's vague and messy methodology, there is a growing recognition even among oil companies that fossil fuels are of finite supply and that the peak in oil production may indeed be upon us. Certainly, as time moves on, the remaining oil reserves become more expensive as drilling and production activities shift to sites that are more difficult to access and that reside in increasingly sensitive habitats.

Among Hubbert's disciples who also worked with industry heavyweights Texaco and Amoco was Colin Campbell, who published the provocative article "The End of Cheap Oil" in *Scientific American* in 1998, which concluded world oil production would start its final and permanent decline before 2010. Other oil economists insist the peak will come as late as 2030. A few other figures can help put things in perspective. As of 2007, the world had produced approximately 650 billion barrels of oil, and according to conventional math, another trillion barrels of proven reserves have yet to be developed. Optimists claim that as much as 10 trillion barrels of oil remain in the ground around the globe, though much of this additional resource requires enhanced recovery methods that are typically more expensive (but that were also pioneered in California).

The Pros and Cons of Oil

+ It is a versatile resource serving as the feedstock for a plethora of different products with a multitude of energy and nonenergy applications.
+ Massive infrastructure investments already in place reduce current exploring, refining, and delivery costs.
+ Industry employs the vast majority of today's commercial shipping tonnage.
+ Resource is distributed throughout the globe, though unevenly.
+ It provides stable revenues to many governments—Venezuela, Russia, and much of the Middle East—to fund essential government services.
+ It represents the largest item in the balance of payments and exchanges between nations.
+ Service and maintenance infrastructure is widespread and mature.
− Wealth and power are concentrated into a handful of large multinational firms.
− Resource is concentrated in countries with unstable governments or links to current terrorist activity.
− Combustion of oil products is among the prime contributors to global climate change, according to most scientists.
− End-products such as gasoline, kerosene, and diesel are toxic and flammable.

- Diesel fuel is among the dirtiest electricity fuels.
- Extraction and development can impose severe impacts on local communities and ecosystems, though modern approaches reduce these unwelcome impacts.

The Future of Oil

California was the center of the nation's most aggressive efforts to tap natural resources such as oil and natural gas during the early part of the twentieth century. Nonetheless, California is also the state that helped shut the door on further development as a dramatic cultural shift occurred after World War II. Greed and rampant and sometimes reckless exploitation gave way to conservation and a NIMBY (Not In My Back Yard) view of the world. While California oil fields rank with the most productive in the world, the state's strict environmental regulations have frustrated efforts to boost in-state production. Map 5 shows the locations of California's existing oil (and natural gas) fields.

Today, roughly 400 companies based in California are still involved with oil and natural gas exploration. They range from familiar giants—such as Chevron (a company tracing its roots back to 1879 with discoveries in Los Angeles County), Shell, and Conoco–Phillips—to small, independent firms akin to Mom-and-Pop shops. Roughly half of today's oil production in California comes from Kern County. As in the electric utility industry, several mergers of once-familiar names have occurred, but on an even grander and global scale. For example, the company known as Chevron was once part of Standard Oil, which was started up by the Rockefeller family and was broken up into thirty-four different companies by the U.S. Supreme Court in 1911 under the Sherman Antitrust Act.

Successor companies of Standard Oil, which once controlled 88 percent of U.S. oil flows, were once commonly known as the "Seven Sisters" and include familiar names such as Exxon, Mobil, BP, Shell, Gulf, Mobil, and SoCal (the latter also known as Standard Oil, and ultimately Chevron, and the

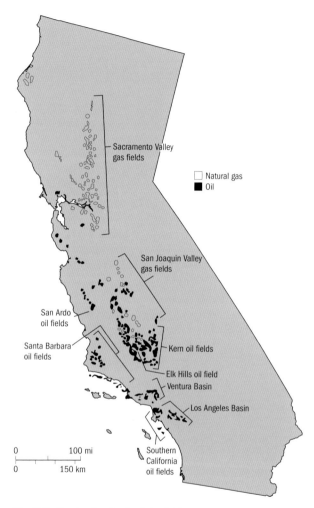

Map 5. California oil and natural gas fields.

only one of the seven to be based in California). The sequential subsuming of Gulf (1985), Texaco (2001), and then Unocal (2005) allowed Chevron of San Ramon, California, to become the second largest oil company in the world, though ExxonMobil of Irving, Texas, can still lay claim to being the largest.

In terms of hard numbers, California's oil industry peaked in 1985. Despite the ups and downs (and mostly ups) of recent oil prices, California production continues its downward slide. There are a few signs of hope. Among the new techniques designed to access sources currently unavailable in California is accessing the oil in diatomite rocks. Named after microscopic organism fossils that comprise these source rocks, they offer a unique challenge. Unlike most porous rocks, which act like a sponge since the openings are interconnected, the diatomite rocks feature individual, disconnected pores full of petroleum. Current R&D efforts are designed to unlock this resource, which is also located in the San Joaquin Valley.

Over the past few decades, Washington, DC, has been much more hospitable to the oil industry than Sacramento; however, with the sudden popularity of climate change as a rallying cry for green energy sources as well as the 2008 price explosion in which crude oil prices rose from $100 to nearly $150 a barrel in four months, oil industry heavyweights are diversifying and moving into biofuels and other lines of business involving energy.

Natural Gas

Natural gas is the generic term used for the mixture of vapors that result from the same decomposition of plant and animal materials over millions of years that creates crude oil. The primary component of natural gas is methane, a hydrocarbon that is cleaner than oil or coal when burned.

Plate 44. Natural gas pipelines and compressors.

Nevertheless, methane is 20 to 40 times more potent than carbon dioxide in contributing to the climate change conundrum. Therefore, controlling leaks and emissions into the atmosphere at natural gas wells and production facilities is a top priority (pl. 44).

Ironically enough, natural gas was vented when California's first oil fields were discovered. It was viewed as an annoying by-product by the state's early petroleum prospectors, who were much more interested in the liquid black gold they could touch directly with their fingertips.

Although natural gas is marketed as a "clean" fuel for both electricity generation and transportation alternative fuel, reserves of natural gas—as with other fossil-based fuels—are finite. Therefore, it is not considered a renewable resource. That said, the combustion of natural gas produces only a fraction of the nitrogen oxide and carbon dioxide emissions of oil and coal. Natural gas has therefore become an attractive "transition" fuel as the energy supply shifts away from heavily polluting conventional coal toward cleaner, renewable energy technologies.

The Development of Natural Gas in California

The earliest recorded use of natural gas in California dates back to 1858 and the city of Stockton. Water wells dug in the vicinity also tapped in natural gas deposits, which were then used to provide lighting at the local municipal courthouse. In 1887, pipelines were installed to bring natural gas to Stockton's residents and businesses. However, it was not until PG&E built high-pressure pipelines to transport this fuel over longer distances that a natural gas industry could take hold in California. The utility was motivated to go in this direction, because electricity had displaced their gas lighting business. Along with industrial applications, PG&E began to market natural gas as ideal for heating and cooking, applications well-suited to this versatile energy source.

Since the evolution of southern California gas utilities has already been described in the Overview, it is suffice to say that the evolution of natural gas development followed the same path as electricity: large centralized production facilities connected to customers via transmission lines. Whereas the public power movement made a significant dent into private ownership of electric utilities, the large and savvy natural gas utilities were quite successful in defeating any large-scale municipalization efforts on the natural gas side of the energy business (map 6).

Responding to widespread flaring of natural gas into the atmosphere, California and several other states began prohibiting this practice in 1911, the same year that electric utilities came under state regulation. Companies soon began viewing this "waste" as a viable energy source in its own right. As was the case with hydroelectric sites, natural gas fields were also often located in isolated spots far from customers. California entrepreneurs again rose to the occasion, developing new technologies to transport energy from where it

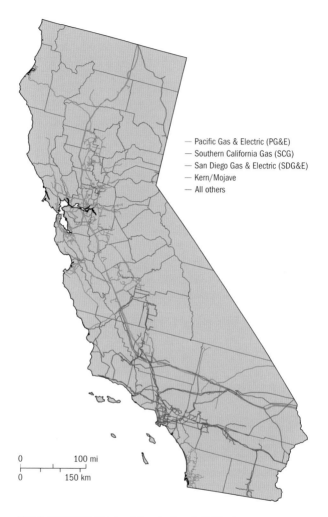

- Pacific Gas & Electric (PG&E)
- Southern California Gas (SCG)
- San Diego Gas & Electric (SDG&E)
- Kern/Mojave
- All others

0   100 mi

0   150 km

Map 6. Ownership of natural gas pipelines in California.

was generated to where it was consumed. At this point, however, supplies of natural gas still greatly exceeded demand. Then, it was discovered that natural gas could make "natural" gasoline. This was welcomed news. The state's heavy crude oil required extra processing to produce gasoline, for which demand had skyrocketed because of the growing popularity of motor vehicles.

The advent of underground storage by Shell and Union Oil in 1928 in conjunction with the Signal Hill oil field near Los Angeles made natural gas more attractive. Still, roughly a third of California's natural gas was still being flared as late as 1930. While other states and nations surpassed California on the natural gas development front in the 1930s, approximately 70 percent of California homes were using natural gas by the 1940s. In 1947, the first pipelines were built to begin importing natural gas from Texas and New Mexico to serve the California energy market.

The focus of natural gas discoveries shifted north to the Sacramento Valley in the 1950s all the way through the 1980s (pl. 45). By the beginning of the twenty-first century, California was importing over 80 percent of its natural gas from Canada and other states that now include Oklahoma, Kansas, Utah, and Colorado.

Natural Gas Today

Like other fossil fuels, natural gas can be used as a fuel in conventional steam boiler generators. However, new technologies using natural gas as their primary fuel are far more efficient than older combustion technologies. New state-of-the-art combined-cycle plants operate at efficiencies surpassing 50 percent, cutting fossil fuel use by as much as 40 percent.

Combustion turbines (CTs), or gas turbines, are jet engines modified to generate electricity. With this technology, the natural gas is burned, creating superheated gas, which is then used to drive the turbine. As the turbine spins in the

Plate 45. This natural gas–fired power plant is located in an industrial corridor in Contra Costa County near the Sacramento River Delta.

generator, electricity is produced; the turbine also drives a compressor to pressurize the incoming air. Combined cycle (CC) technology is really the coupling of two electric generation technologies, which boosts efficiency by producing power twice from the same fuel. In the first phase, natural gas is burned to heat air to drive a combustion turbine. After the heated air is used by this turbine, that air, which still retains very high temperatures, is used to heat water in a boiler. That water creates steam, which is pressurized in pipes and drives a second, electricity-generating turbine.

Natural gas can also be used in fuel cell technologies that rely upon chemical reactions to create electricity at much higher levels of efficiency than can be obtained from fossil fuel combustion. The by-products of these reactions are water, small amounts of CO_2, and electricity. Fuel cell technology is commercially available, but cost-effective applications are still quite limited in scope.

The technology to convert natural gas into electricity is quite mature. The bigger questions center on available natural gas supply. World natural gas resources are estimated to exceed 5,000 trillion cubic feet, most of which have yet to be developed. Experts forecast demand for natural gas will jump by 70 percent by 2030. It is this huge growth in demand that has California exploring new sources of natural gas, including imports of liquefied natural gas (LNG)—a technology discussed in the Challenges part of this book.

The Pros and Cons of Natural Gas

+ It is the cleanest form of fossil fuel combustion.
+ On a Btu basis, natural gas combustion generates about half as much CO_2 as coal, less particulate matter, and very little SO_2 or toxic air emissions.
+ Variety of technology formats offers good fits for round-the-clock or peak demand applications.
+ Fuel supply is abundant globally, but finite.
+ It can be installed on-site or in central power station modes.
+ When cleaner natural gas generation permanently offsets older fossil generation with high CO_2 emissions rates, natural gas fuels reduce the climate change threat.
+ Natural gas power plants do not require fuel storage space and produce no significant amounts of solid waste.
+ Small combustion turbines do not use significant quantities of water, since cooling needs are modest.
− Exploring and drilling for natural gas can damage wilderness habitat, wildlife, surface and groundwater water supplies, and public open spaces.

- Drilling operations can also release toxic substances—cadmium, lead, and benzene—as well as naturally occurring radioactive materials such as radium, radon gas, and their decay products.
- Natural gas combustion can produce nitrogen oxides (NO_x) and carbon monoxide in quantities comparable to coal burning.
- Ongoing use of natural gas inevitably results in emissions of methane, a very potent greenhouse gas contributing to climate change. (Greenhouse gases and their effects are discussed in detail in the Challenges part of this book.)
- Carbon monoxide emissions can escape from gas-fired plant stacks at rates three times that of coal plants, and this may become an issue in regions that are having trouble complying with federal, state, and local air quality standards.
- Gas-fired power plants can consume significant quantities of water, challenging aquatic life forms and ecosystems.
- Methane can be toxic, especially if it seeps into groundwater supplies.

The Future of Natural Gas

Over the last decade, natural gas prices increased dramatically. From the mid-1980s until 1999, natural gas supply prices were well below the heat equivalent of oil (and nearly equivalent to coal). Given all of the other advantages natural gas offered compared to coal, natural gas was a "no-brainer" investment—if projections on price had held true. The reason natural gas prices were so low was the so-called "gas bubble." For 15 years, North America had more gas capacity than demand, so gas-on-gas competition drove prices down. However, this bubble burst in 1998/1999, when supply fell short of demand just as the natural gas combined-cycle technology boom began (which then accelerated the gap between natural gas supply and demand).

A substantial amount of natural gas capacity was built between 1999 and 2004. This spending binge on natural gas-fired capacity is now haunting electric utilities. Eight or ten years ago, many industry experts predicted that natural gas fuel was central to the future of electricity generation. The arguments seemed sound. Natural gas was cheap, efficient, more environmentally friendly than oil or coal, and did not require large capital expenditures. This large commitment to natural gas is now becoming a burden: It is safe to say that no single company expected as much total investment in natural gas as has actually occurred. This glut of gas-fired capacity helped fuel, ironically enough, the run-up in natural gas prices.

Since oil is the logical substitute for natural gas when there is a shortage, natural gas prices then became coupled to oil prices, which also started a run-up in price, pulling natural gas along behind it. These long-term high prices are, in part, due to increase in demand both for direct consumption and for fuel for electricity production. The domestic cheap sources of natural gas have been largely tapped, and existing LNG import facilities are operating near maximum capacity.

Coal

Coal, like other fossil fuels, is a consequence of geologic time. In fact, most of the coal found in the United States dates back 300 million years ago, though some deposits are just a mere million years old. To give a sense of what happens over the course of geologic time, it is estimated that 3 to 7 feet of compacted plant matter is required to create 1 foot of the most common kinds of coal.

With a 250-year supply buried beneath the ground, the United States has more coal than any other country on the planet. Unfortunately, coal is the dirtiest of fossil fuels, and coal burning is allegedly one of the prime culprits behind today's climate change challenge.

There are four basic types of coal: lignite, subbituminous, bituminous, and anthracite. Each represents a progressively harder and more energy-intensive form of coal. Generally speaking, the higher the carbon content, the higher the amount of energy found in the coal.

Anthracite—the highest-quality coal—is quite rare and is found only in Pennsylvania. Bituminous is the most common coal found in the United States. Subbituminous is also common. Lignite—also called "brown coal"—is the youngest of the lot, has less than half of the energy content of anthracite and is found primarily in Texas and nearby states.

Though it has lower energy value than bituminous, subbituminous coal also has lower sulfur levels. This means it is cleaner burning. Roughly 90 percent of the country's coal stock falls in the category of bituminous or subbituminous coal, with the latter dominating coal sources serving California.

While coal today is primarily used for generating electricity, coal was previously used directly to heat homes and power young industries. The steel industry, for example, relied upon a coal product known as coke. Hundreds of chemicals distilled from coal in these so-called coke ovens helped create products ranging from nylons to aspirin.

One of the most fascinating aspects of coal is its profound influence on the history of the human condition. Railroads, the rise and fall of the British Empire, the 8-hour work day, and globalization can all trace their roots to this remnant of natural history. Coal mining, for example, spurred on new mechanical lifting, lighting, and ventilation techniques in order for human beings to go hundreds of feet underground to successfully access coal seams hidden beneath the Earth's formidable crust (pl. 46). The steam engine that would soon power industry and transport owes its existence to the need to suck water out of deep coal mines.

Plate 46. Coal miners in Pittsburgh pushing an empty cart in an underground mine.

Coal was then transported on wagon wheels pulled by horses on cast iron rails. Later, coal-fired steam engines would be hoisted on these same rails as locomotive engines emerged as a key transportation power option, facilitating energy growth and bicoastal trade. The coal-fed steel industry then stimulated the development of steel-hulled steamships, which began displacing wind-powered vessels and boosting volumes of trade while shortening travel times. Coal by-products paved the way for the development of the chemical industry as well as textiles and pharmaceuticals. One could argue that coal also brought to the world the concept of the factory, wage earners, and the regimentation of work schedules into the 8-hour day. Before industrialization fueled by coal, time was a notion shaped by an agrarian way of life where work was defined simply by the changing cycles of nature and the need to produce food and other basic necessities.

Coal was indeed king. The world's reliance upon this fossil fuel peaked in the early 1900s. At that point in time, coal generated more than 90 percent of the world's energy, though the United States, and particularly California, relied more heavily on wood and water for energy.

Development of Coal in California

As noted in the Overview, California lacked the coal reserves that served the rest of the nation. It was the gold miners that explored coal first in the 1850s. Despite early optimism, the simple facts were that the few decent coal deposits found in the state were of poor quality. Towns with such names as Coalinga and Carbondale reflect this early history, but in-state coal production never exceeded 30 percent of the state's total consumption. Because imports were of superior quality, even state consumers preferred importing coal rather than complicated new technologies to boost California's coal energy value here. So California's small coal industry began a steady decline in the 1880s.

The lack of in-state coal deposits also impacted the evolution of the state's electricity markets. Despite the fact that state policy makers banned in-state generation of electricity from coal decades ago, the Los Angeles Department of Water and Power (LADWP) and SCE still owned portions of the coal-fired Mohave Generating Station in Laughlin, Nevada. This coal plant has not been in operation since January 2006, as SCE struggled with the decision on whether to add modern pollution controls or to halt its coal imports. Long-simmering controversy has surrounded the power plant as well as Peabody Energy's Black Mesa mine, located on Navajo tribal lands in Arizona. The impacts these facilities and associated nearby mines had on the local tribes has been something less than reassuring. More than a billion dollars' worth of coal has been extracted over decades of time, but a host of maladies have been reported by mine workers there, including blindness, hearing loss, and shortness of breath. Primitive pollution controls and other factors have had a devastating impact not only on the health of Navajo tribes but on their culture as well, as depression and alcoholism are widespread despite the economic benefits these industrial facilities bring to these depressed, desolate parts of the United States. SCE and LADWP (which is attempting to green California's dirtiest power supply portfolio) have walked away from the Mohave facility, signaling an important shift in priorities among California utilities.

Before that closure, coal consumption had increased in California in the early twenty-first century, filling the void in electricity supply as new natural gas and renewable generation facilities were delayed by regulatory bottlenecks. Coal provided as much as 20 percent of our electricity supply—virtually all of it imported—before state regulators virtually banned new coal-fired electricity imports for private utilities in January 2007 and then did the same for municipal utilities in late May of the same year. This partial ban on all new coal-fired electricity for California has not dampened enthusiasm for coal in other states, however, which are researching coal-to-liquid and coal-to-gas technologies as well as ways to store the CO_2 emissions from coal plants in underground caverns. The only way a California utility can now import coal-fired electricity in the future is if new technologies can reduce emissions from a coal plant to those of a state-of-the-art natural gas–fired power plant (fig. 12).

Once again, California is trending in the opposite direction of much of the rest of the country but more in sync with the international community, looking beyond coal out of climate change concerns.

Coal Today

Coal-fired power plants provide roughly half of the nation's electricity. Almost four-fifths of all coal consumed in the United States is burned in power plants to generate electricity.

Given the decline in iron and steel manufacturing in the United States—and the widespread substitution of plastics for metals in growing numbers of consumer products—the prime industries still relying upon coal have been reduced to the cement, glass, paper, and food-processing industries. Only 10 percent of

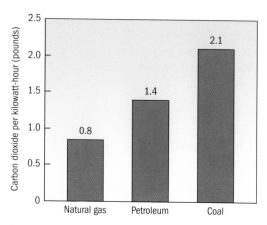

Figure 12. A comparison of carbon dioxide emissions for each major fossil fuel.

domestic coal is exported overseas, so the coal industry is looking to boost consumption here in the United States.

Generally speaking, coal costs five to six times less than the equivalent amount of natural gas. Coal is also cheaper than all renewable energy resources except older hydro projects and new state-of-the-art wind farms in the very windiest spots close to existing transmission lines. Coal consumption by the electric power industry has inched upwards by one percentage point a year beginning in 2002.

Approximately one-third of the nation's coal plants date back from 1970 and earlier; therefore, they have been exempt from many modern pollution controls. Only 12 coal plants have been built since 1990. All told, almost 100 coal plants are currently under construction, with more than 60 or so in the planning or permitting stages. Large new subsidies are helping to fuel this rebirth of the coal industry, as have high and volatile oil and natural gas prices.

The biggest threat to coal is climate change and other environmental issues. To address these obstacles to greater reliance upon coal as an electricity fuel, two key innovations are currently under development. The first are efforts to transform coal into gases or liquids and thereby siphon off some of the toxic and polluting by-products of coal combustion. The second are efforts to sequester the carbon dioxide emissions, permanently storing these emissions.

The Pros and Cons of Coal

+ The biggest plus for coal is its low and stable price. Coal can provide usable energy at a cost of between $1 and $2 per MMBtu compared to $6 to $12 MMBtu for oil and natural gas. (One Btu, or British thermal unit, is the amount of heat required to raise the temperature of one pound of water one degree Fahrenheit; one MMBtu equals one million Btu.)

+ It is a domestic fuel source and therefore contributes to energy security.

+ Improved mining and power generation technologies could extend the nation's reserves to 500 years of supply or even longer.

+ It has a fully commercialized infrastructure and global supply and technology transfer network.

+ It has widespread availability of regional supply, except in states such as California.

+ Modern pollution controls have greatly reduced emissions of sulfur dioxide—the cause of acid rain—and the fly ash that is the dark soot that once plagued communities residing near coal-fired power plants.

− It is the dirtiest of all fossil fuels, carrying major negative impacts on air quality and public health.

− Coal combustion is a prime contributor to the current global climate change threat.

− Pollution controls such as "scrubbers" for sulfur dioxide can cost $100 million a piece and add significant costs to coal plant operations.

− Health impacts and mine worker hazards are among the most severe of all energy sources.

- Impacts of mines and coal-fired power plants alike on ecosystems, wildlife, and the quality of life of nearby human populations can be severe.
- Technological fixes for carbon emissions are still in the development phase.

The Future of Coal

According to the Pew Center on Global Climate Change, reliance upon coal for electricity generation and other applications accounts for 20 percent of global greenhouse gas emissions linked to climate change. In the United States, close to two billion tons of CO_2 are released into the atmosphere annually from coal-fired power plants. At present, coal-fired power plants represent 27 percent of total U.S. CO_2 emissions, and that figure is projected to grow by more than a third by 2025!

A study published by the National Academy of Sciences links a tripling in the growth of greenhouse gas emissions to increases in coal consumption around the globe. From an environmental perspective, perhaps the largest concern over coal is its expanded use overseas in China and India. China's coal output has surpassed that of the United States in recent years, making this Asian giant the world's top source of CO_2 that feeds today's alarming climate change trends. China added enough new coal plants in 2006 to equal the entire U.S. coal plant fleet, the equivalent of almost two new coal plants per week. These facilities alone—representing 90 gigawatts—added 500 million tons of CO_2 to the atmosphere. This figure represents 5 percent of the world's total CO_2 emissions. This is the impact of just the power plants added in a single calendar year.

India's coal consumption is also of concern, as it grew from 360 million tons in 2000 to 460 million tons in 2005. Although India only consumes a fifth of the coal as does its China neighbor, the economy of India is growing at twice the rate of electricity capacity additions, which could be a harbinger of trouble down the road. At present, 68 percent of India's CO_2 emissions are a result of coal burning.

Keep in mind that each of these new coal plants are long-term investments that could lock in carbon releases into the atmosphere for decades to come. The prudent thing to do in order to secure a place for coal in tomorrow's energy economy would be invest heavily in carbon capture and storage technologies. Carbon "cap and trade" programs may also be necessary, but more on these potential solutions will be provided in the Challenges part of this book.

ALTERNATIVES

The Growth of Renewable Energy

UNLIKE FOSSIL FUELS, renewable energy sources are inexhaustible and self-regenerating fuels. While most of these resources also have been shaped by the world's natural history and ongoing natural processes, the majority can trace their origins to the sun. Solar energy, wind power, and biomass resources, which are various forms of plant matter, are all dependent upon that blazing star around which the Earth revolves. Water power also depends upon the sun, as water evaporates and then returns to the Earth in the form of rain. That is when gravity takes over and urges this liquid to flow down rivers and streams, ultimately to reach the ocean and start the whole cycle over again.

In each of these examples—solar, wind, biomass, and water power—the available energy is extraordinary. The challenge is capturing these resources, which often are most abundant in regions far from human beings, though that is not always the case. Solar energy, for example, is indeed everywhere. While these fuels are literally free of cost, the technological gizmos to convert these energy sources into electricity, hydrogen, or liquid transportation fuels require high up-front investments. It is these high capital costs, which need to be invested in the very beginning of the development process, that have made these resources less attractive to a world so preoccupied with the here and now.

Climate change, national security concerns, and other environmental and economic issues have refocused the world's attention on the renewable sources of energy that first allowed humanity to explore the world and to make life easier. From fires to keep us warm and light the night sky to sailboats that allowed ancient civilizations to trade and open their eyes to new cultures, renewable energy sources have long been critical to the advancement of society. They have also allowed contemporary global citizens to walk lighter on the planet and to democratize the energy economy, which has increasingly become captive to large and global corporations.

The first renewable energy resource to be profiled is geo-thermal energy, which actually shares more in common with fossil fuels than its other renewable brethren. Nevertheless, geothermal energy is the unsung hero in California's current efforts to move beyond fossil fuels, and it is projected to be among the top sources of new electricity in California over the next several years.

Geothermal Energy

The natural history of California, with its storied earthquake faults, created ideal conditions not only for fossil fuels such as petroleum and natural gas but also for geothermal steam. A renewable energy resource common throughout the western United States, geothermal steam can be harnessed to gener-ate electricity or to warm your home directly with a technol-ogy called a heat pump.

According to the archeological record, geothermal energy has been tapped for over 10,000 years. Native Americans relied on hot springs for cleansing, warmth, and rejuvena-tion, long before today's swank spas catered to the wealthy leisure class.

The word *geothermal* is derived from Greek terms for Earth (*geo-*) and heat (*thermos-*). Geothermal energy is literally heat from the Earth. At the Earth's core, which lies some 4,000 miles deep, temperatures can exceed 9,000 degrees F. Because of the apparently limitless heat emanating from the center of the Earth's molten core, geothermal energy is considered a renewable energy resource. Pockets of geothermal steam can be found at depths of up to 9,800 feet (3,000 meters), but they may also lie quite close to the surface.

In California, significant volcanic activity has infused the state with some of the world's best geothermal resources, dating their origins back to 20 or even 27 million years. That said, the Clear Lake volcanic region, located about 70 miles north of San

Francisco, is a mere 3 to 8 million years old; the active magma chamber is located down below the Mayacamas Mountains and creates steam when groundwater percolates down into the rock. The heat from the magma transforms this liquid into steam, which then creeps back up to the surface through faults and fractures in the overlying rock. In this region, known as "The Geysers," a permeable rock known as "greywacke" is capped by impermeable rock that traps this geothermal energy.

This colossal one-of-a-kind geothermal steam field spans 30 square miles and straddles the border of Sonoma and Lake Counties. Today, the more than 350 wells generate roughly 1,000 megawatts (pl. 47). That represents the equivalent of a large nuclear reactor or the necessary electricity to power all of San Francisco. Because the capital costs of these facilities have been paid off long ago, this geothermal power house is among the lowest-cost electricity sources operating in California today.

Development of Geothermal Energy in California

The first time electricity was generated from this renewable resource in California was in 1921, when operators at a spa in The Geysers flipped the switch on the nation's first

Plate 47. The Geysers Geothermal power plant, the oldest and largest in the world, straddles Lake and Sonoma Counties.

geothermal power plant. The small 250-kilowatt generator provided on-site electricity for the buildings and streets of this resort.

PG&E began experimenting with this mysterious subterrestrial power source as early as 1950, but the geothermal industry really picked up momentum with discoveries down south. The Kent Imperial Company of Grand Rapids, Michigan, showed up at the Sinclair Ranch in southeastern California in 1957. They had one thing in mind: oil. The well they drilled instead found "only" an enormous basin of volcanically heated water. This discovery of the Salton Sea geothermal field—yet another active volcanic system found within the state's borders—legitimized a whole new industry in California. As time would tell, geothermal resources could also be found in the far north of California as well as down through the central Sierra Nevada. Map 7 shows the known geothermal areas in California.

As noted in the Overview part of this book, geothermal development in California came into its own during the 1980s, with the majority of new development in southern California. Arguments for renewable energy often focus on environmental benefits, but the geothermal capacity operating in Imperial County can make the pure economic claim to have historically contributed roughly a quarter of the county's total tax base, and that percentage is expected to grow in the coming years. Geothermal developer Cal Energy, a subsidiary of MidAmerican Energy Holdings, is Imperial County's single largest private employer, showing how indigenous renewable resources bolster local rural economies.

California still leads the nation in geothermal electricity production with approximately 1,870 megawatts online in 2006. Although commercial geothermal development traces way back, preceding the commercial development of California's other renewable resources by decades, progress stagnated in the mid-1990s. Capacity has actually declined significantly from a peak of 2,686 megawatts in 1989.

Map 7. Known geothermal areas in California.

Some power plants have been retired. Nevertheless, the prime reason for capacity reductions has been the diminishing steam flow at The Geysers. Declining steam levels have been partially arrested through construction of underground pipelines from Lake County and Santa Rosa carrying reclaimed water to recharge the geothermal reservoirs. Upgrades are in the works for some plants at The Geysers, but most new geothermal power plant capacity in California will be using the more common hot water reservoirs in other parts of the state.

Geothermal Energy Today

Today, geothermal power plants are a fully mature, commercialized electricity generation technology. Without subsidies, geothermal power plants can generate electricity at costs averaging 8.5 cents per kilowatt hour, depending upon the particular technology employed and the quality of the steam field. That price estimate reflects a 25 to 35 percent cost increase in recent years, largely due to increasing costs for steel and other metals.

Luckily, California, as well as much of the western United States, is blessed with a variety of excellent geothermal

---

GEOTHERMAL HEAT PUMPS

Perhaps the least utilized form of geothermal energy is the ground source heat pump, a technology that relies upon the heat lying in the Earth to heat your home without conversion to electricity.

Typically, such a system relies upon two closed-loop pipe systems. Each system carries liquids—a mixture of water and glycol, similar to the coolant in a car engine—that are heated and cooled as the liquids flow through a series of heat exchangers and compressors. A circulation pump continuously drives the liquid through tubes in the ground. Once the solution comes back up from the ground, it is heated naturally.

The ground loop sends coolant down 200 to 300 feet into the Earth, where it is warmed up to roughly 60 degrees as it absorbs the Earth's natural geothermal heat. This liquid then passes through a heat exchanger to pass its heat on to a closed-loop system that contains a refrigerant that can boil at a temperature lower than water. The refrigerant is a cooled gas that does not mix with the liquids being sent back below. Instead, it goes to a compressor, which transforms the gas into a liquid, further increasing its temperature. Meanwhile, the liquid heads back down into the Earth to be heated again, and these loops repeat themselves over and over again (fig. 13A).

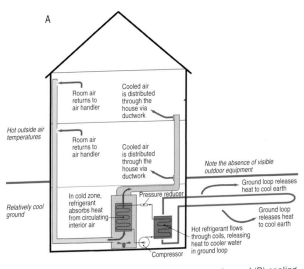

Figure 13. Geothermal heat pumps providing (A) heating and (B) cooling services.

These heat pumps work best when there are wide temperature swings, which is not always the case in California, thereby limiting widespread applications. Advocates point out that since every kilowatt hour of electricity used for pumping and compression in the process generates more than three times as much heat as it would in a conventional heating system, these geothermal heat pumps are highly efficient and should be more widely incorporated into new homes. The primary obstacle to more widespread reliance on heat pumps is drilling costs, which can reach as high as $15,000. Heat pump advocates are lobbying to change state laws requiring special licenses for drillers. While much of the state features mild temperature swings that might not justify the expense of a heat pump, in regions such as the Central Valley—where temperatures swing wildly between summer and winter—heat pumps might make sense, because they can also provide cooling services (fig. 13B).

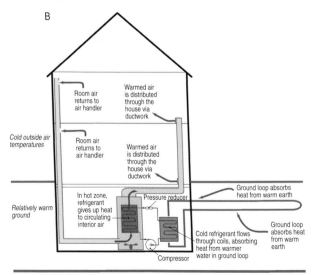

B

Cold outside air temperatures

Room air returns to air handler

Warmed air is distributed through the house via ductwork

Room air returns to air handler

Warmed air is distributed through the house via ductwork

Relatively warm ground

In hot zone, refrigerant gives up heat to circulating interior air

Pressure reducer

Ground loop absorbs heat from warm earth

Ground loop absorbs heat from warm earth

Cold refrigerant flows through coils, absorbing heat from warmer water in ground loop

Compressor

resource fields. Although wind power is often touted as the cheapest current renewable energy resource, geothermal power typically comes in second. Unlike wind, however, geothermal power plants can produce power on a consistent round-the-clock basis and can be turned on quickly to respond to changing market demand conditions, making them extremely valuable in the bigger scheme of things.

At present, geothermal steam is the largest single renewable fuel in the state's supply portfolio, providing nearly 5 percent of the state's total electricity supply. (The large-scale hydro facilities that make a large portion of PG&E's supply—approximately 20 percent—are not considered "renewable" under California's legal definition of "renewable" resources.)

The Pros and Cons of Geothermal Energy

+ A renewable energy source, it is geographically dispersed throughout California.
+ It can operate at over 90 percent of the time, making it an ideal direct replacement for fossil steam power plants.
+ Emissions from stacks are primarily water vapor, with only trace elements of toxics that plague fossil facilities.
+ New technologies can access lower temperature fuels.
+ Generally speaking, it does not require large amounts of imported water for cooling.
+ It provides well-paying jobs in typically rural depressed areas.
− Resources may be located in scenic/protected wilderness sites.
− Drilling and well infrastructure construction impact the local ecosystems, and these are costly endeavors.
− Available remaining steam wells could require more costly extraction and electricity conversion technologies.
− Groundwater contamination has happened in rare instances in the past.

– Transmission costs are often high because of remote steam field locations.

The Future of Geothermal Energy

Over twenty countries around the world derive some portion of their electricity from geothermal steam. The Philippines— located within the so-called ancient volcanic "Ring of Fire," which rims the Pacific Ocean—obtains more than a quarter of its total electricity from this renewable energy source. The United States is the world leader in geothermal electricity generation in terms of total capacity, with approximately 2,800 megawatts currently online. By generating some 15 billion kilowatt hours annually, these facilities displace the equivalent of 9 million barrels of oil or 2.5 million short tons of coal.

The U.S. Geological Survey estimated that 95,000 to 150,000 megawatts of total domestic geothermal electrical capacity is available throughout the nation. Much of this potential will never be realized, of course. The Western Governors' Association expects that 13,000 megawatts of new geothermal power will come online throughout the west over the next two decades. If federal production tax credits for geothermal are sustained, over 5,000 megawatts of new geothermal power are expected over the next five years, a large portion in California.

The technical geothermal capacity opportunity for expansion of all three kinds of geothermal capacity in the state is about 2,862 megawatts, with the vast majority of this new capacity coming in the form of dual flash power plants in the Imperial Valley. The Salton Sea geothermal resource area alone offers as much as 2,000 megawatts of potential new and clean energy.

Geothermal electricity generation is anticipated to play a major role in providing bulk energy to the grid under California Renewable Portfolio Standard (RPS), the law requiring California to derive 20 percent of its electricity from renewable resources by 2010. Because of this advantage, geothermal steam may provide the majority of California's future renewable supply over the next five years.

Solar Energy

It was the Greeks who first systemically viewed the light and heat poured out, seemingly endlessly, from this enormous fusion reactor we call the sun as a source of energy that could be managed and exploited by humanity.

The first written account of harnessing the power of the sun dates back to the fourth century BC, when a scarcity of wood prompted Greece to seek alternatives to importing timber from the Middle East. A short time thereafter, the great philosopher and inventor Socrates laid out the fundamental principles of what is now called "solar passive design," the practice of designing buildings to take advantage of heating and cooling caused by the daily and seasonal patterns of the sun's orbits (fig. 14). Entire Greek cities were planned and designed according to these basic guidelines as early as 400 BC.

It was the Romans who greatly expanded uses of solar energy, but not until after Archimedes of Greece used solar

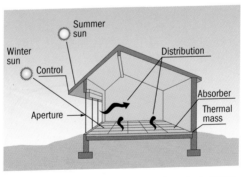

Figure 14. Key design elements in passive solar buildings.

energy as a weapon against Rome in 212 BC. According to legends, Greek soldiers allegedly helped destroy the Roman Navy by reflecting sunlight off of their shields to burn the sails of Roman ships.

Solar technologies received a major boost from the famous inventor Leonardo da Vinci in the 1500s, when he conceived a parabolic mirror that concentrated solar energy for clothes dyes. Two hundred years later, Antoine Lavoisier constructed a solar furnace that could reach high enough temperatures—3,236 degrees F—to melt platinum. Later in the eighteenth century, Horace de Saussure invented the first flat-plate solar collector, a little box with several glass tops that captured enough solar energy to boil liquids. The first electricity generators relying upon turbines driven by solar-heated steam were pioneered in Egypt in 1912.

The discovery of solar photovoltaic (PV) systems harks back to the efforts to link Europe and the United States by way of the telegraph. Selenium was being used as a testing device, and telegraph company representatives discovered that when sunlight hit selenium, conductivity went haywire. In 1876, researchers verified that an electric current could be produced when sunlight interacted with selenium. Henri Becquerel is credited with discovering the so-called "photovoltaic effect," the production of electricity directly from sunlight. Selenium cells produced weak currents that were not originally used for power but for such purposes as indicating light levels for photographers and detecting motion across a light beam in security systems.

Modern PV technology was developed initially for the space program over 50 years ago and relies on silicon transistors. Because these solar transistors were so expensive, it took the emergence of the satellite industry in the 1950s to create a demand for such wireless electricity generators to find a cost-effective application. To operate satellites, the space industry needed remote power sources that did not require copious quantities of stored fuel. Solar PV panels filled a

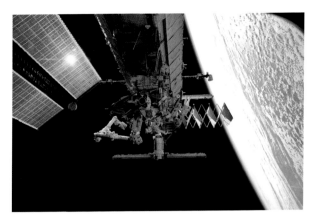

Plate 48. From Vanguard 1 to the International Space Station (shown here), Solar PV panels have been used to provide power in outer space for fifty years.

unique, but quite specialized and very limited, market niche (pl. 48), beginning with the second U.S. satellite, Vanguard 1, launched in 1958.

Rather than converting heat and mechanical energy into electricity as traditional power plants do, PV technologies rely upon chemical reactions to generate electricity. When sunlight strikes the semiconductor, chemical reactions occur between the materials in the PV cell, releasing electrons and creating an electric current. The small amount of current from each individual PV cell migrates along wires connecting the cells. When aggregated, the current generated by the PV cells produces enough electricity to power a small home or business. This power can also be fed into the existing electricity transmission and distribution grid.

The Development of Solar Energy in California

Although solar PV panels are probably the sexiest and most popular solar products on the market today, California's early energy history was dominated by other, simpler technologies, solar hot water heaters among them.

Over time, the flat-plate design by Saussure was improved by placing tanks of water inside the glass enclosures (which were also painted black, so they would absorb more heat). First-generation solar hot water heaters became big hits—first in southern California at the end of the nineteenth century and then later in Florida early in the twentieth century. Relying upon the sun to heat water was common practice in the southwestern United States as far back as the late 1800s. At one point, almost a quarter of the residents of Los Angeles relied upon the sun to heat their water with rooftop solar thermal systems.

It was a Californian by the name of William J. Bailey who devised the basic architecture of many of today's typical solar hot water heaters. The primary problem with the first-generation systems was that the water in the tank would cool down at night, releasing the heat stored up during the day. Bailey simply separated the heating from the storage functions. He also narrowed the pipes of water to be heated, which resulted in a much quicker heat-up rate. Modern solar thermal systems are used to heat water for residences, swimming pools, and commercial enterprises.

It was a company from Israel that helped make solar thermal electric power a commercial reality in California. LUZ International was formed in 1980 by Israeli scientists, and their first power plant was completed in the Mojave Desert in 1985. Although LUZ went bankrupt in 1992, its solar-thermal electricity-generating facilities continue to operate and represent the largest solar generation plant in the world. Eight different facilities total over 350 megawatts, enough electricity for an entire city. Key members of this firm reentered the market under a new name, BrightSource Energy. In the summer of 2007, they announced the development of an even larger solar farm project in the Mojave Desert that will feature a new "Power Tower" design. Dubbed "Solel-MSP-1," the project will, ironically enough, take advantage of transmission infrastructure once employed by the Mojave coal plant, which was shut down as a result of California's new climate change policies and lingering concerns over public health impacts.

Concentrated solar power (CSP) plants—the preferred contemporary term for solar thermal electric facilities—require higher concentrations of sunlight, since they can generate electricity only from direct-beam radiation (pl. 49). (Solar PV panels, on the other hand, can be installed virtually anywhere because they produce electricity from direct, scattered, and reflected rays of sunlight.) Since the most efforts to promote solar energy today focus on solar PV, the majority of this solar section will address this technology, one of the world's fastest-growing power sources.

One of the few bright spots to emerge from California's radical experiment with so-called deregulation on the power supply front was the emergence of

Plate 49. The world's largest solar power complex relies on parabolic trough technology and is located in the Mojave Desert near Barstow.

a vibrant solar PV market. When consumers were no longer allowed to choose "green power" because of the collapse of the wholesale market and the state's two major private utilities toying with bankruptcy in 2000–2001, the only option for Californians looking to lessen their environmental impact was small, on-site distributed generation sources such as solar PV. The fact that the California Energy Commission paid for half of the upfront costs through a popular rebate program helped, as did the skyrocketing wholesale energy prices. From that point forward, momentum kept building to make California the center of the U.S. effort to reduce costs of solar PV and incorporate these microelectricity generators into an overall energy plan tilted toward renewable energy supplies.

Solar Energy Today

The price of various solar energy technologies varies immensely, with solar PV still ranking as the most expensive power source: costs range from 27 to 40 cents per kilowatt hour. CSP technologies vary considerably too, but they hover closer to 7 to 11 cents per kilowatt hour.

Solar technology costs have declined substantially. Solar PV costs, for example, are only about one-twentieth what they were 20 years ago. The demand for PV has risen rapidly, however, and because of silicon shortages and corresponding lags in production, prices climbed up despite (or perhaps in response to) aggressive subsidy programs. After reaching a low point of $2.70 per watt in 2004, solar PV prices rose to $4.00 per watt in early 2006. In 2007, prices fell just below this benchmark and are projected to fall to roughly $2.00 per watt by 2010.

Although it is growing at a pace of 30 to 50 percent every year, solar energy is just a drop in the bucket when it comes to our global energy supply. In 2006, solar PV produced 0.04 percent of the world's electricity, according to the International Energy Agency. All told, the cumulative solar PV production has grown to 12,400 megawatts, enough electricity to power 2.4 million U.S. homes.

Despite its relatively small contribution to the global energy economy, solar PV is the fastest growing power source in the world. California is now the technology's leading mover and shaker. At present, over 336 megawatts of solar PV have been installed in the Golden State, and that number will no doubt grow by leaps and bounds in the coming years. Worldwide manufacturing capacity has grown from just 300 megawatts of solar panels per year to 3,800 megawatts in 2007. Revenues for the solar industry reached $15.6 billion in 2006. According to Clean Edge, these numbers could grow to $69.3 billion by 2016.

All solar power generation technologies share many important qualities that will make them increasingly attractive over time. They can generate electricity far away from electric distribution lines or fuel supply sources (examples include solar-powered water pumps on ranches or remote buildings located in wilderness areas). They can also be installed as very small power supplies where local conventional grid connections are inconvenient or expensive (PV-powered roadside communication systems are a great example of this kind of application).

Solar electric technologies produce no air or water pollution. These modular power sources can also be viewed as a strategic on-site response to global climate change by individual residences, businesses, or governments (pl. 50). The sun drives demand up in California; with solar PV the sun can then drive supply up as well. It is often the least costly substitute for other generation methods when electricity is needed in areas without access to the bulk power grid, which represents huge residential and small business populations worldwide.

Solar PV systems remain among the most expensive power supply options and, generally speaking, produce power the least amount of time on any single day of any of our current supply choices. Intermittency has been the prime objection

Plate 50. Large-scale commercial solar PV system at the Richmond, Virginia, campus of Berlex, a unit of German drugmaker Schering AG.

to all forms of solar energy. That said, variability in solar radiation is far more predictable than in other intermittent renewable resources such as wind power, which can be available at unpredictable times at night and day.

In fact, solar PV generates reliable electricity often when we need it most: during summer peaks in demand, when consumers crank up their air conditioners. The U.S. Department of Energy's (DOE) National Renewable Energy Laboratory underscored the benefit of installing solar PV. Seven major outages were analyzed from the perspective of the solar resource's quality during the exact times of power blackouts. Not surprisingly, in all but one of the outages, conditions for optimal solar electricity generation were above 90 percent.

This makes inherent sense. It is typically sunny days that lead to heat waves that stress our electricity delivery infrastructure. Why not rely on the same sun that helped create the crisis to solve the power supply problem? Interestingly, solar conditions were close to perfect (99 percent) for generating electricity from the sun on June 14, 2000, the day 100,000 customers in San Francisco lost power.

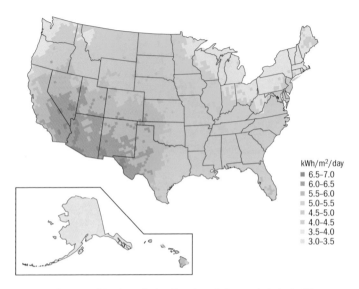

kWh/m²/day
- ■ 6.5-7.0
- ■ 6.0-6.5
- ■ 5.5-6.0
- 5.0-5.5
- ■ 4.5-5.0
- ■ 4.0-4.5
- 3.5-4.0
- 3.0-3.5

Map 8. Annual PV solar radiation (flat plate, facing south, latitude tilt) available for power generation throughout the United States.

The Pros and Cons of Solar Energy

+ It is easy to install.
+ There are no moving parts.
+ There are no operating or maintenance costs.
+ It does not require fuel delivery support.
+ Modular technology allows for flexibility in design and expansion.
+ There is a small environmental footprint when installed as an on-site distributed generator.
+ Site restoration is less complicated and less costly than with any other power source.
– It has the highest cost of all electricity generation options, including other renewable choices (even with government subsidy programs).

OTHER FORMS OF SOLAR ENERGY

Some of the most logical applications for solar energy have nothing to do with electricity. The intense energy of the sun has long been used to heat liquids and warm buildings. As far back as the late 1800s, relying upon the sun to heat water was common practice in southern California. Photos can be found showing pioneer families proudly showing off new homes equipped with solar water heaters. At one point, almost a quarter of the residents of Los Angeles relied upon the sun to heat their water with rooftop solar thermal systems. Modern solar thermal systems are used for heating water for residences, swimming pools, and commercial enterprises. Today's solar thermal heating systems are often competitive with traditional natural gas heating. Solar thermal technologies actually deliver almost the same amount of energy globally—70,000 megawatts—as wind power did in 2007.

An even simpler use of solar energy is the concept of "solar passive design." This method of capturing solar energy is really more a matter of architecture than dynamic technological devices. Dating back to ancient Rome, and more fully developed in Europe in the eighteenth century, solar passive design concepts rely upon glass windows and closed rooms to provide heat and light.

Both of these forms of solar energy are the most cost-effective ways of harnessing the immense energy of the sun. In addition, solar thermal systems can be sited and installed in a very short period of time, obviating the need for upgrades to existing natural gas pipeline and storage facilities. Whereas passive solar design requires up-front planning before the construction of residences or commercial buildings, solar hot water systems can be added on later.

Among the prime benefits of both of these solar technologies is reducing emissions of air pollution associated with natural gas heating systems. Given record high prices for natural gas over the past few years, these price savings add up to a major boon to California's economy.

- If configured as a "central station" system, it has a very large environmental footprint.
- There is minor exposure to hazardous materials in PV manufacturing cells.
- The efficiency in converting sunlight directly into electricity is low. The highest PV cell efficiencies are approximately 35 percent, but the vast majority of PV modules installed in a commercial setting report efficiencies ranging from 6 to 19 percent.

The Future of Solar Energy

The enormous quantity of solar energy reaching Earth far exceeds what the United States—or even the world—could consume for electricity, heat, and light. Did you know that all of the nation's electricity needs could be met from the solar energy striking a relatively small area of U.S. land—100 square miles in an extremely sunny region in California, Nevada, or Arizona—if that energy could be efficiently and economically converted into electricity?

Contrary to popular conception, solar energy is widely available in all parts of the continental United States, including the northeast. The amount of available sunlight in the contiguous United States varies by only 25 percent (map 8), a fact that renders solar PV technologies as a viable alternative almost anywhere in the country.

Optimists hope for the emergence of some "disruptive technology" in the solar PV sector that suddenly makes solar affordable for the majority of consumers. Most solar industry experts do not see that happening, but there is evidence pointing to parallel growth in the "thin-film" sector, a solar option that some insist is the wave of the future. The silicon shortage is driving investor interest in these emerging amorphous thin-film solar and so-called "organic" dye solar PV technologies. Theoretically, these technologies should cost less, because less silicon material is employed. The trade-off is that they are also therefore less efficient in converting sunlight into electricity.

By integrating nanotechnology into production processes, these high production costs can be reduced, rendering thin-film solar PV technologies as a more affordable solar energy option. The key for these products is the integration into roofing and other building-integrated applications.

In spite of the fact that solar consistently ranks as the top power supply choice by consumers, the DOE projects that even as late as 2030, solar technologies will only be supplying 2 or 3 percent of the nation's total energy supply.

The nations most aggressively promoting solar energy are Japan and Germany. Polls conducted by the Public Policy Institute of California and the Charleston Research Company in 2004 showed over 80 percent of Californians supported a campaign pledge by Governor Schwarzenegger to have half of all new homes equipped with solar panels beginning in 2005. While the Schwarzenegger administration did not follow through on that bold proposal, a comprehensive state solar program was put in place in 2006. Ratepayers in California (already the nation's largest solar PV market) will invest $3 billion over 11 years to add 3,000 megawatts of solar energy technologies to its grid by 2016, the year that optimists claim solar PV will no longer need large public subsidies.

In California, there has been a surprising resurgence of interest in CSP technologies too (map 9). Each of the state's major private utilities has entered into contracts for new CSP

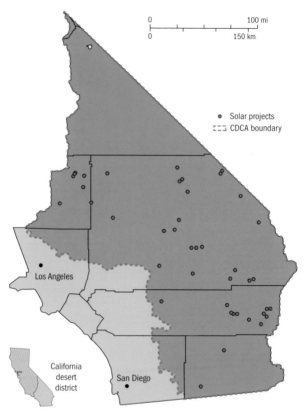

Map 9. Concentrated Solar Power (CSP) technology projects are proposed throughout the California Desert Conservation Area.

technologies, though many experts are skeptical that all of these projects will materialize any time soon. Both SCE and SDG&E have signed contracts for Stirling solar dish technologies (pl. 51) that could total 500–850 megawatts and 300–900 megawatts. A Stirling solar dish keeps sunlight focused on a working fluid that drives a generator using a combustionless piston engine. However, as of summer of 2007, the company

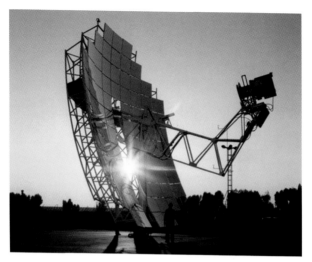

Plate 51. Stirling solar dish technology could finally enter commercial production in California.

promoting this technology had failed to line up financing and had yet to validate the commercial viability of this nascent form of solar energy. PG&E is going with a different CSP technology—the mini-power towers of BrightSource—and has committed to well over 500 megawatts. According to Solar Millennium LLC, another CSP developer with ties to LUZ, 2,000 megawatts of CSP are expected to come online in California by 2010, and another 8,000 megawatts by 2020. All told, if all of the currently proposed CSP capacity were to come online, California would become the clear world leader on solar thermal electric technologies.

Wind Power

The wind is a form of solar energy. The uneven heating of the Earth's surface by the sun results in air movements as the atmosphere engages in a continual effort to reach equilibrium. The tilt of the Earth, its daily rotation around the sun, large bodies of water, and geographic contours of landscapes each contribute to creating regions of the planet where winds blow frequently enough to be harnessed as fuel.

The wind has been tapped as a source of mechanical power for centuries. Yet its variability and potentially destructive nature have, until recently, hampered any modern comprehensive long-term program to convert this free and abundant fuel into a major source of electricity. The winds blowing on just 6 percent of the nation's windiest land sites (excluding Hawaii and Alaska) could theoretically supply one-and-half times the entire United States' electricity needs. Yet today, wind supplies roughly 1 percent of the nation's total electricity and roughly 1 percent of California's current electric supply.

Wind carries kinetic energy. When captured by the spinning blades of a wind turbine, the wind's kinetic energy is transferred to the rotor, which turns a shaft attached to a transmission, which then turns an electricity generator.

The Middle East, which is best known today for its role in providing global oil supplies, was also the setting for the earliest windmills. Located on the border of Iran and Afghanistan, these crude vertical-axis mills looked like merry go-rounds (pl. 52). Windmills then spread to China before making their dramatic arrival in medieval Europe, where historians have credited the windmill with everything from the birth of capitalism to a new world view of nature as a vast cosmological reservoir of forces that could be put to work to meet human needs and desires.

Between the fourteenth and nineteenth centuries, wind provided as much as a quarter of Europe's total energy needs. Until the industrial revolution, windmills ranked second only to wood fuel as a source of power.

Plate 52. Ancient windmill in Afghanistan.

It was during the latter half of the nineteenth century that America became the center of windmill technology advances. Smaller, lighter designs for water pumping began to pop up in the Midwest, the Great Plains, and, ultimately, California, providing roughly a quarter of America's nontransportation energy (table 2). By the early twentieth century, a few off-the-grid farmers began tinkering with these windmills by installing simple automobile generators, producing direct current (DC). Marcellus Jacobs was the most famous and successful of these early pioneers. He established the basic architecture of the American small wind turbine between 1920 and 1960. His small 1- and 2-kilowatt wind turbines featured a horizontal three-bladed rotor, a term referring to the blades connected to a central hub, looking similar to a helicopter rotor stood up on its side, facing into the wind. In the wind industry, this is referred to as an "upwind" rotor.

The first grid-connected wind turbine in the United States to sell electricity to a utility monopoly was erected in 1941

TABLE 2 Estimated California Windmill Power, 1855–1950

Year	Total Windmills	Output
		(thousand HP hours per year)
1855	200	100
1860	1,000	500
1865	2,520	1,260
1870	2,847	1,424
1875	4,350	2,175
1880	7,187	3,594
1885	11,000	5,500
1890	13,246	6,623
1895	18,600	9,300
1900	21,763	10,882
1905	28,000	14,000
1910	30,869	15,435
1915	41,200	20,600
1920	47,068	23,534
1925	47,743	23,876
1930	40,703	20,352
1935	30,072	15,036
1940	19,899	9,950
1945	13,891	6,946
1950	6,858	3,429

Source: Williams 1997:368.

on Grandpa's Knob in Vermont. The machine was immense. Designed and built by leading engineers and scientists from Massachusetts Institute of Technology (MIT) and GE, the Smith–Putnam wind turbine was over 1,000 times larger than the original Jacobs wind turbines. The wind turbine, which featured a rotor 140 feet wide that faced downwind, operated until February 1943, when a main bearing broke. Two years later, after refinements and installation of new parts, the machine started up again. However, a 120-mph wind broke a blade in March 1945, and the machine never was started up again.

The next surge in interest in wind power in the United States occurred after the energy crisis of 1973. Between 1974 and 1990, U.S. taxpayers invested $450 million in R&D funding through the DOE effort to develop a 1-megawatt or bigger wind turbine (about the same size as the Smith–Putnam machine) that would appeal to utility monopolies. Not one commercially viable machine emerged from the federal government's forays into developing a wind turbine based on sophisticated aerospace engineering science. Meanwhile, Danish taxpayers invested about $52 million during that same time period, most of which helped develop much smaller-scale machines that could be used to supply power to rural farms and villages.

The Development of Wind Power in California

California's natural history, with its sharp signatures on the land, played a fundamental role in setting the stage for wind power development. Most wind resource regions in California are located in narrow passes between coastal mountain ranges. Cool winds off the Pacific Ocean flow through these passes like "rivers of air" toward hot inland valleys and desert areas (map 10).

At the peak of the state's global leadership on renewable energy technologies in the mid-1980s, California once had 90 percent of global wind power capacity. State wind power development has been concentrated in four primary wind resource regions: the Altamont Pass (582 megawatts), Tehachapi (620 megawatts), San Gorgonio (355 megawatts), and the Montezuma Hills (500 megawatts).

California does not possess extraordinary wind resources. In fact, it is ranked 17th in the nation, sandwiched between Illinois and Wisconsin (table 3). The reason California was such a leader on wind was its pioneering public policies,

Legend:
● Wind Farm Locations

Wind Resource Areas
□ 11 to 14 MPH
■ Above 14 MPH

Byron
Livermore
Tracy
Hollister

Tehachapi
Frazier Park
Mojave
Lancaster
Newberry Springs
North Palm Springs
San Gorgonio Pass
Desert Hot Springs
White Water
Palm Springs
San Diego

0   100 mi
0   150 km

Map 10. California wind resources, based upon annual wind speeds at the elevation of 70 meters.

TABLE 3 Top 20 States for Wind Energy Potential

Rank	State	Wind Energy Potential
		billion kWh/yr[a]
1	North Dakota	1,210
2	Texas	1,190
3	Kansas	1,070
4	South Dakota	1,030
5	Montana	1,020
6	Nebraska	888
7	Wyoming	747
8	Oklahoma	725
9	Minnesota	657
10	Iowa	551
11	Colorado	481
12	New Mexico	435
13	Idaho	73
14	Michigan	65
15	New York	62
16	Illinois	61
17	California	59
18	Wisconsin	58
19	Maine	56
20	Missouri	52

Source: An Assessment of the Available Windy Land Area and Wind Energy Potential in the Contiguous United States, Pacific Northwest Laboratory, 1991.

[a]Factoring in environmental and land use exclusions for wind class of 3 and higher.

entrepreneurial culture, and legacy as a place where new energy technologies were embraced with unparalleled enthusiasm.

Much of the history of California's wind power development during the 1980s was chronicled in the first section of this book. California's wind power history can be divided into four distinct periods. The early 1980s was a time of raw experimentation fueled by the generous federal and state tax credits with turbines ranging from 25 kilowatts to 120 kilowatts in size. In the late 1980s and early 1990s, more wind turbines were erected, and turbines grew in size to 200 to 300 kilowatts. In the late 1990s, older turbines began to be changed out with turbines in the 600- to 800-kilowatt range.

After each of these cycles, the recently installed turbines experienced mechanical breakdowns. In response, the owners and operators worked to develop solutions to the problems to ensure the turbines were available to generate electricity over 95 percent of the time. The fourth period of wind power development in California is the present moment. Wind turbine technology has matured, and machines have grown to as large as 5 megawatts a piece. Yet regulatory bottlenecks and lack of adequate transmission are thwarting development despite California state policies such as the Renewable Portfolio Standard. This law requires California to boost overall renewable energy production up to 20 percent by 2010.

Ironically, Denmark and the rest of Europe benefited more than anyone else from California's aggressive pro-wind policies in the 1980s. Today, 90 percent of the world's wind turbine manufacturers are based in Europe, with Denmark remaining the world's dominant supplier of wind turbines.

To learn more about California's early wind power history, please see my book *Reaping The Wind: How Mechanical Wizards, Visionaries and Profiteers Helped Shape Our Energy Future* (Asmus 2001).

California lost its long-standing national wind power lead to Texas in 2006. As of the end of 2006, California's 2,323 megawatts of wind power represented approximately 3 percent of the global market, which now exceeds 74,223 megawatts, with Germany (20,261 megawatts) and Spain (11,615 megawatts) now ahead of the United States (11,603 megawatts). Denmark, nevertheless, generates more than 20 percent of its total electricity from wind power, the highest percentage of any country in the world, and that percentage is quietly climbing to 25 percent over the next several years.

Wind Power Today

Wind power is the lowest-cost renewable energy source currently available; the cost of electricity generated at individual wind projects can range from 4 to 8 cents per kilowatt hour depending, in large part, on the nature of the wind resource. In proceedings in key states such as Texas, Colorado, and Minnesota, regulators declared wind to be the lowest-cost electricity source, given the recent volatility of natural gas prices just after the turn of the last century.

Nevertheless, the transmission expense involved with bringing wind-generated electricity to urban centers of high energy demand adds a layer of cost that often prevents wind power from truly competing with fossil fuels on a broad basis. Ironically enough, wind power costs have gone up over the past few years because of a turbine supply shortage due to skyrocketing demand for this climate-friendly power source.

Today's state-of-the-art wind power generator is a "variable-speed" turbine, which can generate electricity from a wider range of wind speeds than the constant-speed rotor, which dominated early California wind farms. With variable-speed technology, the rotor of the wind turbine can speed up or slow down to optimize power production. In the past, constant-speed wind turbines had to be turned on and off if the wind blew too hard or too little, the rotor rarely turning at the precise speed that provided the maximum amount of electricity. Variable-speed technology can boost power production by 4 to 6 percent, an increase that can represent the entire profit from a major wind farm.

Although variable-speed technology was originally developed by Enercon of Germany and Kenetech in the United States, the majority of new wind turbines feature some form of this important innovation.

Keep in mind that a rotor cannot extract all of the kinetic energy contained in winds. The best theoretical conversion efficiency of this renewable energy resource into electricity is 59 percent; most state-of-the-art wind turbines operating today convert 35 to 40 percent of the kinetic energy in wind into electricity. The other thing to keep in mind is that the nature of a wind resource can determine which type of turbine design would be most cost effective. Some wind turbines work better in a wind regime that is smooth, whereas others can better address wind turbulence.

Wind turbines on the market today look virtually identical: three-bladed machines that face into the wind, the same architecture that the Danes put forward over 25 years ago (pl. 53). The fundamental design of wind turbines has been standardized, though new vertical axis and two-bladed downwind machines are still being developed by entrepreneurs seeking a major breakthrough. There is even a new design of a vertical-axis machine that is being incorporated into urban buildings in downtown San Francisco.

A diversity of wind turbine products available today makes this renewable energy source a versatile choice in

Plate 53. Modern wind turbines spin while sheep graze nearby.

ANATOMY OF A "WIND FARM"

Utility-scale wind systems, often referred to as "wind farms," typically cluster a number of wind turbines into a single power generation facility. An accurate assessment of the wind resource serves as the foundation of any viable wind farm.

While the DOE has developed wind resource maps that identify wide swaths of land the feature Class 3, 4, 5, and 6 wind regimes (classes that correspond to minimum and maximum average wind speeds necessary to develop a viable wind project), micro-siting issues still need to be addressed to make a wind farm successful. A Class 3 wind resource has average wind speeds of 6.4 to 7 meters per second. Most wind projects are sited in Class 4 (7 to 7.5 meters per second) and Class 5 (7.5 to 8 meters per second) wind regimes.

The power output from any given wind turbine is proportional to the *cube* of its speed. This means that a doubling of wind speed yields an *eightfold increase* (2 × 2 × 2 = 8) in power production. A 10-mph wind generates almost *twice* the power as an 8-mph breeze. This formula illustrates how critical an accurate assessment of the wind resource is to predicting annual power production figures.

Generally speaking, wind resource data are monitored from a potential wind farm site via several meteorological towers over a two- to three-year period. The data collected from these towers—typically measured at heights of 10, 30, and 60 meters—are used to calculate the "wind shear," a term that refers to the rate of increase in wind speed with height. Among the other parameters that must be measured before installing wind turbines are wind speed and direction and the density of turbulence (a measure of frequency of changes in temperature and direction).

Even within a known wind resource area, the wind can vary immensely due to the local terrain. The shape of a hill, trees, or rocks can arrest wind and create "wind caves." After screening a region according to annual average wind speeds, local measurements of wind are then required to ensure that each wind turbine is installed in the best possible site to take advantage of seasonal and daily fluctuations.

Wind farms are typically operated remotely and controlled by way of computers via a telecommunications link. The operational status of each individual wind turbine in a wind farm is continuously monitored and can be controlled to respond to changes in weather over the course of each day. Maintenance crews of "wind smiths" are dispatched only on an as-needed basis when alarms go off indicating mechanical or electrical problems.

increasingly segmented power markets. Smaller wind turbines can be installed as off-the-grid power systems in remote villages in the developing world or in rural America. Utility-scale wind turbines can deliver large amounts of bulk wholesale electricity to the nation's transmission grid. Wind seems to offer the greatest modularity among the range of renewable sources. From 1-kilowatt machines for remote off-grid desert villages to 7.5-megawatt machines located in the ocean, turbines can generate electricity from the wind.

Small wind turbines are also expected to play an increasingly important role in supplying electricity to both domestic and overseas markets. Wind turbines are available as small as the tiny 400-watt Air 403 turbines manufactured by Southwest Windpower for residential and even mobile applications. Sizes of small units range up to 10-kilowatt turbines manufactured by Bergey, Jacobs, and Southwest Windpower; these are most commonly used on small ranches and farms.

The small wind turbine market is the only renewable energy technology dominated by U.S. manufacturers, who have captured 60 to 70 percent of the global small wind turbine market.

The unsubsidized cost of electricity from a 10-kilowatt small wind turbine falls in the 8- to 12-cent kilowatt per hour range. With new and improved terms for net metering—the process whereby the turbine owner barters its electricity production with the host utility—the value of grid-connected wind turbines to state end-users has increased dramatically. In some cases, the capital costs of between $15,000 and $22,000 have been paid off in less than five years. The largest concentration of small wind turbines in the United States is San Bernardino County, where approximately 100 small wind turbines have been installed as a result of local zoning laws, aggressive installers, and a good wind resource (pl. 54).

Plate 54. Small wind turbines in San Bernardino County, the nation's center of small wind power development.

The Pros and Cons of Wind Power

+ It is the lowest-cost renewable energy supply.
+ It has zero fuel costs.
+ It has virtually zero air pollution and therefore no climate change impacts.
+ Wind farms provide economic benefits to landowners in the form of "wind royalties," which can often provide large annual revenues to supplement farm income.
+ It creates good-paying jobs in rural and often depressed regions.
+ Modularity offers designs for wholesale power as well as on-site power production.
+ Construction and grid connection can be performed in very little time, making it easy to bring large amounts of new power supplies online very quickly.
– Intermittent and somewhat unpredictable power production can make it less appealing to grid managers.
– It has high upfront capital costs.
– Large visible presence raises aesthetics and NIMBY issues.
– It could have impacts on local bird and bat populations.
– Infrastructure for wind projects can carry other ecosystem impacts such as erosion caused by service roads.
– Majority of manufacturers are no longer based in the United States.
– Potential interference with radar has emerged as an issue of national security (though the wind industry is working to resolve this limiting factor on future wind development).

The Future of Wind Power

Wind power not only displaces conventional pollutants such as nitrogen oxides and particulates, but it also does not generate any direct emissions of carbon dioxide (CO_2), methane, or other greenhouse gases. Consequently, it is viewed as the top supply-side greenhouse gas emissions reduction technology throughout the world.

Deep concerns over the contribution of fossil-fueled power plants to global climate change have rendered a political environment in Europe that is very supportive of wind power. Europe has set a goal of obtaining 20 percent of its total electricity supply from renewable sources by 2020, up from 6 percent today. Wind is expected to play the leading role. As of 2006, Europe had installed 46,972 megawatts of wind power.

Although the United States has been slow to embrace wind power, it took the lead in global annual capacity additions in 2006 when 2,454 megawatts of new wind came online, the vast majority outside of California. Still, the lack of a clear, long-term commitment to wind and other renewable energy technologies has hampered the industry in the United States as it ramps up to become a mainstream power supply choice. The lack of a consistent federal policy on wind power—with production tax credits periodically starting and then stopping—has taken its toll, as firms providing up to 8,000 different components struggle to scale-up to meet burgeoning demand for products and services.

Along with concerns about climate change and air quality, the future prospects of wind power hinge on economic development opportunities in rural, typically depressed parts of the state and nation. According to the American Wind Energy Association, every 100 megawatts of wind power development generates roughly $1 million in property tax revenue and 500 job-years of employment.

In California, the key for future wind development is developing transmission access to prime wind resource areas such as the Tehachapi Mountains in Kern County, where at least 5,000 megawatts waits to be constructed and brought to market. A series of other more esoteric regulatory issues also stand in the way. California's top wind resources are offshore and in the Sierra Nevada, which are places currently off-limits to development.

Successful offshore wind development in California would require the development of new and innovative foundations. Winds blowing off of the Pacific Coast north of San Francisco offer some of the highest wind power densities in the continental United States. Nevertheless, the sea floor features slopes that are too steep for the installation of bottom-mounted wind turbines. The working depths between San Francisco and central Oregon are typically 30 meters, which exceeds the maximum depth to install traditional monopile foundations. Focused R&D projects investigating innovative foundations tailored to deep water could greatly expand California's wind power potential. It is doubtful that wind development would ever encroach upon the Sierra Nevada.

Biomass and Biofuels

The majority of biomass and biofuels can also be considered a form of solar energy, because it is the sun that provides the energy for all trees, plants, and other forms of vegetation to grow (pl. 55).

The term "biomass" encompasses diverse fuels ranging from simple fuel wood to sewage sludge and even cow manure. Given the ability of forests and other biomass to renew and regenerate, energy crops such as firewood are considered renewable. Crop residues, municipal garbage or sewage, and manure are all wastes continually generated by activities of daily human living and so are also considered renewable (if anything, they increase as the population grows). In large part they too are derived indirectly from plant material.

Plate 55. Large dead and twisted pine tree on the western slope of Mount Tamalpais in Marin County appears to be an organic sculpture, but it also represents a potential source of clean energy.

"Biofuels" is a term that typically refers to biomass resources that are converted into liquid fuels needed for transportation. Among these are ethanol and biodiesel. In some cases, both electricity and liquid transport fuels can be produced from the same fuel feedstock at the same facility.

Early humans relied on their own muscles to provide mechanical power and then turned to harnessing animals, using food and fodder as biomass fuel. For activities requiring heat, wood was their first biomass fuel of choice. It was the dominant fuel for Native Americans and the first European settlers in this country. Primary uses included heating and cooking. The first New World industries also relied upon wood-fired steam generation, as did key transportation businesses such as trains and ships.

Transportation "biofuels" received an early boost when Samuel Morey developed an engine that relied upon a fuel mixture of turpentine (derived from trees) and ethanol (derived from corn). Nicholas Otto, the German engine inventor best known for the theory behind the modern internal combustion engine (known as the Otto Cycle), also used ethanol in one of his engines in 1876. In the United States, the high costs associated with the Civil War prompted the Union Congress to adopt a $2.00 per gallon tax on ethanol, which had been used widely in lamps. This high tax rendered illumination applications of ethanol obsolete. At the very start of the twentieth century, however, ethanol was still competing with gasoline to become America's dominant transportation fuel.

About the same time, the widespread shift to higher-intensity fuels such as coal doomed the previous dominance of the wood-based biomass power industry, except in California. Most rural homes in this country, however, still relied upon wood for heat until the 1950s.

However, the discovery of oil and then natural gas thwarted the biomass industry from becoming a major fuel source in either the emerging electric utility industry or the transportation sector. While the need for transportation fuel in both World War I and World War II spurred on demand for ethanol during times of shortages, this biofuel industry never could sustain itself. From the late 1940s until the 1970s, it was virtually impossible to find ethanol anywhere in the country.

It was not until the "energy crisis" of 1973–74 that interest in ethanol and other biofuels picked up. However, by 1980, fewer than 10 ethanol plants were up and running and producing roughly 50 million gallons of ethanol on an annual basis. After a series of other subsidies, the number of ethanol plants peaked at 163 in 1984. As has been the case with the fate of many alternative fuels, low oil and natural gas prices resulted in many ethanol producers going belly-up. However, that dynamic has reversed itself in the latter half of the current decade.

The Development of Biomass and Biofuels in California

It was also the energy crisis of the 1970s that spurred on the development of the biomass electricity generation business in response to the passage of the Public Utility Regulatory Policies Act (PURPA) in 1978. Federal policy on biomass and other "alternative" energy sources was supplemented by state incentives, particularly in California, which added 850 megawatts of new biomass capacity (primarily forestry and agricultural wastes) as a result of lucrative long-term utility power purchase contracts pegged to projected prices of oil as high as $100 per barrel. (Although such price projections ultimately came true in 2008, current utility purchasing procedures no longer rely upon this pricing model.) These contracts ultimately became political targets, and biomass power plants began closing as subsidies declined over time.

California remains the nation's top producer of electricity from biomass with approximately 625 megawatts of capacity currently online. Over 4 million "bone-dry" tons of biomass fuel are currently being consumed annually by 28 surviving biomass power plants. Another 360 megawatts of capacity is also online generating electricity from landfill gas and biogas from sewage treatment facilities, food processing waste, and livestock manure digestion (map 11). Therefore, the total biomass capacity is around 1,000 megawatts.

Biomass facilities currently account for more than 2 percent of California's total electricity consumption as well as a minor, yet quickly growing, share of liquid transportation fuels. Although electricity-generating capacity in the solid-fuel biomass combustion sector has declined since the 1990s, increases in landfill gas-to-energy capacity kept the total biomass sector nearly constant at roughly 1,000 megawatts. Biomass facility closures have resulted in

Power Plants

■ Biomass

⬢ Landfill gas

0 ——————— 100 mi

0 ——————— 150 km

Map 11. Biomass and landfill gas power plants in California.

greater amounts of biomass being sent to crowded landfills. Some biomass is still being burned in open fields in locations such as the Central Valley, which is one of California's most polluted air basins.

Of the 625 megawatts currently operating, many of these plants cannot afford any new capital investments and are closing down if they do not receive any additional subsidy. Many cannot afford to operate during off-peak hours, because energy prices are too low at those times of the day. Many in the biomass industry sense there is little or no possibility of any new biomass power plants ever coming online in California. A series of delays on distributing long-term funding has created great uncertainty within the ranks of biomass power plant operators. Once a biomass power plant shuts down, it is very difficult to get it back online. Once the plant closes, the fuel supply infrastructure disappears. On top of that, once a plant is mothballed, it typically costs too much money to bring the facility back into working condition. Many air quality management districts worry that if additional biomass power plants shut down, air quality in places such as San Joaquin County will deteriorate significantly as a result of increased open-field burning of agricultural wastes.

According to the California Biomass Energy Alliance, a total of 19 biomass power plants have closed over a 13-year period, which translates into a loss of 230 megawatts of renewable energy capacity. In response to the state RPS, state utilities have signed 14 contracts for seven new biomass power plants and are starting seven existing facilities. However, many of these facilities may never come online, because the energy prices in those contracts may be too low to support ongoing operations. One solution would be to remunerate biomass facilities for the nonenergy benefits they provide. At present, these facilities consume the equivalent of a quarter of the total waste deposited in California's landfills every year.

Over 70 million bone-dry tons of gross potential biomass fuel still can be found throughout California. Municipal solid wastes are the largest category (50 percent), followed by agriculture (30 percent) and forestry (20 percent) wastes. Unlike other renewable fuels, the biomass industry also offers the opportunity to coproduce transportation fuels, chemicals, and a wide variety of other value-added products.

Yet, absent new public policies and support programs, the only type of biomass facilities expected to come online in response to the RPS are smaller landfill gas projects.

Biomass and Biofuels Today

At present, biomass plants represent well over 11,000 megawatts of electricity—the second largest amount of renewable electricity generation in the nation (hydroelectric power is No. 1). One of the primary challenges with converting biomass to electricity is the cost of gathering and managing fuels. That said, biomass facilities are valuable in a power supply portfolio, since they offer the greatest array of public benefits attached to renewable energy resources. Like other renewable resources, biomass fuels can reduce greenhouse gas emissions contributing to global climate change as well as reduce our dependency on imported energy sources such as oil. Like most renewable fuels, biomass can, if managed properly, improve air quality. However, particulate emissions from first-generation systems can contribute to local air pollution woes.

Pros and Cons of Biomass and Biofuels

Since the pros and cons of each category of biomass and biofuel technologies are so different, each major fuel/technology will be treated individually below. Although power plants burning municipal solid waste as fuel are sometimes included in the "biomass" category, California's tight environmental restrictions—as well as NIMBY concerns—have prevented the development of this potential energy source here, so the history and pros and cons of this "renewable" resource are not included in this section.

Forestry and Agricultural Wastes

Most biomass electricity-generating facilities operating in the United States today burn lumber, agricultural, or construction/demolition wood wastes. These facilities are also known as "direct combustion" power plants. They burn the biomass fuel directly in boilers that supply steam for the same kind of steam-electric generators used to burn fossil fuels.

With "biomass gasification," solid biomass is converted into a gas (methane) that can then fuel steam generators, combustion turbines, combined cycle technologies, or fuel cells. The primary benefit of biomass gasification, compared to direct combustion, is that extracted gases can be used anywhere gas fuels can be used in a variety of power plant configurations. These facilities can also coproduce transportation fuels. The pros and cons:

+ Because these power plants use combustion processes to produce electricity, thermochemical conversion systems can generate electricity at any time, in contrast to wind and most solar technologies, which produce electricity only when the wind is blowing or the sun is shining.
+ Open burning of forestry and agricultural wastes emits higher levels of air pollutants than does controlled combustion in biomass power plants and other conversion methods (fig. 15), and it does not yield any useful energy or products.
+ When biomass fuels are obtained from forestry and agriculture wastes, the net environmental impact is often minimal, because less-desirable waste disposal methods can be avoided.
+ Biomass fuels can be derived from supplies of clean, uncontaminated wood wastes that serve no useful

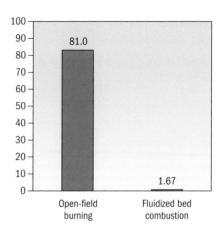

Figure 15. Comparing emissions between fluidized-bed biomass power generation and open-field burning of agricultural wastes.

purpose and would otherwise end up in landfills as solid waste.

+ Wood waste streams are diverted from landfills, which reduces the production and atmospheric release of methane, a potent greenhouse gas.

+ The thinning of forests can improve the health of forest ecosystems while suppressing the potential for catastrophic forest fires.

+ Biomass and biofuels development also offers new economic opportunities for agriculture and related industries.

− Emissions of nitrogen oxides (NO_x) vary significantly among combustion facilities depending on their design and controls, but they can be higher than in other combustion technologies.

− Carbon monoxide (CO) is also emitted from some biomass power plants, sometimes at levels higher than those of contemporary coal-fired power plants.

− Biomass plants also release carbon dioxide (CO_2), a primary greenhouse gas.

- Another air quality concern associated with biomass plants is particulates, emissions readily controlled by conventional technologies. Few biomass power plants have installed advanced particulate emission controls.
- Significant adverse impacts on local ecosystems could occur if the fuel production and harvesting are not done properly.
- Because biomass fuels require comparatively large volumes of fuel to produce the equivalent amount of energy generated by burning fossil fuels, land resource impacts could be extraordinary.

Landfill Gas

Large municipal or industrial landfills produce gas that can also be tapped to generate electricity. Microorganisms that live in organic materials such as food wastes, paper, or yard clippings break these substances down in the anaerobic conditions that exist in a landfill. While decomposing, these organic materials produce "landfill gas," which is typically composed of roughly 60 percent methane and 40 percent carbon dioxide (CO_2).

Methane is a major culprit of global climate change, having about 23 times the negative impact on a pound-by-pound basis as CO_2. Combusting landfill gas produces some CO_2, but these global climate change emission impacts are offset many times over by the methane emission reductions. Though not technically a renewable resource, landfill gas will be in great supply absent major innovations in solid waste management systems (pl. 56).

The methane and CO_2 that are produced by landfills either seep out of soil covers into the atmosphere or are collected in pipes and then diverted so that the methane can be flared or put to some other use. Since this methane gas is highly flammable, it can serve as a fuel to generate electricity. Landfill gas has only about half the combustion value as natural gas; therefore, it is typically used only in smaller electricity generators.

Plate 56. Yolo County bioreactor.

Most landfill gas electricity generators use diesel engine technology. These relatively inexpensive generators are easy to transport and install. Unfortunately, they are also inefficient and tend to produce comparatively high levels of air pollution. Some landfills generators employ cleaner gas turbine technology. Landfill gas can also be used in fuel cell technologies, which rely upon chemical reactions other than combustion to generate electricity. Fuel cells convert landfill gas directly into electricity at much higher efficiency levels than combustion technologies. Instead of air pollution, the by-products of the chemical reactions in fuel cells are water, small amounts of CO_2, and electricity. Using landfill gas in fuel cells is no doubt among the most environmentally benevolent choices to generate electricity available. The pros and cons:

+ Landfill gas electricity generation offers major air quality benefits where landfills already exist or where the decision to build the landfill has already been made. (A landfill gas power plant burns a waste—methane—that would otherwise be released into the atmosphere or burned off in a flaring process.)
+ Employing landfill gas as a fuel source can also reduce odors and other regulated pollutants, such as volatile

organic compounds, which make smog and ground-level ozone.

+ Because these power plants tend to be very small, their cooling towers, which consume local water supplies, are typically quite modest. Polluting discharges to local lakes or streams have been rare.

+ Landfill gas power plants produce no significant land impacts. Located at the landfill site, generators require little, if any, additional land.

− The tiny modified diesel generators that are used at most landfill sites tend to have comparatively high NO_x emission rates.

− Landfill gas includes uncombusted nonmethane organic compounds. The combustion of these compounds could produce trace levels of dioxin emissions or other air pollutants under certain conditions.

− Air pollution and other environmental impacts are associated with the collection and transportation of solid waste from widely distributed fuel locations.

− Leaking landfills can damage water ecosystems (although this impact is really linked to the landfill itself, not the power generator added on after the fact).

Ethanol

Historically, ethanol (also referred to as grain alcohol or ethyl alcohol) is derived from any starch- or sugar-based feedstock. So far, corn has been the most popular feedstock in the United States, whereas sugar cane is the top choice in Latin America. The fundamental process of producing this biofuel used in the transportation sector is to break down simple sugars and starches and then ferment them to produce alcohol. Whether produced through distillation or microbe fermentation, the end result is a liquid fuel that contains about two-thirds of the energy of an equivalent volume of gasoline.

Newer technologies are emerging that can break down more complex sugars from other parts of plants, such as husks, grasses, and stalks. Converting these sources of "cellulosic" biomass into ethanol is opening up whole new markets to this alternative transportation fuel as new conversion systems access the same forestry and agricultural wastes now typically burned in biomass electricity-generating facilities.

Throughout time, the popularity of ethanol has gone up and down, largely correlated to fossil fuel shortages. Today, however, the primary drivers behind the push for ethanol include air emission reduction strategies, rural economic development, strategic diversification of transportation fuels, and mitigation of global climate change. At present, ethanol is replacing methyl tertiary butyl ether (MTBE) as the primary additive to reduce emissions and increase fuel octane rating in cars and trucks; that is this alternative fuel is blended in with traditional fossil fuels. The federal government's emphasis on biorefinery development is intended to provide an economic platform for a variety of higher-value products along with alternative fuels. The pros and cons:

+ The prime application of ethanol over the past decade has been as an oxygenate that reduces ground-level ozone.
+ Burning of ethanol in internal combustion engines in motor vehicles also reduces levels of carbon monoxide as well as other toxic air pollutants.
+ Since the biomass basis for ethanol absorbed CO_2 when it was grown, switching to ethanol transportation fuels adds no net carbon to the atmosphere, a plus from the perspective of global climate change.
+ Beyond environmental benefits, ethanol can also boost engine performance if blended with gasoline, preventing engine knocking.
+ Since ethanol can be produced domestically and in rural depressed economies, ethanol can boost rural economic development in the same way that other biomass fuels and technologies can.

- Depending upon the precise blend of ethanol and gasoline used as a transportation fuel, ethanol can raise levels of NO_x that come out of the tailpipe. NO_x is a major contributor to urban smog and lung disease.
- Because of its lower energy content, the efficiency of vehicles fueled by ethanol is less than that of a vehicle fueled exclusively by gasoline.
- Ethanol production derived from corn is very energy intensive. In some cases, the amount of energy needed for farming and making fertilizers to grow ethanol feedstock can supersede the amount of energy contained in the end-product fuel.
- When ethanol is transported through a pipeline, it picks up water and can cause corrosion. Research into dedicated ethanol pipelines made of special materials is just beginning. Transporting ethanol by truck or train uses up some of the fuel the ethanol was intended to save.

Biodiesel

The other primary biofuel attracting attention today is biodiesel, which can be produced from any vegetable oil or animal fat (fig. 16). Biodiesel contains no petroleum itself, but like ethanol is typically blended with petroleum diesel for use in traditional diesel engines, often with virtually no modifications. Biodiesel is simple to use, biodegradable, nontoxic, and virtually free of sulfur and aromatics.

Glycerin is separated from fat or vegetable oils during a chemical process known as "transesterification" to create biodiesel. In the United States, roughly half of biodiesel production is from soybean oil; the other half comes from old cooking oil from restaurants. Typically, fats and oils are combined with an alcohol and a catalyst (most often sodium or potassium hydroxide), which then produces fatty acid methyl esters and glycerol, the latter a valuable by-product that can be used in soaps in other products.

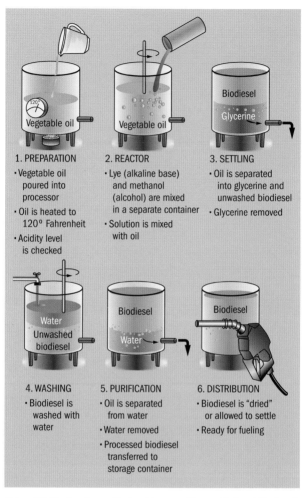

1. PREPARATION
- Vegetable oil poured into processor
- Oil is heated to 120° Fahrenheit
- Acidity level is checked

2. REACTOR
- Lye (alkaline base) and methanol (alcohol) are mixed in a separate container
- Solution is mixed with oil

3. SETTLING
- Oil is separated into glycerine and unwashed biodiesel
- Glycerine removed

4. WASHING
- Biodiesel is washed with water

5. PURIFICATION
- Oil is separated from water
- Water removed
- Processed biodiesel transferred to storage container

6. DISTRIBUTION
- Biodiesel is "dried" or allowed to settle
- Ready for fueling

Figure 16. Biodiesel: new life for old grease. Source: National Biodiesel Board.

Biodiesel is less toxic than table salt and biodegrades as fast as sugar. It is the only alternative fuel to have completed the health effects testing required by the 1990 Clean Air Act Amendments. The pros and cons:

+ Biodiesel extends the energy capacity of finite petroleum-based fuels, increasing national security while improving regional air quality.
+ Biodiesel can also be used as home heating oil.
+ If a transportation fuel contains 20 percent biodiesel, CO_2 emissions will be reduced by 15 percent. Emissions of particulates, carbon monoxide, and SO_x are also reduced.
+ Biodiesel is less toxic and combustible than petroleum, making it a safer alternative during transport and storage.
+ When spilled, biodiesel breaks down at roughly four times the rate of petroleum diesel.
− When used in diesel engines, biodiesel combustion results in higher NO_x emissions than traditional transportation fuels (though these emissions are not typically released when used in residential heating applications).
− When burned as regular diesel, biodiesel emits the same amount of hydrocarbons as regular diesel petroleum fuels.
− Pure biodiesel has a high "clouding" point. In other words, liquid biodiesel begins to thicken into a solid at cold temperatures. Among the implications of this phenomenon are that biodiesel is limited to warmer climates or requires additional costs to keep in a liquid form.

The Future of Biomass and Biofuels

If you take the big picture, biomass energy's share of global energy consumption has remained roughly the same over the last 30 years, accounting for more than 10 percent of final energy consumption, according to the International Energy Agency. This compares to electricity's 15 percent and natural gas's 16 percent shares of final energy consumption. Nevertheless, much of biomass's market share is represented by inefficient, polluting, and highly destructive practices in poor, developing countries with few other energy supply choices. One of the often unrecognized benefits from better fuel collection and conversion systems for biomass is improving the quality of life for women and children in the developing world. The intense burden placed on women and children to forage for free fuel can take up long stretches of every day and prolongs cycles of poverty.

While abundant and diverse, biomass energy resources are not uniformly distributed. Successful energy conversion strategies hinge on cultural and social issues as well as land use patterns. Biomass is "free" in many parts of the developing world, but this "free" energy comes at the unrecognized costs of deforestation, global climate change, extreme poverty, and rampant inefficiency.

When it comes to generating electricity from biomass in California, this sector of the renewable energy industry has never been the most popular with environmentalists. Part of this lack of support from renewable energy advocates stems from the fact that some biomass power generation facilities are owned by lumber companies that have been the targets of boycotts and protests from environmental activists over the years. In addition, first-generation systems were somewhat crude and often still lack state-of-the-art pollution controls.

That said, biofuels have never been more popular as grassroots entrepreneurs get into biodiesel, and large oil companies such as BP and Chevron explore opportunities with a broad range of biofuels. Growing investor and consumer interest in biomass and biofuels is driven by some unique attributes of this alternative fuel. Among them is that this fuel can deliver energy in all forms: heat, liquid, gaseous, and electricity. Biomass and biofuels can provide energy around the clock, reducing poverty in the developing world, while restoring and increasing biodiversity, soil fertility, and water retention.

As far as California is concerned, biomass resources are more evenly accessible throughout the entire state of California than are wind, solar, hydro, or geothermal resources. Biomass resources can be found in both northern and southern California as well as in rural, suburban, and urban counties. One of the primary challenges with converting biomass to electricity is the cost of gathering and managing fuels. Still, biomass facilities are valuable in a power supply portfolio, since they, like geothermal power plants, can operate virtually 24/7. They also offer some one-of-a-kind benefits, such as support and integration into solid waste management systems. Like most renewable fuels, biomass can, if managed properly, improve air quality. Particulate emissions from first-generation systems, however, can also contribute to localized air pollution level.

The eventual role of biomass and biofuels in the U.S. and California energy supply depends upon advances in fuel processing technologies and the prolonging of today's steep electricity and fossil fuel prices. Estimates show that biofuels are likely to make a greater contribution to our transportation sector inventory than to our electricity supply mix. Even without major improvements, experts estimate biomass could supply 10 percent of our current national gasoline consumption. If a major conversion to energy crops took place on marginal lands as part of a major federal strategy to shift to a bioeconomy, biofuels could supplant as much as 45 percent of our national gasoline consumption.

Water Power

The Earth is, after all, the water planet, so it should come as no great surprise that hydropower has been the world's most popular renewable energy source.

Like many other renewable energy resources, water power has an innate and intimate relationship to natural processes involving our sun, our atmosphere, and our natural history. The sun shapes our weather as it interacts with our revolving planet and its oceans and the terrestrial geography. As the Earth spins around the sun, heating and cooling air, clouds ultimately develop, sprinkling precipitation in the form of rain and snow, which, in turn, recharges lakes, rivers, and streams. Forces of gravity then push this water to fall to lower elevations through canyons holding rivers and streams (pl. 57). The premise of hydropower is to intercept this falling water and convert this mechanical force into electricity.

Plate 57. Sierra Nevada mountain stream.

Because the sun's energy causes water to evaporate, which, in turn, creates clouds accumulating moisture that then falls again back to the Earth in the form of rain and snow, hydropower is considered a renewable energy source. Hydropower taps into the hydrologic cycle, which serves as sort of a natural engine, continually recycling energy through natural transfers of energy. This eternal cycle serves as the genesis of an industry now grappling with a lack of strong governmental support and increasing criticism from environmentalists wanting the industry to atone for past sins that include devastation of fish and other aquatic life.

Ocean wave and tidal power are emerging forms of hydropower. The physics underlying ocean power resources are simple. Waves are created by wind blowing across the ocean (therefore, wave energy can also be considered a form of wind energy, which, in turn, is a subset of solar energy). The circular motion of water molecules that create the waves on the surface then continues below the surface, swirling with loads of kinetic energy that may be captured by turbines. Tides are the result of the gravitational pull of the moon on the Earth. Ocean water on one side of the Earth is closer to the moon than the center of the Earth is, so it is pulled more strongly toward the moon, and the sea level rises. The moon also pulls the center of the Earth more than it pulls the more distant ocean water on the opposite side, so the sea level rises there too. As the Earth rotates, therefore, the sea level at any given location rises and falls twice each day, producing currents which humans can tap in bays and harbors.

Harnessing the energy contained in flowing rivers is an age-old practice. Some historians trace early hydropower innovations back to the Greeks, who built aqueducts and used water to power their gristmills. The Romans built some of the world's first irrigation systems, and the Japanese also tapped running water for a variety of purposes around AD 610.

Although the first waterwheel was built around 200 BC, it was not until the nineteenth century that water was used to generate electricity. Before then, water was used primarily for milling and pumping. The first hydroelectric plant in the United States began operating in September 1882 on the Fox River in Appleton, Wisconsin. No doubt the most famous of early hydroelectric plants was the plant located at Niagara Falls, New York. It relied upon a Westinghouse polyphase AC system to transmit electricity to Buffalo, New York, in 1896, one year after Sacramento's celebrated successful demonstration of long-distance transmission from the Folsom power-house on the American River (pl. 58).

One of the first widespread methods of generating electricity in the United States, hydropower supplied as much as 40 percent of the nation's electricity in the early part of the twentieth century. In California—and throughout the west—hydropower provided roughly three-quarters of

Plate 58. The interior of the Folsom powerhouse today.

the total electricity supply as late as World War II. Today, 10 percent of the United States' current electricity supply—and 80 percent of the nation's current renewable electric supply—comes from hydroelectricity.

The Development of Water Power in California

The first Californians to tap water power looked to the ocean first, before trying their luck with Sierra Nevada streams. A logging and sawmill operation located along the rugged Mendocino coast constructed a "tide mill" in 1851. (The next effort to tap the energy of ocean water flows occurred much later at the Cliff House in San Francisco, when a one-of-a-kind pendulum was thoroughly trashed by the raging Pacific in 1889.)

It was an inventor by the name of Lester Allen Pelton, migrating to California from Ohio during the great gold rush of 1849, who accelerated hydroelectric development in California and the rest of the west. His major contributions to the evolution of river-based hydropower in California were chronicled in the Overview section of this book. The Pelton water wheel (pl. 59) captured an incredible 90 percent

Plate 59. Historic photograph of the interior of a PG&E hydroelectric station featuring Pelton water wheels.

of the available energy contained in moving water, while his nearest competitor captured approximately 76 percent.

Given the widespread early development of hydro sites throughout California, there has been little interest in further large-scale development. Instead, the focus of today's hydro industry is smaller projects and improvements to existing facilities. Unlike most of electricity sources, hydro plants fall under the jurisdiction of the Federal Energy Regulatory Commission (FERC). These facilities are allowed to operate on the nation's rivers, streams, and lakes in a license akin to a rental agreement. FERC grants these licenses for terms ranging from 30 to 50 years.

Most current hydro facilities operating in California and elsewhere were developed with few environmental safeguards factored into their design and standard operating practices. Recent laws now require FERC to factor fish and wildlife impacts when renewing these licenses. Environmentalists hope to improve the environmental performance of the nation's hydroelectric fleet as these licenses come up for reauthorization. In extreme cases, dams and their associated powerhouses can be removed altogether.

At present, California does not consider the vast majority of hydropower serving the state as "renewable." Since California was the state that most aggressively sought to develop a voluntary green power market under the 1996 restructuring law, it grappled with defining what power sources could legally be called "renewable." In the case of hydro, only projects below 30 megawatts in size are included in the definition of "renewable," though a case can be made that larger hydro projects could be "green." California receives roughly 20 percent of its electricity from hydroelectric facilities. Yet, the vast majority of this power does not count toward the goal of obtaining 20 percent of the state's electricity from renewable resources by 2010. Indeed, less than 2 percent of the state's current hydroelectric supply qualifies as "renewable" energy.

The San Francisco-based Center for Resource Solutions played a large role in the development of the Low Impact Hydropower Institute, which certifies hydropower facilities as being sustainable energy sources by scoring each facility according to the following criteria: river flows, water quality, fish passage and protection, watershed protection, threatened and endangered species protection, cultural resource protection, and recreation. Facilities recommended for removal due to severe negative environmental impacts are obviously not certified by the Low Impact Hydropower Institute. These low-impact hydro standards have been adopted by environmental groups across the country as they pass judgments on hydroelectric facilities that differ greatly in technology, scale, and operations. Generally speaking, facilities that have come online since 1987 are better environmental performers. It is in that year that FERC began factoring environmental considerations in licensing new power plants.

The greatest interest in California today with water power is among unconventional water power technologies such as tidal power or wave, also referred to as hydrokinetic power technologies.

Water Power Today

California has 386 existing hydroelectric power plants representing 14,116 megawatts, which represents 26 percent of the total installed capacity in the state. Since most hydroelectric facilities were built long ago, they are the cheapest renewable supply, with costs close to just 1 cent per kilowatt hour.

The category of hydropower actually consists of three major categories of power generation technologies: storage projects; run-of-river; and pumped storage.

The vast majority of existing hydroelectric facilities fall under the category of *storage* projects. A dam is constructed to create a reservoir, which periodically releases impounded water to flow through turbine generators to create electricity (pl. 60). Storage and release cycles can vary, with some

Plate 60. Exterior of Feather River hydroelectric facility.

large projects operating over multiyear cycles, managing stored water in wet years to offset shortages during dry years.

Run-of-river projects rely on smaller dams, where the amount of water running through the turbine generators is dependent upon natural river flows. Generally speaking, these facilities do not hold water back in a reservoir; therefore, they do not impact stream flows as significantly as storage hydro projects. The disadvantage of this technology is that electricity generation depends solely upon the levels of water flowing through the river.

Pumped storage projects are the last major category and are the least common. They rely upon off-peak, low-cost electricity to pump water from a lower to an upper reservoir. During periods of high electricity demand, the water is released back down to the lower reservoir. Less than 50 pumped storage projects exist in the United States today, though some are quite large. These projects are 80 percent efficient, as some power is lost during the conversion-to-storage process.

In terms of ocean resources, the two primary technologies are tidal turbines and wave energy technologies. Among all supply-side sources, ocean-based technologies are now the most expensive of all supply options as they try to become a commercial reality. Capturing the energy in tides dates back centuries to Europe, where such systems often operated like dams, capturing water in high tides and releasing it after tides fell. Today's technologies are far more sophisticated. The turbines placed underwater are typically horizontal axis, though vertical-axis designs are also under development (fig. 17).

Whereas tidal power technologies often look suspiciously like wind turbines placed underwater, wave energy technologies often look more like metal snakes that can span nearly 500 feet, floating on the ocean's surface horizontally or standing erect vertically (fig. 18).

Some conventional hydroelectric plants have spawned ecological disasters. Efforts are underway to modernize the water power industry and to reduce its negative environmental impacts.

> Imagine that someone built a power plant that set your heater to 97 degrees F year round, randomly cut off all of your water for hours or days on end, and placed a giant impassible wall through the center of your home, making it impossible for you to get to the kitchen or your bedroom. (Hydropower Reform Coalition 2007, www.hydroreform.org)

According to Hydropower Reform Coalition, this describes what happens to a river and its inhabitants with a typical poorly run hydroelectric plant. Since many of these facilities still employ nineteenth-century technology, they have never been brought up to modern environmental standards. The coalition offers the following suggestions to reduce environmental impacts of hydropower systems:

- Alter the schedule of power generation to more closely mimic a river's natural ebb and flow.

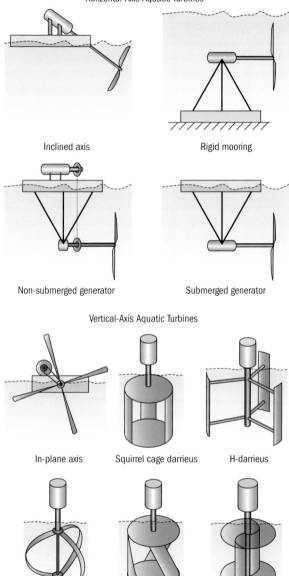

Figure 17. Illustrations of aquatic tidal turbine designs.

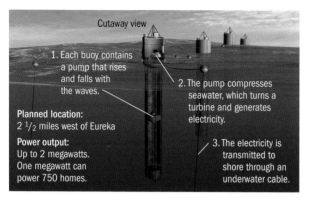

Figure 18. Vertical wave power collector developed by Finavera Renewables.

- Manage lake levels and water releases from dams to limit erosion of shorelines and riverbanks.
- Change out turbines with newer, more efficient equipment.
- Restore habitat for fish and wildlife.
- Tweak operations and instill measures that stabilize river temperatures and oxygen levels.
- Increase access and manage water to allow more fishing, boating, and swimming.

Although hydroelectric operators worry about the loss of revenue if nonenergy considerations shape the management of their power plants, a study conducted by FERC found that facilities that did upgrade operations to meet modern environmental standards lost only 1.6 percent of their previous levels of electricity production. If that level of power generation were applied to the entire fleet of the nation's hydroelectric facilities expected to receive license renewals between 2000 and 2010, the total amount of capacity lost would amount to just 0.04 percent of the nation's energy supply.

When compared to other renewable resource, hydroelectricity offers many advantages. For example, if paired with wind farms, pumped storage facilities can serve as batteries to store wind energy in the form of water power to be utilized at times when demand is highest. Though hydroelectricity is technically a "renewable" source of energy, critics claim it is among the most damaging of all electricity resources. The survival rate for fish passing through large turbines varies, but the rate averages approximately 90 to 95 percent. If sensitive juveniles must pass through multiple dams with multiple generators, long-term populations can dwindle over time. Large dams have, no doubt, forever altered waterways and lands, especially in the west and in California. The steep declines in salmon populations in California and the Pacific Northwest are a direct result of the region's heavy reliance upon hydroelectricity.

The Pros and Cons of Water Power

+ Hydropower plants are often the lowest-cost resources on the system.
+ There are zero fuel costs.
+ If developed properly, hydropower can be a noncarbon, renewable source of electricity.
+ Storage systems can serve as giant batteries, storing clean energy for later use.
+ There are low maintenance requirements.
+ There are quick ramp-up and ramp-down operation times.
+ It provides a plethora of nonenergy benefits, including flood control, irrigation, and recreational opportunities.
– Storage projects require flooding of entire valleys, destroying scenic areas as well as historical human communities.
– It causes major impacts on fish, waterfowl, and aquatic populations.

- River flow changes can carry long-term ecosystem impacts.
- Dams could block contaminated sediment from upstream sources, compromising water quality and damaging habitat.
- Flash floods are a rare, but potentially catastrophic, outcome from an earthquake.

Because tidal and ocean wave power have yet to be fully commercialized, they are not included in this weighing of water power pros and cons.

The Future of Water Power

Looking at the big picture, water power currently provides one-fifth of the world's electricity, with the United States being the largest consumer: 12 percent of the global water power total. The United Nations projects that the total "technically exploitable" potential for hydropower is 15 trillion kilowatt-hours, equal to half of the projected global electricity use in the year 2030. Of this vast resource potential, roughly 15 percent has been developed so far.

While there is a common perception that the United States has tapped out its hydropower resources, the Electric Power Research Institute (EPRI) disputes this claim. According to the EPRI's assessment, the nation has the water resources to generate from 85,000 to 95,000 more megawatts from this noncarbon energy source, with 23,000 megawatts available by 2025. Included in this water power assessment are new, emerging technologies such as ocean energy technologies. In fact, according to the EPRI, ocean wave energy will match conventional hydropower in new capacity additions between today and 2025.

The largest share of the future conventional hydropower market is small hydro, a sector of the water power industry still poised for major growth. (Interestingly enough, more than half of the current small hydropower capacity is in China.) A new debate in California is whether upgrades squeezing more energy out of existing large hydro projects not recognized as "renewable" under state standards should be labeled as such from this point forward. The hydroelectricity lobby not only wants these incremental upgrades to existing facilities to be counted as renewable resources in state RPS procurements, but they also want new hydroelectric generators at dams not currently generating power and new ocean-based water power technologies to be eligible for renewable energy status. These new technologies are just beginning to be investigated on the West Coast.

Although neither wave nor tidal power technologies are considered fully commercial at this point in time, smaller, more powerful turbines and advances in marine cables and new anchoring techniques have all rendered these emerging water power options as intriguing future sources of energy for California. To date, the greatest interest has been in tidal power, with one experimental project that could generate as much as 35 megawatts under consideration near San Francisco's famed Golden Gate Bridge. According to some energy experts, the San Francisco Bay is the largest tidal power resource in the lower 48 states, and the entire northern coast of California offers prime tidal power development sites. (Alaska is the national leader, with approximately 90 percent of the total tidal energy resource.)

The notion of wave power has also captured the imagination of California firms (pl. 61). Among them is PG&E—California's leading hydro utility—and it has already filed permits with the FERC to invest $3 million to develop projects off of the Mendocino coast at Fort Bragg and the Humboldt Coast at Eureka by 2010. The PG&E applications are the first in North America to showcase competing wave energy technologies, and each site could provide up to 40 megawatts each of clean, nonpolluting, and carbon-free electricity. Waters in both locations range from 60 to 600 feet deep.

One reason there is so much interest in these new forms of water power is that water is denser than air. As a result, the amount of extractable energy in any given volume of

Plate 61. Finavera pilot project featuring solar, wind, and wave power generation technologies, deployed near Newport, Oregon.

water is 800 times greater than that of the same amount of air. Unlike wind power—the world's current most popular form of renewable energy—waves and tides can be tapped for electricity virtually 24 hours a day. Data have also been collected by federal agencies and others on wave height and tidal patterns, information that serves as resource assessments for interested power plant developers.

Tidal and wave energy may be the next big energy rush in California, rivaling early wind power development in this state with its cast of characters and deal-making shenanigans. Wave energy, although variable, can be predicted days in advance. Tidal power, also variable, can be predicted into the indefinite future. This predictability is important to electrical grid dispatchers, who must balance the changing demand with the supply. Ocean energy resources are powerful and predictable. California's long coastline could clearly become the national testing grounds for this emerging renewable energy technology.

Nuclear Power

While it was ancient Greek philosophers who first came up with the notion that all matter is composed of tiny particles called "atoms" (from the Greek word for "not cut," meaning the smallest possible particles into which a substance could be divided), it was not until the dawn of the twentieth century that scientists realized that these atoms, despite their name, could be split, producing enormous amounts of energy.

Brilliant scientists such as Albert Einstein contributed to the understanding of the physics behind mass and energy, but it took Enrico Fermi of Italy to demonstrate in 1934 that when bombarded with neutrons, uranium released elements lighter in weight than expected. The loss of weight suggested an energy transfer of some sort. Four years later, German scientists such as Otto Hahn, Lise Meitner, and Fritz Strassman continued doing similar research, finding even lighter residual elements after splitting atoms. These discoveries laid the groundwork for U.S. research into this immensely powerful source of power from tiny atoms just at the start of World War II.

Fermi began working with other scientists for a uranium chain reactor in 1941; one year later, they began construction of the world's first nuclear reactor, then known as Chicago Pile-1, constructed beneath the University of Chicago's athletic stadium (which had not been used for games since 1939). On the morning of December 2, 1942, Fermi and his associates transformed scientific theory into a technological reality, when they successfully demonstrated a self-sustaining chain reaction. Yet the initial use of this major advance in energy was the development of atomic bombs in the United States under the code name of the Manhattan Project.

Plate 62. The morning sun illuminates the Diablo Canyon nuclear power plant.

After the conclusion of World War II, Congress created the Atomic Energy Commission to promote civilian applications of nuclear energy, laying the groundwork for the commercial nuclear power industry (pl. 62). The first electricity generated from a nuclear power plant occurred in December 1951 at the Experimental Breeder Reactor I near Arco, Idaho. In 1957—the same year that California generated its first civilian nuclear power in Santa Susana, California—the world's first large-scale nuclear reactor also began operating at Shippingport, Pennsylvania.

Like fossil fuels, uranium is a finite, nonrenewable resource. Though it is possible to extend the life of uranium fuel through reprocessing and "breeding," the United States abandoned a breeder reactor program well over a decade ago. Today, there is a global resurgence in interest in developing new techniques to extend the world's uranium resources.

Nuclear fusion is another form of nuclear reaction that produces energy. Instead of heavy atoms splitting, light atoms are driven together so that they fuse into heavier nuclei. Nuclear fusion is the process that powers the sun, the Earth's dominant energy source. The most promising nuclear fusion fuel for power on Earth is an isotope of hydrogen known

HOW DOES A NUCLEAR REACTOR WORK?

More than any other single power generation source, nuclear power is the object of extreme loyalty as well as utmost disdain. Beyond the politics revolving around atomic and nuclear power, what is the precise science behind the most complex—and dangerous—power plants in the world?

Nuclear fission power plants are fueled by uranium, a naturally occurring element found in the Rocky Mountains and other countries such as Canada, Australia, and South Africa. Known as a "heavy" element since each atom of it comprises a high number of atomic protons and neutrons, uranium is usually found in one of two forms (called isotopes), labeled by the combined number of the neutrons and protons (or atomic weight). The unique properties of each atom type—uranium-235 and uranium-238—make nuclear power possible.

When an atom of uranium-235 is struck by a stray neutron, it spontaneously decays or splits into two smaller nuclei; that is, it undergoes a fission reaction, and uranium-235 is therefore known as a "fissile" isotope. This fission reaction releases a great deal of energy, mostly in the form of heat, and it also releases neutrons, which can then collide with other fissile nuclei to cause a chain of further fission reactions.

Uranium-238, which makes up over 99 percent of natural uranium, is not fissile, but it can sometimes absorb an extra neutron from the fission reaction and, by emitting a couple of electrons, turn into plutonium-239, which shares the fissile properties exhibited by uranium-235. This process is known as "breeding," and uranium-238 is said to be a "fertile" isotope.

For use as fuel, uranium ore is extracted from other minerals, enriched (the concentration of uranium-235 is increased above naturally occurring levels to increase fission activity), pelletized, and loaded into tubes called fuel rods. The fuel rod assemblies are positioned inside a nuclear reactor, where the rate of fission can be controlled. The fuel assemblies are placed in water and separated by control rods containing cadmium, which absorbs neutrons that otherwise would cause fission. The rate of the chain reaction, and therefore the amount of power produced, can be adjusted by pushing the control rods into the reactor core or pulling them out. When there are just enough neutrons available to keep the chain reaction going, the reactor is said to be "critical." (The water surrounding the fuel rod assemblies absorbs the heat from the fission reaction and carries it away to do useful work rather than melt the reactor core.)

There are two types of commercial nuclear reactors operating in the United States today. In one kind, called a boiling-water reactor (BWR), the water that carries away the heat from the nuclear fission is allowed to boil, creating steam under high pressure, which directly drives the turbine that spins a generator to produce electricity. The second and more common kind is a pressurized-water reactor (PWR), in which the primary coolant (the water that carries the heat from the nuclear fission) is kept under high pressure so that it does not boil even though it is hotter than the boiling point in open air. The hot, pressurized water passes through a heat transfer system known as a steam generator, where it gives up heat to a separate secondary coolant loop. The secondary coolant water (which is not radioactive, unlike the steam and the turbine in a BWR) boils and creates the steam that is used to drive the turbine and generator.

as deuterium. Fusion reactors would create less radioactive waste than fission reactors, but scientists have not yet been able to produce a controlled fusion reaction that could generate cost-effective electricity from this other form of nuclear power.

Development of Nuclear Power in California

As described in the Overview, California was among the states that most enthusiastically espoused the virtues of nuclear power before this technology became a lightning rod for the nascent environmental movement. In 1976, the California government set in place a long-standing ban on new nuclear plants in the state until "there exists a demonstrated technology for the permanent disposal of spent fuel." Efforts to establish such a site at Yucca Mountain in Nevada (pl. 63) have run into continuous delays and controversy,

Plate 63. View of the rear of the tunnel boring machine at Nevada's Yucca Mountain, showcasing the laser guidance system in operation.

as have all other efforts to enact a comprehensive national waste disposal program in the United States.

However, the recent rise in concern about global climate change has led to fresh efforts to restart the nuclear industry throughout the nation, including California. For example, nuclear advocates in the State Legislature have vowed to overturn the effective state ban on nuclear power via a 2008 ballot measure after state legislation died in 2007, but the measure failed to get on the ballot.

At present, California obtains about 14 percent of its total electricity from the two in-state operating nuclear reactors, Diablo Canyon and San Onofre, as well as imports of nuclear power from Arizona and elsewhere. To address the existing ban due to waste disposal limitations, some argue that dry cask storage, a technique already in use at Rancho Seco, could safely stock wastes for 100 years, at which point long-term storage technologies may be in place.

If California overturns its current ban on nuclear power, it could open the floodgates for new kinds of nuclear power technologies. Nuclear power plants are already on the drawing boards of utilities in several other states. Given the aggressive carbon reduction goals contained in the Global Warming Solutions Act of 2006, the nuclear industry is set to invest considerable time, money, and effort into reopening the door to this controversial power source in California.

Nuclear Power Today

There are currently 103 commercial nuclear power reactors operating in 33 states. No new nuclear power reactors have been ordered since 1978. Globally, there are more than 435 nuclear reactors operating in 30 countries with a total capacity of approximately 370,000 megawatts, which represents 16 percent of the world's total electricity. In addition, more than 50 countries operate "research" reactors, and another 220 reactors currently power submarines and ships.

In terms of cost, advanced nuclear power plants could be among the cheaper supply options, but massive subsidies are required before developers will move forward. At present, more than 30 new nuclear reactors are under construction around the globe, with another 70 new reactors in the planning stages.

Though virtually no reactors have come online between 2000 and 2006, increased efficiency in power production has increased overall output of the world's nuclear fleet to the equivalent of 30 new nuclear reactors. Today roughly a third of all reactors operate more than 90 percent of the time, and more than two-thirds operate greater than 75 percent of the time, a vastly improved performance profile compared to 1990. The top 25 performing nuclear reactors are dominated by U.S. units, including California's Diablo Canyon, with Japan coming in second place.

Calls by U.S. President George Bush to restart a major nuclear power program in response to concerns about global climate change and dependence upon foreign sources of energy have prompted a reexamination of an electricity generation technology that California helped shut the door on some 20 years ago. The DOE has, for example, launched a "Nuclear Power 2010" program that hopes to jump-start a moribund nuclear industry. As much as $50 billion in loan guarantees for the nuclear industry was also slipped into the national energy bill in 2007, which the industry claimed was vital to plans to add 28 new nuclear reactors to the U.S. power supply portfolio. Each one of these power plants represents a $4 to $5 billion investment.

The Pros and Cons of Nuclear Power

+ Nuclear power plants do not directly release the "traditional" power generation pollutants, namely sulfur dioxide, nitrogen oxides, carbon dioxide, carbon monoxide, and particulates or toxics, such as mercury.

+ Nuclear power plants are, generally speaking, the largest power generation technology available; therefore, they are capable of adding significant power supply from a single, centralized location.

+ Because of massive public subsidy, nuclear power plants can be competitive with fossil fuel power plants.

+ Nuclear power plants can directly displace fossil fuel generation, since they can operate essentially around the clock.

+ New designs allegedly boost efficiency, safety, and modularity.

− Uranium is a finite fuel source.

− Nuclear power plants require about two-and-one half times as much water for cooling purposes as is required for a same-size coal plant.

− Nearly 90 percent of the United States' uranium deposits have been found in the Rocky Mountain States, and the vast majority resides on Native American lands, raising environmental justice issues.

− In the nuclear fuel processing process, the uranium enrichment process depends on huge amounts of electricity, the majority of which is currently provided by dirty fossil fuel plants releasing all of the standard air pollution emissions not released by the nuclear reactor itself. Today, two of the nation's most polluting coal plants in the United States generate electricity primarily for enriching uranium.

− The operation of nuclear power plants releases dangerous air emissions in the form of radioactive gases that include carbon-14, iodine-131, krypton, and xenon.

− Uranium mining is nearly identical to coal mining; therefore, similar issues of local land and water resources contamination arise, as well as unique radioactive contamination hazards for both mine workers and nearby populations (pl. 64).

Plate 64. Pit 3 at the Midnite uranium mine on the Spokane Indian Reservation—a Superfund cleanup site.

- Human exposure to radioactive particles can cause cancer and genetic anomalies.
- Exposure to radiation in the general environment will also have consequences on flora and fauna, impacting the ability of natural resources to sustain life.
- Catastrophic accidents could easily kill as many as 100,000 people or more.
- Abandoned mines used as storage facilities for high-level radioactive waste can continue to pose radioactive risks for as long as 250,000 years after closure.
- Increasing nuclear power plant capacity also exposes the world to greater risks of proliferation of nuclear bomb-making capacity by unstable or unfriendly governments.

The Future of Nuclear Power

The International Atomic Energy Agency predicts as many as 100 new reactors could come online over the next two decades, increasing annual demand for uranium from today's 40 million pounds to 240 million pounds. While this agency projects sufficient uranium fuel to meet this huge increase in demand, others are waving warning flags. Some go so far as to say that the world's uranium consumption could permanently outstrip supply within 50 years.

A recent study by MIT, for example, calculated that current global uranium production can only meet 65 percent of the industry's fuel needs. In fact, the domestic nuclear industry has been surviving off of government and commercial reserves that have dwindled down to next to nothing. This shortage of uranium fuel has fueled a huge run-up in the costs of nuclear fuel, jumping from just $7 per pound in 2000 to as much as $120 per pound in 2007. "Just as large numbers of new reactors are being planned, we are only starting to emerge from 20 years of underinvestment in the production capacity for the nuclear fuel to operate them," noted Thomas Neff, a MIT research affiliate. "There has been a nuclear industry myopia; they didn't take a long-term view," he added. Interestingly enough, roughly half of the United States' fuel for its fleet of reactors comes from obsolete Russian nuclear missiles.

Despite these fuel supply concerns, nuclear advocates are pinning their hopes on an improved technology known as a pebble bed reactor (PBR), also known as very high temperature reactors, under active development in South Africa and China. Instead of relying upon water as a coolant, these more advanced reactors rely upon an inert or semi-inert gas such as helium, nitrogen, or carbon dioxide. These gases are heated to extremely high temperatures to drive a turbine directly, eliminating today's elaborate steam management system, which boosts overall thermal efficiency by as much as

17 percent. In other words, less fuel is required to produce the same amount of power. Another advantage is that nonuranium fuels can be used in the PBR; materials such as thorium and plutonium could also be tapped to generate electricity.

Since the gases used for cooling do not dissolve contaminants or absorb neutrons, as is the case with water used as coolant, radioactive wastes are reduced. This, in turn, improves the economics. Although first pioneered in Germany, the technology was abandoned there, since that country is phasing out nuclear power in response to safety and environmental concerns. General Atomics is the only United States–based firm investigating the development of this nuclear option, though MIT is also involved. A 110-megawatt prototype is moving forward in South Africa, which will also desalinate seawater. Despite stiff opposition from local environmentalists, this helium-cooled reactor passed key regulatory hurdles in January 2007.

These reactors are also "modular" in the sense that several small reactors would be comprised in each power plant. In fact, PBRs could power cars. A firm called Romawa B.V. in the Netherlands is promoting a 24-megawatt modular design dubbed "Nerreus" that can power ships; serve as an off-grid, stand-alone power plant; and serve as a backup generator.

Hydrogen

The idea of a global hydrogen economy is hardly new. Jules Verne declared water "to be the coal of the future" back in the 1870s, and, a decade later, William Grove was already experimenting with primitive fuel cell technologies that ran on hydrogen.

However, the first applications of hydrogen were related to war. Shortly after the storming of the Bastille and the toppling of the monarchy during the French Revolution, a chemist named Guyton de Norveau sought to generate hydrogen to fill reconnaissance balloons. In 1794, the world's first generator of hydrogen was therefore constructed on the outskirts of Paris in an army camp as warring factions sought to take control of France.

California also played an early role in the development of hydrogen. A Canadian firm sold the first commercial electrolyzers—contraptions that could split water (H_2O) into hydrogen and oxygen—to a U.S. firm based in San Francisco in 1920. Shortly thereafter, the British biologist John Burdon Sanderson Haldane argued that liquid hydrogen was "weight for weight the most efficient known method of storing energy as it gives about three times as much heat per pound as petrol." Hydrogen could decentralize the global economy, since the costs of power production could be equalized throughout each country and, ultimately, the world, he predicted.

It is important to note that like electricity, hydrogen is a secondary energy medium. Unlike primary sources of energy that can be used directly, such as gasoline you put in your car, hydrogen has to be generated from a primary fuel source. Like electricity, hydrogen is a carrier of energy, and like electricity, the conversion to hydrogen entails a large energy loss. The principal advantage hydrogen has over electricity is that it can be stored in a liquid form; therefore, it can be used both as a transportation fuel and as a medium to displace current electricity applications.

When looking at transportation options needed to address climate change and air quality challenges, an important advantage of a hydrogen fuel cell over its internal combustion engine counterpart is simplicity. Internal combustion engines are complicated. In fact, a fuel cell propulsion system will likely have only a tenth of the moving parts required in today's conventional car engines.

At the start of the twenty-first century, it seemed the most powerful corporations in the world suddenly discovered hydrogen: General Electric, DuPont, BP, Shell, and all of the major car companies. The Bush administration pledged

$1 billion for hydrogen over a 5-year period too. All of this activity might imply that a consensus was emerging that hydrogen is the way to go. In reality, there are vastly different views of how to get to the holy grail of the hydrogen economy. As time has moved on, political and popular support for hydrogen has waned. Even environmentalists, many of whom have touted the hydrogen economy as the ultimate solution to the conundrum of energy, now wonder whether the costs of implementing the so-called "hydrogen economy" in the United States (estimates range from $20 billion to $100 billion) are commensurate with its purported clean air benefits.

Development of Hydrogen in California

The election of Arnold Schwarzenegger as governor certainly intensified the debate over hydrogen in California, since he originally picked one of the nation's leading hydrogen advocates, Terry Tamminen, to the top post at the California Environmental Protection Agency. When heading up Environment Now, Tamminen pushed hydrogen state legislation that then served as the centerpiece of the governor's environmental platform. This platform boasted that California will feature the nation's first "hydrogen highways" by 2010. By that date, each of the state's 21 major interstate highways is supposed to feature hydrogen fueling stations every 20 miles.

Other states have put some generous subsidies on the table, among them Ohio and Michigan. Connecticut state lawmakers approved a $1 billion package of incentives that stretches over the next 10 years. Texas is also big on hydrogen. General Motors announced the largest hydrogen fuel cell transaction in the world, selling over 250 of its prototype 75-kilowatt fuel cells to the Dow Chemical Company's Freeport, Texas, facility. The largest chemical plant in the world was looking for a way to make the most of hydrogen, a by-product of its chemical processes. Texas Governor Rick

Perry boasted that the GM–Dow deal allowed the Lone Star State to take a national lead on hydrogen fuel cells.

The hydrogen industry is looking for a state to become the next Silicon Valley for hydrogen. Jobs hang in the balance, but there is a more parochial concern in California. "We need to reduce California's air pollution by 50 percent by 2010 or we will be facing some significant fines for non-attainment with federal air quality standards," remarked Tamminen. "The beauty of hydrogen is that it can come from so many sources. The wasted electricity and waste sewage from Los Angeles County alone could produce enough hydrogen to fuel 100,000 cars."

California's tough air quality laws and zero-emission vehicle regulations have created a testing ground for hydrogen fuel cell technology today (pl. 65), much as the Golden State served as the laboratory for renewable energy technologies in the 1980s. The California Air Resources Board (CARB)

Plate 65. Stationary fuel cell at California State University at Northridge.

was driving this market for zero-emission vehicles by way of its tough mandate for zero-emission cars in the smoggy Los Angeles basin before it relaxed this mandate in early 2008.

Analogies are often made between these fuel cell vehicles (FCVs) and electric vehicles (EVs), which failed to grab the hearts, minds, and pocketbooks of southern Californians over a decade ago. Of course, the difference is that all of the auto companies are seeing a potential to get fuel cell vehicles on the road (pl. 66). While operating under different time frames, each major car company is involved with the Fuel Cell Partnership Program, which has been based in West Sacramento since 1999.

It is GM that is taking the biggest gamble. GM has fought against CARB's mandates for cleaner cars for years, but it dropped a long-standing lawsuit in its efforts to develop better relation with California regulators. GM lost on EVs, because although it was the first car company to deliver a commercial electric car to the California market, these EVs

Plate 66. Ford Focus hydrogen fuel cell.

failed to attract the hearts, minds, and pocketbooks of consumers. GM has already committed to being the first car company with a million fuel cell vehicles on the road, though progress is lagging behind the firm's ballyhooed projections. At one point, GM devoted 40 percent of its R&D budget to hydrogen.

Then there are the oil companies. The European firms such as Shell and BP are talking up hydrogen and renewable energy, whereas American oil giants such as ExxonMobil prefer to wait and watch and pump more oil before jumping into hydrogen markets. An exception to this generality about U.S. firms is San Ramon–based Chevron, which has taken the step of installing a fuel cell and developing a hydrogen refueling station in Richmond.

However, even if CARB's clean air and climate change goals could be met with hydrogen-powered cars and trucks, questions remain as to whether the environment will reap the full potential benefits of hydrogen. Here is the key issue: Although hydrogen is everywhere, it rarely exists as a free-floating element. It needs to be extracted from either water or hydrocarbons, hence the "black" versus "green" hydrogen scenarios.

Hydrogen Today

Fuel cells can work in stationary as well as mobile applications, thereby making them very attractive to both emerging electricity markets and long-term transportations options in California. These distributed systems rely upon an electrochemical process to convert chemical energy into electricity and hot water and generate electricity at a cost of approximately 10 to 12 cents per kilowatt-hour. Though capital costs are extremely high, $4,000 per kilowatt, they have the highest fuel-to-electricity conversion ratio of all energy sources.

Fuel cells operate more or less like a battery and run on hydrogen to create electrical, rather than mechanical, energy. Unlike a battery, fuel cells do not need to be recharged. They will produce electric power as long as there is hydrogen fuel and oxygen (from the air) available. They are classified according to the type of electrolyte employed. The electrolyte is the component through which the disassociated positive ions travel between the positive and negative electrodes, while the electrons travel through the external circuit and do work. The four primary types of fuel cells are proton exchange membrane (PEMFC), phosphoric acid (PAFC), molten carbonate (MCFC), and solid oxide (SOFC) fuel cells. Each fuel cell uses a specific set of electrochemical reactions to produce electricity, operates at a specific range of temperatures, and employs a specific catalyst.

Despite critics who contend that the hydrogen economy is fraught with problems—a huge price tag, energy losses in converting electricity to liquid hydrogen fuel, and even some fears of increasing the size of the ozone hole—California and other states continue to push fuel cell technologies, though performance and cost have lagged behind expectations and hype. The target price for power from a fuel cell is $50 per kilowatt. At present, the cost of generating electricity from a fuel cell hovers around $500 per kilowatt.

The Pros and Cons of Hydrogen

+ It can be employed as micro-power plants or as propulsion systems for automobiles.
+ It can be generated from a variety of fuel sources, including both renewable energy sources as well as fossil fuels.
+ It offers the most efficient conversion ratio of fuel to energy of all energy sources.
+ It offers clean on-site power generation.
+ Water consumption, as well as discharge, is minimal.
+ It can help solve California's prime climate change challenge: emissions from the transportation sector.
+ Hydrogen allows renewable energy to be stored, addressing one of the prime obstacles to widespread reliance upon intermittent but clean energy sources.

- It augments and supports trends toward a decentralized power grid featuring smaller and cleaner generation sources.
- Cost is currently too high for widespread deployment in either mobile or stationary applications.
- Fuel cell power plants contain high concentrations of hydrogen, which presents fire and explosion risks.
- Fuel cell power plants require raw fuel cleanup to protect the reformer and stack from catalyst poisoning.
- Fuel cell power plants take up more space than combined-cycle power natural gas–fired power plants and could disturb habitats.
- Changeover to hydrogen infrastructure is costly and time-consuming.
- If hydrogen is employed to power a motor vehicle, as much as 80 percent of the original energy is lost in conversion processes.

The Future of Hydrogen

"Hydrogen is the most dangerous of all fuels and could be a boon to terrorists. We need major technological breakthroughs, and whole new materials, for hydrogen to make sense for consumers."

These are the words of Joe Romm, a physicist who worked on developing fuel cell technologies under the Clinton administration and author of the book entitled *The Hype About Hydrogen*. Romm sees a hydrogen conspiracy at the federal level of government. He, and other cynics, claims the federal Bush administration is pushing a "black hydrogen" agenda based on traditional energy sources such as nuclear and coal, not the clean renewable energy fuels that have long been envisioned as the feedstock for the hydrogen economy.

"The Bush administration is essentially designating hydrogen as the winner, the silver bullet to our air pollution problems. Since the hydrogen economy will be here in 10 to 15 years, we don't have to do anything about global warming between now and then," said Romm. From his point of view, introducing a hydrogen car before 2030 would actually "undermine efforts to reduce greenhouse gases contributing to global climate change. Why? Hydrogen will only penetrate the transportation sector in significant numbers after 2035. It is not the easiest, nor the cheapest way to gain near-term air pollution benefits or to wean us off of foreign sources of oil," he said. It took wind and solar technologies 20 years to drop tenfold in price, reductions inspired in large part by California's energy policies. Romm claims that a fuel cell is 100 times more expensive than the good old-fashioned internal combustion engine.

To many of California's long-time hydrogen backers, today's debate over hydrogen is both exhilarating and a bit frustrating. "We need to get some private capital involved to make things happen. In essence, we need to let greed rule," commented Alvin Duskin, a California wind power pioneer. His comments reflected a view that shaped the Jerry Brown administration's program for jump-starting the global wind power industry through lucrative tax breaks and other incentives. Duskin maintains that a $1.00 per kilogram national subsidy for hydrogen (or $1.00 tax per gallon of gasoline) would enable large-scale wind farms at America's best wind sites in the Great Plains to generate hydrogen cost-effectively.

Radical environmental activist Randy Hayes, who helped launch a national "green" hydrogen campaign with Duskin dubbed "The Conversion Project," sees cities being the early adopters, ordering fleets of first-generation hydrogen fuel cell vehicles. The San Francisco Board of Supervisors has already declared San Francisco to be a "Hydrogen City" and has plans on the drawing boards for three hydrogen fueling stations and solar, wind, and tidal power pilot projects that could generate the electricity to create hydrogen.

Nevertheless, Peter Schwartz, executive director of Oakland-based Global Business Network, believes nuclear and more traditional sources of power will have to play a role in the hydrogen economy. "Silly" is the word he used to describe those believing that all of our future hydrogen fuel can be derived from renewable energy sources. He predicts natural gas, a fuel already in tight supply, will be the dominant source of hydrogen over the next 10 or 15 years. "Few people realize that a small hydrogen economy already exists," he said. "Hydrogen is used in refineries and is a by-product of several plastics and food production processes. In the near-term, hydrogen will be extracted at refiners, gas pumping stations and chemical plants."

What does this all mean for California, you might ask? According to conflict negotiator Bill Shireman, CEO of Future 500, a San Francisco-based organization that works out collaborations between corporate players and environmentalists, California could shape the nation's hydrogen economy by tilting toward renewable energy sources—such as wind and solar power—that are so abundant in the Golden State. "What's interesting about the battle over hydrogen and fuel cells is that it has the potential to draw together long-time adversaries," commented Shireman. "It meets environmentalist demands for zero-emission cars. It also aligns with the ten-year objectives of the biggest auto companies. It could represent a breakthrough achievement for the Schwarzenegger administration."

So far, California is falling woefully short on transportation-related hydrogen development, according to CARB. "While substantial progress has been made," claims CARB, "simultaneously achieving performance, durability and cost objectives continues to be a difficult challenge. In addition, the cost, weight and volume of adequate on-vehicle hydrogen storage and availability of hydrogen production and infrastructure remain major barriers to commercialization," reads a status report issued by the state agency. The Hydrogen Highway project is also lagging behind schedule.

While the goal of this highly publicized initiative was to have 50 to 100 hydrogen filling stations scattered throughout California by 2010—designed to support at least 2,000 hydrogen vehicles on the road—progress thus far falls "far shy" of this goal. In light of this delay, fuel cell and car manufacturers are concerned that the necessary infrastructure for the hydrogen economy will be insufficient in the short term to deliver on the promises surrounding the hydrogen economy.

CHALLENGES

The Risks of the Status Quo
and Systems Overhaul

MANY OF THE MOST forward-looking U.S. leaders on energy issues call California home, and many cut their teeth here, venturing into the great unknown with a bold sense of what was possible. Without this human ingenuity and public policy acumen on the part of activists and politicians alike, California's natural history might have underwritten a much different story on energy.

Jan Hamrin (pl. 67) began working in the electricity business in 1964, peddling new electric kitchen appliances and food recipes on TV shows for a New Mexico electricity utility. The goal of electric utilities back then was to promote gizmos that increased electricity consumption. With a degree in home economics, she never dreamed she would spend her entire career promoting renewable energy and energy efficiency in California and the rest of the world. Since her career path chronicles, in a sense, the evolution of California's electricity markets over the last three decades, her story is presented here as a convenient way to set up

Plate 67. Jan Hamrin and former state senator Herschel Rosenthal, holding resolutions commending the Independent Energy Producers Association.

this overview of California's energy challenges. (Hamrin was recognized for her role in developing renewable energy sources by the American Wind Energy Association and the California Energy Commission in 2007.) Her story sums up the modern human history embedded in California's efforts to meet daunting energy challenges with novel and enlightened solutions.

Hamrin's first direct exposure to renewable energy came when she pursued an advanced degree in biological ecology, with a special emphasis on environmental policy, at the University of California at Davis in 1975. She began studying solar energy just as the first energy crisis hit the nation in the mid-1970s. What she discovered was that Village Homes, a small community located in Davis that featured passive solar systems and other energy conservation measures, fared better on reducing energy consumption than a community in Hemet, located in San Bernardino County, that was outfitted with fancy active solar heating and cooling systems. "In Hemet, people just assumed technology would take care of everything, whereas in Village Homes, people became more aware of their energy usage and closed the shades and did other small tasks that saved considerable energy," reminisced Hamrin.

Shortly thereafter, Hamrin began working with the Energy Extension Service, which operated through the University of California system. Her goal was to ensure that energy research conducted at the eight campuses and three national laboratories "was relevant to commercial applications of renewable energy technologies." Impressed by the Japanese, who sought to apply solar research into intermediate products, Hamrin was worried about researching solar energy to death without delivering useful products to the marketplace. Her advocacy, nevertheless, raised eyebrows with a few folks in academic circles, among them Edward Teller, the so-called "father" of the hydrogen bomb and a staunch nuclear power advocate. "In those days, folks thought this solar stuff was small and not very macho," she recollected.

Her next stop was the California Energy Commission, where she took over management of solar programs. (Back then, most of the attention with solar was on hot-water systems, not solar PVs.) Among her accomplishments was development of a new state incentive for solar energy. One night, after dining with her new colleagues (and a few glasses of wine), they somehow came up with the appropriate level for state solar tax credits. "People would be surprised to know how often much good public policy has been devised over a good dinner," she chuckled. "It's often not about theoretical economic analysis. It's passing the laugh test while still accomplishing something."

Her partner at the time (and current husband), Tim Rosenfeld, then began developing a small wind farm to get into the business side of California's emerging shift to smaller and cleaner power sources. He became increasingly frustrated with the protracted bad faith negotiations on the parts of private utilities. After nearly two years of wrangling with utilities who were begrudgingly required by law to buy the output from his wind farm—and still no fair power purchase contract—Hamrin suggested to him and other energy entrepreneurs that they create a trade group to represent all of the developers flocking to California to build renewable and cogeneration projects. "I told Tim and others that they needed a third party to negotiate contracts so that they were not the bad guy. You can't go up to the California Public Utilities Commission and play hardball with utilities, and then do business with them as a buddy. I didn't think that would work," she said. Her condition for taking on this challenging assignment: "I would take the high ground. As a trade organization, we would only advocate good public policy. I was not interested in representing short-sighted, get-rich-quick kind of companies."

Hamrin soon found herself head of the Independent Energy Producers Association (IEP), which brought wind, solar, geothermal, biomass, and natural gas–fired cogenerators all under one big roof. "Most people thought that these small power plants authorized by the federal PURPA law would be developed by small operators. But once the state tax credits were combined with PURPA and federal tax incentives, well-heeled financiers suddenly wanted to get into the energy business. People who were tinkerers—with the next greatest invention in their garage—also wanted to get into the action," she recalled. "To be successful a company had to have both—the techies and the financial wizards. Unfortunately, the industry learned that lesson the hard way."

Her proudest accomplishment during this pivotal period for the world's renewable energy industry was her negotiation of the Standard Offer No. 4 contracts, precursors to the feed-in tariffs that have been so successful in developing renewable energy projects so quickly in Europe. These contracts locked in fixed payments for the first 10 years of a project's life based on estimates of what a utility might pay to bring an equivalent amount of power capacity online. With the promise of a long-term price and a solid revenue stream in hand, private developers could find banks willing to invest in new technologies. That is why California was able to bring over 6,000 megawatts of new power supply online within six years at prices below those estimated by the same utility's resource plans.

She ultimately left IEP in the early 1990s "when the attorneys began to take over the membership." She went on to write a series of guidelines to state legislators and regulators to ensure that renewable-energy generators would not be pushed out of deregulated markets. She survived the collapse of California's power markets during the brief heyday of deregulation, though her take on those times is surprisingly upbeat. "Nothing will ever be perfect the first time out of the chute," she recalled. "But with AB 1980, the restructuring law, there was no room for adjustments. All of the economists assumed a world with perfect competition. But there is no such thing!" she laughed. "The whole system was designed assuming prices would go down. When prices went up, the system imploded itself," she explained further. Ironically enough, while many perceive that nascent green power program as a major failure, Hamrin disagrees. "The green power market was the one aspect of our restructured electricity market that was working," she claimed. The problem, in reality, was that the price for green power was pegged to natural gas, which was the lowest-cost resource at that time, because utilities wanted to pay as little as possible for renewable power. When natural gas prices went through the roof, so did the price of green power. This pricing approach denigrated one of the primary advantages of renewable sources: that they can unhook our electricity costs from fossil fuel price swings.

Soon thereafter, Hamrin began to work internationally more often, helping China develop its first renewable energy law. After a few more energy gigs with federal agencies and national organizations, Hamrin ended up designing her current job during the state's experiment with deregulation. The notion of green power was so new to consumers that she saw a need for someone somewhere to create standards and to certify that, in fact, electricity that was sold as "green" was indeed green. "I really did not want to get into the certification business, it is really hard work, and seems to be something government should do. But nobody else was stepping up to the table," she said.

The end result of Hamrin's efforts was the creation of the San Francisco-based Center for Resource Solutions (CRS) and the Green-e certification program. The one advantage of having a nonprofit serve as a certification body, argued Hamrin, "is that we can be more flexible and make adjustments quickly as markets change and new kinds of products emerge." CRS is currently developing a certification system for products promising to offset carbon emissions linked to global climate change. "Environmental markets will only succeed if the products being sold are credible," Hamrin chided. "Making them credible is one of the roles we seem to

Plate 68. Jan Hamrin standing inside a wind turbine tower.

have carved out for ourselves." Hamrin stepped down from the CRS executive director position in early 2008, but has not slowed down in her efforts to move renewable energy sources into the mainstream (pl. 68).

Hamrin believes California is still an energy leader, "but not internationally like we were in the 1980s. We had it all, but it came to a screeching halt in the 1990s." Still, she observed that California is viewed as a country unto itself by energy experts around the world. "California is still the state people love to hate. This is still the wild, wild West, where people are willing to try new things. People are fascinated. They want to see what happens as long as it's not them doing the experimenting! But can we deliver. . . that is now the challenge in California." There is a bit of this bravado today in California, with the passage of the Global Warming Solutions Act of 2006. Unfortunately, "there are no widgets that can simply solve the climate crisis. We have to transform the entire system, the technology as well as the infrastructure."

As Hamrin's career clearly shows, the energy business is full of unforeseen risks and is fraught with unexpected twists and turns. California's wild experimentation on the energy front—exemplified by the rolling blackouts in 2000 and 2001—has earned the state the reputation as a pioneer, but such forays into the great unknown can also have severe consequences. Because energy reaches into so many aspects of our daily lives, the challenges are immense. They cover a broad spectrum of economic, environmental, and social issues. As the first decade of the twenty-first century draws to a close, all eyes are again focused on California and its radical reformist agenda.

Here are just six among many challenges California is facing today:

- Global climate change
- Finite, polluting, and often imported fossil fuels
- The question of nuclear power
- The terrorist threat, national security, and energy reliability
- Variability, cost, and NIMBY challenges of renewable energy sources
- A dumb electricity grid

The Latin roots for the word "challenge" is *calumnia*, a word that can be translated as "deception." We in the United States and the rest of the West typically look at challenges as obstacles to overcome on the path to some righteous goal. Yet another way to look at challenges/deceptions is that they are merely natural responses in self-regulating systems bumping up against the limits of current growth patterns. Therefore, we could turn the notion of challenge on its head, recognizing that the identification of a challenge is merely another opportunity in the ever-present natural evolution of complex interactive systems.

In *The Dance of Change: The Challenges of Sustaining Momentum in Learning Organizations*, a book by MIT professor Peter Senge—a devout disciple of "systems thinking"—and a number of colleagues sum up their views on challenges in this way:

> The stronger a learning or change initiative, the stronger the challenge seems to be, because they represent natural systemic responses to maintaining balances threatened by the initiative. At the same time, the earlier and more clearly that you can anticipate these challenges, the easier it becomes to deal with them. You don't have to wait until the challenges become visible; the best time to prepare for them is before they have appeared. They require investments of time and energy that may not be possible once you are facing the problems directly.
>
> As leaders at all levels deal with these challenges (and others) regularly, they may gradually cease to appear as challenges at all. They will become aspects of life, episodes that bolster and strengthen those committed to genuine change, bringing new capabilities and new understanding.
>
> —*Senge et al. 1999:30*

Senge and his cohorts operate within the realm of business, but the perspective of "systems thinking" extends well beyond the confines of the corporate boardroom. Nations, forests, the nuclear family, and our atmosphere are all systems.

Challenge 1: Global Climate Change

If we could suspend gravity and walk vertically out from the Earth (instead of being limited to horizontal travel on the Earth's surface), it would take us just two hours to reach the edge of the troposphere, the bottom layer of our atmosphere where most weather happens (pl. 69). When we fly in a jetliner, we occupy the stratosphere, the next layer of sky, which extends to about 30 miles out. Outer space is approximately

Plate 69. View from the stratosphere. Most weather happens in the lower layer, the troposphere.

200 miles out. The hot debate on climate change is focused on this thin layer of atmosphere where we all live.

Our atmosphere provides a broad range of services we have come to take for granted. Not only does it protect us from ultraviolet light rays thanks to ozone (a job now in jeopardy due to air pollution), but our atmosphere also provides fresh water in the form of rain, delivers the oxygen we need to breathe in order to survive, and recycles virtually everything. Radio signals, airline flights, and sailboats all work thanks to the ecosystem services our atmosphere supplies. Our dear friend, the atmosphere, has kept processes in balance that have supported myriad forms of life for millennia.

In the book *Who Owns The Sky? Our Common Assets and the Future of Capitalism,* author Peter Barnes observes that what we humans commonly call "sky" is a phenomenal gift of nature and a highly refined system:

> Like an orchestra, a system is an ensemble of many parts, with a set of rules and feedback loops that, most of the time, help the parts work together smoothly. There are, however,

two types of feedback loops: a virtuous kind and a perverse kind. In virtuous loops (which scientists, oddly enough, call "negative"), if one part of the system gets out of line, another part of the system brings it back. In perverse loops (which scientists call "positive"), one bad event triggers another, and the whole system can spiral into disequilibrium.

—*Barnes 2001:23*

Global climate change is the classic perverse feedback loop. Barnes goes on to note that the fundamental issue facing the planet is not sources of materials (e.g., metals or silicon). It is the sinks that accumulate wastes. "The problem is, where do we put our voluminous wastes? Molecules never disappear; they always go somewhere, and gravity keeps them tied to earth," Barnes writes. So the ability of the biosphere to absorb them must always be taken into account. "How do we store radioactive wastes for ten thousand years when no government has ever lasted more than a thousand?" He goes on to note that the bigger the difference between inflow and outflow, the bigger the imbalance in our atmosphere and other living systems linked to planet Earth.

What, then, is the science behind climate change, and what are the imbalances between inflow and outflow that threaten such an impact on our future? The most important imbalance is not in urban garbage or nuclear waste but in energy.

Science tells us that the energy contained in radiation increases as wavelengths get shorter, with gamma rays, x-rays, and ultraviolet light having the shortest wavelengths and infrared and radio waves having the longest. Most of the radiation coming from the sun into our global climate has wavelengths in the range from violet at 400 nanometers to red at 700 nanometers, which we call visible light because our eyes evolved to see best at these ranges. Our atmosphere is largely transparent to radiation at these wavelengths. The most common light wave making its way from

Plate 70. Earth at twilight, as seen from the International Space Station orbiting at an altitude of 211 nautical miles. The sunlit half receives visible light energy from the sun. Both the sunlit and dark halves emit invisible infrared energy into space.

the sun to Earth is yellow-green in color and approximately 500 nanometers in length.

The Earth radiates energy just as the sun does. The total amount of energy entering the Earth's climate (mostly from the sun) must be balanced by the total amount of energy the Earth radiates back into outer space (pl. 70). The temperatures on Earth average around one twentieth the surface temperature of the sun, illustrating the energy loss that occurs as solar energy makes the 92-million-mile trip to our dear planet. The cooler surface of Earth radiates energy at a slower rate and a much longer wavelength—that is, in the infrared range—than radiation from the sun.

Composed primarily of three gases—nitrogen, oxygen, and argon—our atmosphere has done an incredible job of maintaining a stable environment to foster a plethora of life forms. The Earth's atmosphere has little effect on the mostly visible radiation arriving from the sun beyond scattering the shorter, bluer wavelengths, making the sky look blue and the sun look yellow. Yet some of the molecules in the atmosphere—among them carbon dioxide, ozone, and water vapor—absorb infrared radiation emitted by the Earth. The molecules that do so are those that have more than two atoms or contain atoms of more than one element, such as CO_2. Such molecules trap the energy from infrared radiation in the form of vibrations in the bonds between the atoms. Eventually the gas molecules radiate this energy, too, but only half of it is emitted into outer space; the other half is radiated in the other direction, back to Earth. The natural result of this phenomenon is that the temperature of the Earth's global climate is higher than it would be without these gases. They are called greenhouse gases (GHGs) because they behave exactly like the glass in a greenhouse window does. Some amount of the greenhouse effect is necessary for life on Earth, because without it the water on Earth's surface would freeze. If the amount of GHGs in the atmosphere increases, however, more and more energy becomes trapped by the translucent blanket that is our atmosphere.

As far back as 1890, scientists raised the question of whether burning fossil fuels was increasing levels of CO_2 and other molecules that would augment the naturally occurring greenhouse effect, resulting in a rise in overall temperatures, thereby altering the complex weather systems that shape and influence all life forms on Earth. A worldwide growth in CO_2 was first documented in the 1960s, with evidence accumulating over subsequent decades. There is a growing consensus that society is facing, in essence, an increase in the greenhouse effect— commonly referred to as "global warming" or "global climate change"—fueled by our century-plus–long, ever-rising consumption of petroleum, natural gas, and coal.

What consequences does California face from global climate change? Consider the following summary presented by several leading scientists in the book *Global Climate Change and California: Potential Impacts and Responses*:

> If projections of global climate change are correct, the natural ecosystems of California might undergo major changes during the next century. Such changes might include large economic losses in timber, fisheries and recreation; major changes in our national and state parks and forests and in our nature preserves and conservation areas; increase in extinction of endangered species; loss of large areas of existing habitats; and development of new habitats whose location and areal extent can only be surmised. Many areas currently set aside for the conservation of specific ecosystems might no longer be suitable to them. Yet, in spite of the potential seriousness of these problems, which could dwarf all other environmental changes, California is at present in a poor situation to project what the effects of global change on its natural ecosystems might be.
>
> —*Knox and Scheuring 1991: 123*

This assessment was made in 1991. At that point in time, scientists were already projecting that forests throughout California (pl. 71) might no longer be sustainable, "since a tree seed that might germinate in a suitable climate in one decade might reach maturity in a climate no longer suitable to its growth or the germination and survival of its seeds." The book goes onto note that if these conditions were to occur, "only the shortest- and longest-lived tree species might persist. Trees common over much of California's landscape today might be no longer viable" (Knox and Scheuring 1991).

Because of California's multitude of physiographic regions, and its complex flora and fauna, research going on in other parts of the country could not be extrapolated to apply to California. Research was more advanced in understanding how climate change might impact the east, Midwest, and south. California has since pioneered research on climate change and now leads the nation in terms of state research programs designed to shape future state energy, land use, and transportation policy. Among the research completed to

Plate 71.
A meadow
in Sequoia
National Park.

date is a historical review of sea level rise along the California coast (fig. 19), a challenge facing the state as three of its largest cities—Los Angeles, San Diego, and San Francisco—are located near the Pacific Ocean.

In 2003, a virtual research center was created with the help of state funding. Known as the California Climate Change Center, it comprises core research efforts at Scripps Institution of Oceanography in La Jolla and the University of California at Berkeley, as well as substantive complementary research activities at other research institutions.

The California Climate Change Center has installed meteorological and hydrological sensors in key remote areas to better understand and document how the climate is changing in our state. Sensors have been installed in Yosemite National Park, the Santa Margarita Ecological

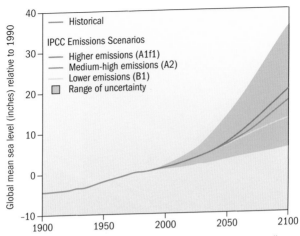

Figure 19. Projected sea level rise scenarios for California's coastline.

Reserve, and the White Mountains. Research using data from this sensing infrastructure is contributing to our understanding of important processes such as how snow melt conditions are impacted by elevation. This information will be crucial to project the effects of climate change on water and other state resources. Scientists from Scripps have shown, for example, that more and more of the precipitation falling in the Sierra Nevada is rain instead of snow. This fact has significant implications for water storage in California. The World Resources Institute declared this work one of the major breakthroughs in climate change science in 2005. The same Scripps group published a paper in *Science* (Westerling et al. 2006) reporting an increase of large forest fires in the western United States. The researchers demonstrated a statistical association between large fire events and the early onset of snow melt caused by higher ambient temperatures (fig. 20).

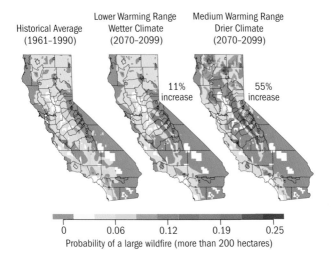

Historical Average
(1961-1990)

Lower Warming Range
Wetter Climate
(2070-2099)

11%
increase

Medium Warming Range
Drier Climate
(2070-2099)

55%
increase

| 0 | 0.06 | 0.12 | 0.19 | 0.25 |

Probability of a large wildfire (more than 200 hectares)

Figure 20. Earlier spring runoff from snow melt in the Sierra Nevada, due to climate change, leads to drier conditions and increased fire risk in summer.

The research has also discovered major challenges facing the state's future energy strategy. For example, climate change will increase demands for air conditioning in summer but reduce needs for heat in winter. Changes in precipitation also impact hydropower availability, both positively and negatively. Among the major concerns, for example, is the lack of a snow pack during winter months, which has traditionally served as a form of storage for spring runoff and hydroelectric production. With less snow, the existing assumptions about hydroelectric availability will no longer hold, and total hydropower production would be expected to shrink.

Scientists examined stream flow data for more than 300 river systems between 1848 and 2002. Of the snowmelt-dominated gauges, which totaled 241 in number, two-thirds had an early spring onset date of more than three days.

California's utilities are already cleaner than those of the rest of the country, so it is our motor vehicles and buildings (as well as everyday habits) that will have to play major roles in forging solutions. Because the rest of the United States burns so much more coal than California—and coal is the least climate-friendly electricity fuel source—carbon reductions will come easier for other states. Large reductions on carbon can be secured by switching to renewable and other noncarbon sources. Meanwhile, California will have to focus on the transportation and building sectors, which together account for roughly 80 percent of California's total energy consumption (fig. 21).

Climate change is clearly a challenge facing the entire world. The United States has been the major laggard in pursuing policies and programs to address this potential environmental catastrophe, largely because of coal and inefficiency. With just 5 percent of the world's population, the United States pumps out almost a quarter of the world's CO_2. Even California, with its aggressive renewable energy targets on paper (20 percent of total electricity supply by 2010), today imports twice as much coal-fired power as it generates from modern renewable energy facilities. California is exporting nearly $30 billion every year—that is $2,500

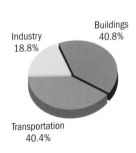

Figure 21. California energy consumption in 2003. Transportation and building sectors offer equally large targets to reduce fossil fuel energy use.

from every Californian household—to buy imported fossil fuels.

Challenge 2: Finite, Polluting, and Often Imported Fossil Fuels

Global demand for oil is 84 million barrels *every day*. The United States consumes an estimated 20 million of those barrels. About two thirds of it goes into our gas tanks and the fuel tanks of trucks, trains, and airplanes, but oil is ubiquitous in contemporary life; for instance, you will find petroleum in many chemicals, medicines, synthetic fabrics, and almost everything plastic. We have to import approximately 13 million of those barrels, and at an ever-rising cost. Roughly a quarter of our balance of trade deficit is due to our purchase of foreign oil. As economies grow in India and China, so do emerging middle classes there, who are buying more cars, pushing demand for oil higher and faster than ever before.

For more than a century, U.S. energy and foreign policy has been based in part on petroleum: where it is geographically and which countries are sucking it out of the ground. As much of the world's oil production comes from nations that are culturally at odds with our own, the United States is caught between an insatiable demand for this "black gold" and upholding democratic principles that are ignored and even scorned by the oil-producing countries, some of which are unstable or controlled by brutal dictators or religious extremists (pl. 72).

The United States has a diverse economy, but petroleum and other fossil fuels still play a fundamental role. Unfortunately, the United States does not sit on enough oil to satisfy our current needs. Even if we suspended all environmental protections, even if we could extract every drop beneath us, we would not produce enough to meet our own energy needs over the long term. Meanwhile, supplies of drillable oil worldwide are declining. While some

Plate 72. A flame from the Baji oil refinery in Iraq illuminates fuel storage tanks, with armed guard in the foreground.

oil giants such as the Russians and the Saudis have substantial deposits, there will soon come a time when the cost of extraction will force prices higher and higher. There still will not be enough, regardless of the price, to meet the world demand.

The debate over available supply of the three primary fossil fuels driving today's economy—oil, natural gas, and coal—certainly offer California challenges as it attempts to make the transition to a more sustainable energy economy.

Petroleum remains California's leading source of energy, and the volatility of the global oil market will no doubt carry major repercussions for state businesses and residents. Beyond concerns over global climate change are major questions about short- and long-term price. Rich Ferguson (Ferguson 2007), research director for the Center for Energy Efficiency and Renewable Technologies, points out that as crude oil prices increased between May 2004 and

January 2007, profits to oil producers increased on the aggregate level by approximately $1.5 trillion.

This transfer of wealth has led to efforts at the federal level of government to reduce subsidies to the oil industry. Some have gone so far as to suggest new taxes to siphon off industry profits and direct them to the development of alternative fuels. However, one such effort in California, ballot measure Proposition 87 in 2006, failed.

"The concept of less oil even at high prices is a difficult one for modern individualistic Westerners to grasp," comments Ferguson. "We are used to thinking that almost *anything* can be obtained if we have enough money. This may be true for individuals but not necessarily true for society at large. Rich individuals will still be able to obtain plenty of fuel even if global oil supplies begin to decline and prices increase. But *collectively*, people will have to learn to live with less oil" (Ferguson 2007).

Ferguson spins this scenario:

Less oil to burn would mean that there would be less transportation and less motorized equipment available. Cars, trucks, airplanes, railroad trains, and ships would be able to travel fewer miles. Farm and construction equipment would be able to do less work. This would happen if there is less fuel regardless of what the price of fuel might be—you can't burn oil that doesn't exist.

Cutting transportation by 10 percent suddenly would create economic disaster. Unemployment would become even more widespread. Stock markets would collapse taking 401ks with them. The gulf between the rich and the poor would become a chasm. The global monetary system would be chaos.

Oil would become the de facto global currency—if it hasn't already. U.S. dollars, the currency used by international oil markets in the last century, would become increasingly worthless.

> Only a handful of countries produce more oil than they
> burn, and most of these are in the Middle East. These export-
> ing countries would suddenly be the wealthiest in the world
> as importing countries competed for remaining supplies.
>
> —Ferguson 2007: 5–6

Ferguson's conclusion: "The world is completely unprepared for declines in the crude oil supply." His assertions are backed up by government sources. The U.S. Governmental Accounting Office dropped a bombshell report in February 2007. Among other things, this report warned that there was an urgent need in the United States for a strategic program to develop alternative energy sources. "The United States, as the largest consumer of oil and one of the nations most heavily dependent on oil for transportation, may be especially vulnerable among the industrialized countries of the world."

According to the International Energy Agency (IEA) "Medium-Term Oil Market Report" (International Energy Agency 2007) issued in July 2007, oil, as well as natural gas, will witness tightness in supply beyond 2010. "A stronger demand outlook, together with project slippage and geopolitical problems has led to downward revisions of OPEC spare capacity . . . ," reads the report's executive summary. "Despite an increase in biofuels production and a bunching of supply projects over the next few years, OPEC spare capacity is expected to remain relatively constrained before 2009," continues the report, noting that increasing demand in the developing world will "once more pull [OPEC spare capacity] down to uncomfortably low levels" (International Energy Agency 2007). In other words, the IEA is still worried that supply can keep up with demand and that price volatility will continue in the near future.

The report goes on to note that declines in oil field production have been steeper than expected. The good news is that refinery capacity has increased globally as a result of subsidies and other market incentives (such as high prices), and less attractive sources of heavy/sour oil are now being processed as a result of new technologies. Still, the IEA notes that the situation with natural gas is even tighter than that with oil through the end of this decade, and this factor further increases the risk that high prices will stick.

> Over the past 25 years there has been a substitution away from fuel oil and towards natural gas. However, when natural gas supplies have been insufficient or there have been supply problems (such as those seen following Hurricanes Katrina and Rita in 2005, Russia in 2006), fuel oil has been the natural substitute. By the end of the decade, such flexibility may be constrained, producing upward pressures on all hydrocarbons.
>
> —*International Energy Agency 2007: 7*

For California, natural gas is still the dominant fuel for new electricity power generation. Current economic and environmental considerations have encouraged natural gas-fueled power plants to become the standard when it comes to constructing new power plants in this country. Natural gas typically has a higher fuel cost than coal, but new gas-fired power plants are generally cheaper to build than new coal plants. The lower capital costs of gas-fired resources stem largely from the lack of need for extensive air pollution controls.

Fuel price volatility and a fairly steady rise in price have made natural gas less attractive this decade. The key to moderating natural gas fuel prices today could be increasing diversity of supply, hence the current debate over liquefied natural gas (LNG) imports (pl. 73). Nevertheless, proposed terminals off of Humboldt Bay, in Long Beach, and off the Ventura coast have all been rejected by local and state regulators. The only successful LNG terminal sited to serve the California market has been constructed in Mexico to serve Sempra Energy's California natural gas customers.

The enthusiasm for LNG has also been tempered by price increases in LNG supply over the past five years. Many of the arguments used by proponents of LNG in the recent past—it

Plate 73. A tanker carrying liquefied natural gas (LNG).

could help decouple natural gas costs from oil—have been called into question as LNG costs have risen at an even faster rate than traditional natural gas supplies, and NIMBY opposition has stalled many terminals throughout the United States.

Then there is coal. The challenge with coal is the opposite of its fossil fuel brethren. Instead of running out of the stuff, which is increasing price, coal is so abundant that it is priced too low, especially in light of its negative environmental impacts. At present, the United States still burns, on average, roughly 20 pounds of coal for every citizen per day. That adds up to over 1 billion tons of coal annually.

Whereas California has, in effect, banned future purchases of electricity generated from coal in other states, there are a number of new coal plants being proposed throughout the west and the rest of the United States. With coal being the lowest-cost source of electricity, you could argue that California has boxed itself in, limiting its access to not only domestic oil supplies just off of its coastline, but also imports of cheap coal-fired power plants that are being built in the southwest, Rocky Mountains, and Pacific northwest.

That said, the Crandall Canyon mine disaster near Huntington, Utah, in August 2007 provided a vivid reminder

THE PROS AND CONS OF LNG

LNG is a liquid form of natural gas that is cooled to minus 259 degrees F. When warmed, LNG returns to its gaseous state and can be used for heating and cooking as well as to generate electricity. There has never been a spill from an LNG tanker over its 60-year history of the industry (although other accidents have occurred). The increased threat of terrorism since 9/11 has helped raise opposition to LNG in the United States, largely because this country, unlike Japan and Australia, has for so long relied upon domestic natural gas sources.

Developers are pushing natural gas drilling activity to record levels just to keep up with current demand. Much of this drilling activity is being proposed in environmentally sensitive regions of the country. North America appears to be running out of inexpensive natural gas, so the big energy companies are pushing imported LNG to fill the gap.

California's traditional prime sources of natural gas have been Canada and the southwest. Prices have escalated and remain volatile because of future supply uncertainty. As a consequence, natural gas prices spiked and are not expected to drop significantly anytime in the near future.

Complicating the debate over LNG is the growing and even greater environmental threat from coal, the dirtiest of all fossil fuels. Utilities are planning a huge number of new coal-burning power plants throughout the western United States. While none are planned for California because of the state's strict air quality and new climate change laws, bringing LNG to California could potentially help displace new coal-fired plants serving the rest of the west.

No doubt there are also serious economic and environmental consequences if California becomes a major LNG importer. Billions of dollars will flow out of the United States to countries that produce the imported LNG, with billions more to be spent for the high-tech terminals and ships needed to get the LNG here. Environmental concerns also play a factor as development of LNG supplies in Bolivia threatens the rainforest, a diminishing resource that helps absorb carbon and therefore mitigates against global climate change.

On the other hand, Australia is developing its LNG export business from offshore gas fields, avoiding some of the ecological disturbances that plague other sources of LNG. A project under development on land in Australia will feature the world's first commercial-scale carbon dioxide injection system. The goal is to re-inject three million metric tons of CO_2 underground. That is the equivalent of removing 250,000 large passenger cars from the road.

---

of one of the downsides of relying upon America's cheapest and most plentiful electricity fuel. Despite technology advances, coal mining can still be lethal occupation. In addition, impacts on the environment can be quite severe. Among the most controversial aspects of coal mining are the mountaintop removal mines (pl. 74) that have already covered over 700 miles of streams and removed 400,000 acres of forests in Appalachia, according to Jeff Goodell, author of *Big Coal: The Dirty Secret behind America's Energy Future* (Goodell 2006). Instead of strengthening regulations to limit this type of coal mining, the Bush administration's response to the need for more energy in these times of heightened national security was to try to gut environmental controls. According to one estimate, if mountaintop removal mining continues at the current clip of development over the next four decades, a region the size of Rhode Island could literally be excavated and forever scarred as a result of our energy

Plate 74. A mountaintop removal coal mining site between Rawl and Buffalo, West Virginia.

supply choices. Albeit an unlikely scheme, this visual image captures what could lie down the road if the United States exploits its cheapest and most plentiful electricity fuel without proper environmental safeguards.

Consider this one fact when contemplating our energy future: In just one year, a typical coal plant emits as much CO_2 as 1 million sport utility vehicles (SUVs). Coal does add diversity to California's power supply, but state regulators have already spoken. The only real hope for coal as an electricity resource for California is for rapid development of carbon sequestering technologies, but more on that later.

Challenge 3: The Question of Nuclear Power

Given bans on coal and off-shore oil, California's prohibition on nuclear power looks short-sighted to growing numbers of Californians. Concerns over climate change have fueled

Plate 75. The shuttered Rancho Seco nuclear power plant, just outside of Sacramento, is the only nuclear facility to be closed by a public vote in the United States.

growing interest in a technology once branded as the ultimate enemy of the environment (pl. 75).

Ironically enough, among the new prime advocates for nuclear power are those who espouse its "green" credentials, with some going as far as wanting to label "nuclear" as a "renewable" energy technology. Those endorsing the process of splitting atoms to generate the majority of our future electricity are the following environmentalists:

- James Lovelock—the fellow from London who came up with the "Gaia" theory of the Earth being a self-regenerating organism—proclaimed that nuclear power was "the only green solution" to our power supply woes, maintaining that there was not enough time to allow renewable energy technologies to fill the gap.
- The Bay Area's Stewart Brand—the utopian thinker behind the *Whole Earth Catalog*—echoed Lovelock's claims, adding that the nuclear power industry's half

century of experience rendered concerns about safety and waste as obsolete.

- Patrick Moore—co-founder of the radical Greenpeace activist group—has proclaimed: "There is now a great deal of scientific evidence showing nuclear power to be an environmentally sound and safe choice."

Just how dangerous is nuclear power?

The impact of radiation on human and environmental health is directly linked to the duration and magnitude of exposure, but it is also a function of the manner in which any one individual reacts to radiation exposure. The issue of chronic or routine exposure to radiation is in addition to the risk of a catastrophe that could result from power plant accidents. Serious accidents could result in environmental and social consequences. These accidents are assigned an extremely low probability of occurring, yet just a single occurrence could be catastrophic.

A significant failure in the plant's cooling systems, such as the rupture of the reactor vessel, could result in a so-called "nuclear meltdown." Without sufficient coolant, intense heat melts fuel rods (pl. 76) within a matter of seconds. The heat from the uncontrolled reaction can melt everything, including the containment vessel and plant substructures, into the Earth below, hence the term "the China Syndrome." The rapid expansion of steam caused by the meltdown of nuclear fuel could breach the containment building and release radiation into the surrounding environment. This is what happened at the Chernobyl nuclear reactor in the former Soviet Union on April 26, 1986.

In addition to environmental impacts from routine operations or accident scenarios, the "life cycle" impacts of nuclear power resulting from the use of uranium as fuel can have acute environmental consequences too. Mill tailings, sands, and liquids left over after the uranium ore has been processed retain 85 percent of the radioactivity of the original ore.

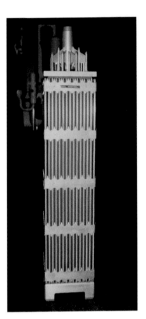

Plate 76. Nuclear fuel rod assembly.

Nuclear power plant operations generate a variety of radioactive wastes, which are typically categorized by their level of radioactivity. High-level waste generally consists of spent fuel rods. Even after their use in power generation, the fuel rods will take hundreds of thousands of years to lose their radioactivity. At present, U.S. nuclear reactors produce about 2,000 annual tons of high-level waste. Spent fuel is now stored at the site of the reactor, as the industry awaits federal decisions on policies for ultimate disposal and safe storage of high-level waste.

Low-level waste consists of any materials that have been exposed to radioactive materials, including worker gloves and safety clothing as well as plant components that become irradiated during the normal course of operations. Management of low-level waste has been assigned to the states. However, to date, no new low-level disposal sites have been opened by any state.

The lack of an accepted plan for long-term, high-level waste storage as well as comprehensive implementation and disposal plans for low-level waste and plant decommissioning increase the level of uncertainty surrounding the total cost of nuclear power and ultimately the risk of exposure to radiation. These precise reasons convinced California to ban future development in the state.

From a portfolio perspective, nuclear power can be attractive, as it adds large quantities of substantial round-the-clock electricity. Because of public subsidies, a next generation of nuclear power plants could be cheaper and safer. Yet at this point in time, these much-ballyhooed nuclear reactors are still in the R&D phase of development. Given the long lead times required to site and build nuclear power plants, skeptics wonder whether time is running out on this technology to be able to contribute to a meaningful reduction in carbon in time to make a difference on climate change.

Challenge 4: The Terrorist Threat, National Security, and Energy Reliability

The unprecedented terrorist attacks on New York City and Washington, DC, on September 11, 2001 (pl. 77), have fundamentally altered the debate over future energy supply in the United States and throughout the world. Just building more fossil fuel power plants and nuclear reactors to deliver electricity could look pretty naïve if you look at the United States through the eyes of a terrorist.

Plate 77. Smoke still billows from the remains of the World Trade Center on September 21, 2001.

Our current energy supply challenges are being amplified by the nation's war on terrorism, revealing the limits of our aging transmission and distribution electricity grid. Our electricity grid, with its emphasis on large, polluting, and centralized power plants sending power long distances over transmission lines, is an artifact that is over 100 years old and is extremely vulnerable to enemy attack. It is also dramatically out of sync with information technologies and the digital economy. The architecture of the existing transmission grid is the antithesis of distributed networks being made possible by the Internet. The future of America's electricity supply can no longer be held hostage to a centralized network of power plants that represent high-profile terrorist targets.

Today, power can be transmitted at a distance of 4,000 miles by relying upon a new wrinkle to electric transmission technology: ultrahigh-voltage DC. Yet the central power plant and long-distance transmission model are still inherently inefficient. On-site distributed generation sources avoid the 7 to 15 percent line loss that plagues the current electricity delivery system. At the wholesale prices witnessed throughout the west during 2000–2001, those losses represented hundreds of millions of dollars. True, new technologies that reduce these losses could help create a kind of World Wide Web of electricity, which could theoretically take advantage of idle power plants on the other face of our planet Earth. Trading energy with China and other Asian countries could reduce the need for new power plants globally. Yet these intercontinental power trades could also be exposed to great risk as real-time trades are secured through global telecommunication and delivery systems.

Beyond electricity, there is also the availability, price, and security of fossil fuel supplies. Today, the costs of military interventions and related national security expenses are not figured into the costs we pay at the gas pump. Granted, the United States and the rest of the industrialized world share large investments in the petro–status quo. However, there are clear signs that new alternative fuels must be phased in as the world moves out from under the shadow of our collective fossil fuel addictions.

Shortly after 9/11, representatives of an oil company acknowledged the national security weak spots our natural gas pipelines represent. In response, the nation's oil and natural gas companies have stepped up security measures on natural gas pipelines to continue to allow these fossil fuels to flow to California. Like our airport security systems, these systems have, nonetheless, never been fully tested during a time of apparent war. According to the Center for Strategic and International Studies, information about the nation's natural gas pipelines is much more widespread since power markets were deregulated, increasing risks of rolling blackouts that could reverberate for days on end.

The additional costs of policing nearly 180,000 miles of natural gas pipelines in this country will be passed along to ratepayers.

Continued dependence upon petroleum to fuel our cars and trucks carries national security risks. The advent of wars over diminishing supplies of oil is not science fiction. Since much of our oil does come from unstable governments with ties to Islamic fundamentalist terrorists, the specter of these organizations holding oil supplies hostage is an unwelcome outcome of our current energy strategy. Oil-exporting countries such as Saudi Arabia, Iran, Russia, Nigeria, Libya, and Venezuela could accumulate wealth from oil revenues, while the rest of the world sinks into economic turmoil as only the rich can afford transportation services we have taken for granted in the United States, and the poor become disenfranchised. "We find ourselves dependent on imports from people who, by and large, are hostile to us," acknowledged Frank Gaffney, former national security advisor to President Ronald Reagan when testifying before Congress in 2004. He cited the growing scarcity of traditional energy resources set against a backdrop of booming population growth creating a perfect storm for global resource wars. "Situations like this have given rise to wars in the past," Gaffney said. A parade of national security experts has echoed his concerns. Yet trying to implement radical changes in direction on energy has bumped up against institutional and cultural roadblocks.

In these dire scenarios painted by bipartisan security experts, the infrastructure supporting our oil-based transportation sector becomes a terrorist target. These security concerns carry over to the electricity sector, as imports of LNG and gas pipelines also become potential magnets for terrorist activity (pl. 78).

Then, there are our nuclear power plants. Most nuclear reactors have been designed to withstand the crash of only small aircraft. Although a nuclear explosion would not occur if a jumbo jet crashed into one of the nation's over one hundred operating nuclear reactors, there are a number of possible

Plate 78. Natural gas pipelines could be terrorist targets.

scenarios where deadly radioactive clouds could cover a region the size of Pennsylvania and create national sacrifice zones.

Shortly after 9/11, SCE, the primary owner of the San Onofre Nuclear Generating Station (SONGS), located on the borders of Orange County and San Diego County (pl. 79), asked the highway patrol to monitor traffic along Hwy. 5 because of security concerns. "I am confident that San Onofre's containment buildings are the strongest structures in all of Southern California," proclaimed Ray Golden, San Onofre business manager for SCE. "They are designed to withstand earthquakes, floods and landslides. But they are not designed to protect against the type of aircraft used in last week's terrorist attacks." Golden pointed out that a nuclear explosion is next to impossible, but radioactivity could leak into the atmosphere if the reactor core cracked open and the emergency cooling water system failed. "We are not certain what could happen to the plant from that type of event," continued Golden referring to the terrorist strikes to the World Trade Center and the Pentagon. "We cannot protect completely against it. Nor, from a security standpoint, are we required to."

Plate 79. The San Onofre Nuclear Generating Station is sandwiched between the Pacific Ocean and Hwy. 5.

The FERC authorized utilities to pass along the costs of antiaircraft and other security systems at the nation's nuclear power plants to ratepayers. In 2007, antinuclear activists petitioned the U.S. Nuclear Regulatory Commission (NRC) to disavow a finding of "no significant impact" for PG&E's plans to store radioactive waste on-site and outdoors at the Diablo Canyon facility. "A terrorist attack on high-level radioactive waste storage containers at Diablo Canyon atomic reactors could unleash catastrophic amounts of deadly radioactivity downwind and downstream for long distances," charged Kevin Kamps, a nuclear waste specialist with the Washington, DC-based Nuclear Information and Resource Service. "These storage containers must be fortified against terrorist attacks, but NRC is derelict in its duty to protect public health and safety and the environment."

You could argue that coal-fired power plants are the answer. However, increasing our reliance upon coal does not address the issue of inefficiency inherent in a central power plant dependent upon long-distance transmission. (If we take a systems view, trade-offs between energy independence and global climate change are really no longer an option.) Yes, it is true harnessing the electricity from excellent wind resource areas would require long-distance transmission too. However, the environmental benefits accrued by introducing large amounts of wind power capacity into the nation's power plant portfolio raise serious questions about the efficacy of future investments in the dirtiest of all fossil fuels. Wind turbines can also be developed in modular clusters, as is the case in Minnesota and Iowa, where a cooperative "community wind" movement has taken hold (pl. 80). They can also be deployed as on-site distributed generation resources.

Plate 80.
A community wind system alongside an old water-pumping windmill in Dodge Center, Minnesota, in winter.

Relying exclusively on long-distance transmission systems to transport electricity from points of production to points of consumption is suspect if the top priority is energy security. With hundreds of new power plants coming online all across the country, the demand for natural gas and other fossil fuels could stay high for years to come. The price volatility, and occasional blackouts, experienced in California, Texas, New York City, Boston, and Chicago in the first part of the current decade reinforce the dire warning signs that we can no longer support the status quo.

The future of the electricity industry lies in better planning in transmission to deliver bulk renewable power generated in remote locations to urban load centers. Nevertheless, policy makers could be spending more time in figuring out ways to foster innovation at the distribution grid. Finding the answers as to how best develop a democratic, decentralized power supply system is one of the most formidable challenges facing reformers. How do we support tiny on-site electricity generators while still maintaining reliability for the electricity grid as a whole?

Distributed renewable energy systems such as rooftop solar PV systems, small wind turbines, and fuel cells suddenly begin to look like an enlightened approach to generating electricity that bolsters national security while addressing global climate change and other environmental concerns. Renewable on-site generation, cutting-edge energy management software, energy efficiency upgrades, and new energy battery storage systems are all technologies that smart corporations should be investigating in light of recent volatility in power markets. It is also important to note that there are no big terrorist targets in a truly decentralized renewable energy system. Now, no one is suggesting dismantling existing transmission lines. In the future, however, the focus of a national energy strategy should be on diversifying risks: economic, environmental, and national security.

The electric utility industry is undergoing rapid changes in response to political, economic, and environmental forces and expectations. California has become a focal point of debate regarding the ability of our existing energy production and delivery infrastructure to provide the kind of reliability required by corporations so dependent upon electricity for day-to-day operations. Consumer lifestyles are also increasingly electric. At the same time, growing concerns over unstable fossil fuel supplies and the national security risks associated with nuclear reactors are increasing the value of renewable energy technologies. Moving from a central power plant model to a more distributed system featuring a greater diversity of fixed-price renewable fuels offers solutions to an array of energy challenges facing companies in the industrialized world, among them the lingering terrorist threat.

The huge potential costs and liabilities linked to large-scale fossil and nuclear-generating sources are avoided entirely with solar PV and other distributed, renewable energy systems (pl. 81). Cost and NIMBY issues associated with these renewable sources remain steep challenges, as is described next. One favor 9/11 might teach us is that our energy supply

Plate 81. The nation's largest solar PV array, located at Nellis Air Force Base in Nevada.

is far too dependent on unnecessary security and military interventions to secure petroleum for our transportation needs. National security concerns should also shape analysis of fossil fuel options, such as LNG imports, on the electricity side of the energy equation.

Challenge 5: Variability, Cost, and NIMBY Challenges with Renewable Sources

Over the past decade, wind power has emerged as one of the fastest-growing electricity resources in the world. California is poised to regain the national lead in total installed wind power capacity, but only if issues surrounding transmission scheduling and planning can be successfully addressed in the near future. NIMBY issues and valid concerns about bird and bat populations must also be adequately addressed before California, and the world, greatly expands its current wind turbine fleet.

The variability of solar and hydro resources can also become an issue for energy planners and managers. However, solar resources are far more predictable than the wind because of the daily cycles of night and day. Clouds and fog impact the quality of solar power, yet technologies such as solar PV panels still generate electricity even when the skies are not blue. In terms of hydroelectricity, precipitation in California is concentrated during winter, and because of dams and other structures, water can be stored and then be released when needed.

So, the largest challenge when it comes to renewable energy sources and the need for a 24/7 power supply rests with wind. The passage of the Renewable Portfolio Standard (RPS), which currently requires California to supply 20 percent of the state's total electricity from renewable resources by 2010,

Plate 82. Modern wind farms feature fewer but larger turbines.

has accelerated efforts to address the grid integration impacts of scheduling variable renewable resources. (This renewable target may reach 33 percent by 2020.) Since wind power is the lowest-cost renewable power generation option currently available, it is projected that as much as 12,000 megawatts of new additional wind power capacity may need to come online in response to the RPS legislation (pl. 82). This total represents five times the amount of wind power California currently has online.

With the help of state funding and a partnership with the wind industry, wind forecasters and the California Independent System Operator (CAISO), the cost of clean, renewable wind power for California ratepayers has been reduced, setting an example of regional forecasting for the nation. (The CAISO was a regulatory institution created by the state's 1996 restructuring law, taking over management and control of the transmission grids of the state's investor-owned utilities.)

Plate 83. Inside the control room of the California Independent System Operator, which manages the state's transmission operations from its offices in Folsom.

The CAISO began to levy relatively large grid imbalance fees upon wind generators. Why? In order to match generation with forecast consumer electricity demand, the CAISO schedules energy production from generators in advance (pl. 83). Because of unpredicted outages, there is always some deviation in power scheduling. With wind power, the actual energy production typically deviates from schedules. The net deviation between scheduled and delivered energy triggered high penalties for wind projects, making them less attractive from a resource scheduling point of view. Since the ratepayer ultimately pays these costs, maintaining this limited arrangement was obviously not in the public interest.

In collaboration with private industry and state agencies, the CAISO created and implemented a new program that simply reworks protocols and payment schemes used by grid operators geared to the operating characteristics of round-the-clock fossil fuel power plants. One of the top goals in this consensus process was to be able to forecast wind energy production far enough in advance to avoid starting expensive and polluting fossil units. A consensus process came up with such an innovative compensation and availability forecasting system for wind power projects that FERC and other grid operators have investigated adopting for use.

Here are some of the key challenges facing the wind industry in California addressed by recent R&D initiatives:

- The ability to forecast predictable generation from wind projects better in a region on a day-ahead and hour-ahead basis
- The ability to integrate wind projects affordably into the transmission grid without having to purchase a significant amount of power from other fossil fuel generators to fill gaps when the wind is not blowing
- The ability to accommodate wind resources if wind projects generate electricity when demand is low
- The ability to provide sufficient transmission as the envisioned and significant but variable wind resources come online

A sophisticated wind forecasting service emerged from this public–private partnership. Instead of being focused on what the wind did the last hour or last 10 minutes, the software developed by AWS Truewind relies upon a weather and terrain analysis to provide forecasts for the hour ahead. Each individual wind project participating in this CAISO program is required to install meters, share in the costs of forecasting, and schedule energy deliveries based on new state-of-the-art predictions of energy production.

The ability of the CAISO grid operators to balance the grid will only get better as data are collected month-to-month and year-to-year for existing and new wind projects serving the California power market. As more wind projects participate in the CAISO program, the benefits to California ratepayers will grow as a result of the increased geographic diversity of wind projects, each with their quantified hourly, daily, and seasonal electricity generation profiles. New advances in wind forecasting technologies and market-based reforms will give CAISO the ability to better understand and manage wind power that best fits into California's power supply portfolio.

Beyond variability, another factor limiting increased reliance upon renewable energy sources is higher costs. Generally speaking, clean, nonpolluting renewable energy resources cost more than dirty, polluting fossil fuel and nuclear power plants. However, what is worse is that renewable resources have high up-front capital costs, whereas traditional conventional power generation options have relatively low up-front capital costs. The advantage of renewable sources—small or nonexistent fuel costs—then must be compared to volatile fossil fuel price risk. In today's world, however, time is money. The required up-front capital costs are the prime limiting factor on solar PV panels, for example. While polls consistently show solar as being among the most popular electricity generation technologies (pl. 84), the required initial investment of $20,000 to $30,000 is often a showstopper for consumers.

The good news for renewable energy advocates is that fossil prices have gone up dramatically since the energy crisis of 2000–2001. Although natural gas combined-cycle power plants were once projected to generate power at a cost of below 3 cents per kilowatt-hour, escalating natural gas prices have more than doubled the cost of electricity from the nation's most popular source of electricity, with gas-fired generators charging 8 cents per kilowatt-hour for electricity. The bad news is that, although modern wind facilities generated electricity at costs between 4 and 6 cents per kilowatt-hour just five years ago, steel shortages and a surge in demand have spawned price increases of similar magnitude as those for wind's natural gas competitor.

Worse yet, geothermal energy costs have also jumped, as have the costs of solar PV technologies. Whereas geothermal power plants in the best sites could generate electricity

Plate 84. Solar PV panels can be integrated into residential rooftops in an aesthetic way.

at roughly 5–7 cents per kilowatt-hour, costs have jumped to 8–11 cents per kilowatt-hour. For solar PV, electricity costs can reach as high as an astounding 40–70 cents per kilowatt-hour. Part of these cost increases can be attributed to a run-up in steel, copper, and other metal prices—and a silicon shortage in the case of solar PV. However, part of the price increase for wind and solar is the sudden phenomenal increase in demand for product, with manufacturers desperately trying to scale up and finally go mainstream. Over time, as the necessary manufacturing capacity achieves economies of scale and maintenance and infrastructure requirements fall into place, these costs will come down, whereas costs for finite fossil fuels will likely stick and eventually go even higher.

From an environmental perspective, renewable energy sources are superior to fossil and nuclear counterparts. Still, the fact of the matter is that all energy sources carry some environmental impacts. Hydroelectric facilities have ravaged California's native fish populations, for example, and some older biomass power plants still emit significant particulates and other pollutants, sometimes in excess of state-of-the-art fossil fuel facilities. Large solar farms can impact ecosystems and endangered species. Perhaps the biggest controversy concerning renewable resources is wind power's impact on birds and bats. Furthermore, could tidal and wave power technologies further threaten our imperiled fish stocks?

The latest obstacle to further wind development in California, and the rest of the United States, is military radar systems. It has recently been discovered that wind farms can interfere with radar tracking systems, though these issues have already been resolved in the UK and other parts of Europe. "We cannot develop one of the last remaining best wind sites in California—near Barstow—[it] is currently off-limits," lamented Michael Rucker, development origination leader for Clipper Windpower Development Co. "Since we cannot move the wind, we are working with stakeholders to find a solution that makes the most sense," Rucker said. One potential solution is curtailing wind farm operations during radar tests, but so far representatives at Edwards Air Force Base and other military bases have not been willing to go that route. "My sense is that the

BIRDS, BATS, AND WIND POWER

Both birds and bats collide with the spinning blades of wind turbines. Other sources of mortality at wind projects include electrocutions at power lines (a source of mortality throughout the country). Less visible and direct impacts come from disturbance of habitats. In the case of both birds and bats, these negative environmental consequences were unforeseen and highlight a dilemma facing environmentalists who tout renewable energy sources as the solution to our power supply woes. Placing electricity generators out in nature does have its benefits as well as drawbacks.

The wind power industry is busy working with scientists to figure out ways to reduce current mortality levels, but this process is arduous. Critics contend the wind power industry is not so green after all and is actually worse than the rest of the power generation business when it comes to complying with the nation's environmental laws.

Consider the following statistics:

- Domestic cats kill hundreds of millions of birds.
- Pesticides add tens of millions of dead birds to the annual U.S. avian mortality total.
- As many as a billion birds die each year in the United States after colliding with human-made structures.
- Communication towers for ubiquitous cell phones and other telecommunications kill up to 50 million birds per year, according to the American Bird Conservancy.

By comparison, the wind industry might kill 40,000 birds every year, an estimate made in 2001 based on data associated with the number of existing projects at that point in time. This figure represents less than 1 percent of total human-related avian deaths.

Nevertheless, the Center for Biological Diversity has filed a lawsuit in the Superior Court of Alameda County, claiming that wind turbines operating there violate several federal laws, including the Bald and Golden Eagle Protection Act and the Migratory Bird Treaty Act. Unlike the Endangered Species Act, neither of these two federal laws includes provisions for "takings"—that is, accidental deaths. The U.S. Fish and Wildlife Service also weighed in, insisting that mitigation steps be implemented sooner rather than later.

The bird mortality problem in the Altamont Pass was first identified by the California Energy Commission (CEC) in 1992. More recent figures compiled by the CEC during a six-year study indicate that 1,766 to 4,721 wild birds are killed at the Altamont Pass every year, the vast majority being raptors (pl. 85), including the golden eagle.

Plate 85. Raptors such as this red-tailed hawk make up the majority of birds killed by California wind turbines.

An internal report circulated by the CEC in 2005 suggested that turbines clearly identified as major bird killers, and representing between 7 and 16 percent of the Altamont Pass's 583 megawatts of total capacity, be permanently retired. Even more drastic, this report also suggested that perhaps the entire fleet of 5,400 wind turbines currently operating at the Altamont Pass be shut down during the winter months, the season when only 16 percent of the gigantic wind plant's energy is generated. This shutdown policy is now in place. California wind projects generally produce the vast majority of their power during the summer, whereas many wind projects in the Midwest and east generate the most power during winter months.

Here is the good news. Given the size of modern wind turbines, one single 3-megawatt turbine could displace 30 of the 100-kW wind turbines that used to predominate in the Altamont Pass as well as the Montezuma hills. The smaller machines spin at a rate of roughly 60 revolutions per minute while today's modern and larger machines feature rotors spinning at speeds of 20 or 30 revolutions per minute. In addition, the fewer the machines, the less the risk, or so implies some recent research. Yet a variety of regulatory and procedural issues have stalled such plans, some of which date back to 1998.

military's perspective is that they see emerging competition for a variety of uses surrounding their sites, and they just say no because they don't want to open the door a crack for potentially incompatible uses," he said. He suggested a high-level political solution might be necessary, but so far no political leader has come forward to challenge the military—a source of local jobs.

Challenge 6: A Dumb Electricity Grid

The far-flung electrification of America was once described by the U.S. National Academy of Sciences as "the greatest engineering achievement of the 20th century." Yet today, in the early twenty-first century, terrorist threats, the digital economy, global climate change, and recent natural disasters such as Hurricanes Katrina (pl. 86) and Ike have all focused attention on the pressing need for an intelligent, nimble, and more reliable power grid. Yet there are some immense challenges ahead when dealing with an electricity infrastructure that, in many respects, has been largely stuck in time.

Consider the following startling facts:

- Electricity is big, big business. With over $600 billion in assets, the nation's electric utilities are twice as large as the telecommunications industry and almost 30 percent larger than the auto industry.
- Roughly 70 percent of these assets are power plants, most of them built in the mid-1960s with 1950s technology. Only 10 percent of utility assets are in transmission facilities, the highways for kilowatt-hours

Plate 86. Natural gas processing plant in Louisiana flooded by Hurricane Katrina.

Plate 87. Clouds highlight the silhouettes of transmission lines.

(pl. 87). The remaining 20 percent of utility assets are in the poles and wires of utility distribution systems that connect power directly to people.

- Between 1975 and 2004, electricity demand grew by over 100 percent, while spending on grid upgrades declined by 50 percent.
- The largest market capitalization for an individual electric utility, Exelon, was about $40 billion in 2008. This compares to a market cap of over $400 billion for Exxon-Mobil. Of the over 5,000 private and public utilities in business in the United States, only 17 boast market caps of greater than $10 billion.

These facts underscore the challenges posed to revamping the highly capital-intensive business of providing a product that has become the elixir of modern life. The stakes are extremely high. All told, it is estimated that today's dinosaur power grid costs U.S. business and residents $100 billion every year. If present trends continue, a blackout enveloping half the continent is not out of the question.

Most of the equipment that makes up California and the nation's grid is reaching the end of its design life after nearly three decades of under investment. During the rolling blackouts in 2003, which started in Ohio, the utilities right next door could not see what was going on. As a consequence of geographical monopolies, which fostered a lack of interaction with competitors or vendors, this blackout in 2003 rolled through 11 states and carried a price tag of $6 billion. There is phenomenal value in enabling companies and customers to interact easily, but the cultures of larger systems, such as electricity monopolies, all slow down efforts to integrate distributed intelligence in our electricity system.

Today the grid is overbuilt in some areas and underbuilt in others. It was hard for utilities to make money off investments in transmission and distribution in a regulated monopoly system, and the result is today's lack of progress. What the system needs now is more sensors tracking temperature, wind speed, and voltage to increase reliability. In premium power applications, the most innovation can be seen: backup power systems, batteries, distributed power generation, and redundant resources. All of these things are being done by the private sector today.

Several strategic public/private partnerships on grid modernization have been launched, and it appears some of the advanced work on grid modernization is occurring in California and the West Coast. Take the Palo Alto–based EPRI's IntelliGrid program, which is dominated by U.S. private and public utilities, but also includes Electricité de France (EDF), the government-owned French utility serving 42 million customers in 22 different countries. In essence, the program pushes an open architecture for electricity, similar to current common-carrier platforms for telecommunications services. IntelliGrid has also been pushing the notion of a "self-healing" grid—one that would respond automatically to limit disturbances and boost both efficiency and performance.

There was a little bit of good news for smart grid enthusiasts in the passage of the Energy Policy Act of 2005, which calls for nationwide reliability standards and other demand response and time-of-use metering provisions that might stimulate innovations inching us closer to the promised nirvana of an intelligent grid. Yet, observers such as Patrick Mazza with Olympia, Washington-based Climate Solutions claimed that significant obstacles remain. "Traditionally cautious utilities tend to hold back until success is demonstrated elsewhere. So technological progress stalls awaiting the courageous act of some early adopter utility, or a public–private partnership to take the lead."

Jesse Berst, president of the Center for Smart Energy, claims we have indeed reached a tipping point. "Computer intelligence is less expensive than old-style capital assets," Berst stated simply. He pointed to studies conducted by Pacific Northwest National Laboratories and the Rand Corporation that show that a shift toward an intelligent system that substitutes bits for iron could save between $50 to $100 billion over 20 years. Berst noted that other studies show a return on investment of $4 to $8 for every dollar invested in a smart grid. "We can't postpone this any longer," Berst said, noting that business-as-usual spending will fall short of what is now needed to make the grid modern. He estimated that investments on the magnitude of $5 to $10 billion annually over current funding levels will be necessary to move closer to a new era of "designer electricity." Trends are beginning to move in a positive direction, he maintained, but there is much work to do.

If history repeats itself, efforts to upgrade and revolutionize our contemporary power transport system will mimic what happened with computers and telecommunications: smaller, cleaner, and smarter solutions. We now have the tools and technologies necessary to propel a revolution in energy that mimics, to a large extent, the evolution in scale evident in telecommunications and computer industries. These new technologies—flywheel storage systems, solar PVs, fuel cells, and wind turbines—are the equivalent to wireless cell phones and portable laptops that replaced traditional grid-connected phones and huge mainframe computers, respectively. Since wireless cell phones appear to be dominating telecommunications in the developing world, wireless distributed power generation systems might also become the preferred option for power supply in these new electricity markets. The future of power generation could indeed evolve into a system where smaller, smarter sources will be dispersed throughout the electric grid—and preclude the need for grids in the developing world, where 2 billion people have yet to experience electricity.

The IEA projects that deregulated energy markets represent a $220 billion market. That is larger than the cellular and long-distance telecommunications markets combined. On a global basis, the potential numbers are staggering. The World Energy Council projects by 2020 the developing world (notably Latin America, Asia, and China) will consume more energy than the industrialized world. Some $4 trillion will be required to build the power infrastructures needed to serve the newly electrified. Distributed generation sources that include solar PVs, fuel cells, and small stand-alone wind turbines will be among the prime beneficiaries of these staggering investments in the future of world electricity supply. With the advent of plug-in hybrids and the next generation of electric vehicles, these renewable resources can not only shrink levels of air pollution but bolster national security by minimizing California's, and the nation's, exposure to finite fuels controlled by powers hostile to the United States.

Peak Power, Water Supply, and Other Challenges

The just-described six challenges facing California on the energy front just begin to scratch the surface of a myriad of issues that all wind themselves around energy production, transportation, and consumption. These issues are also inter-related.

One of the biggest challenges when looking at the state's electricity system is keeping up with peak demands for power. As global climate change increases temperatures, California's boost in energy consumption will accelerate. The energy supply, in turn, is influenced by the state's water supply (pl. 88). Changes in the hydroelectric system as a result of less snow and an earlier onset of spring runoff will then translate into less available noncarbon water power in late summer, when peaks in demand typically reach their highest marks.

Today, most facilities used for peak power or power outages are diesel generators, among the dirtiest fossil fuel power

Plate 88.
Yosemite Falls
in Yosemite
National Park.

supply options. On these hot days that push large jumps in demand from air conditioners, air quality is also poor. Under this current dysfunctional system, demand for peak electricity would threaten reliability as demand exceeds supply, could reduce available water for other higher-end uses (fossil and nuclear plants consume huge quantities of water for cooling), and mar air quality.

These issues are all intertwined. That is why a systems approach is needed to coordinate government, industry, and individual responses to our energy challenges. While the future of California's energy supply might rely more on decentralized systems, that viable yet untested approach will require more sophisticated systems to manage electricity flows.

On top of those consideration, the vision of plug-in hybrid vehicles becoming microelectricity generators for your home is even more challenging, as our transportation technologies take on double-lives as on-site power generators. The vision is compelling. However, figuring out public safety issues, impacts on existing grid infrastructure, and other minute details all require R&D and testing.

The challenges facing California on energy mirror those facing the rest of the nation and the rest of the world. There are some unique twists out here on the edge of Western civilization, some related to our natural history, some to our political preferences, and still others to cultural factors shaped by the gold and oil rushes, the subsequent rise of the environmental movement, and the state's legacy of optimistic entrepreneurism.

The next section of this book examines future solutions to the challenges facing the state on energy, highlighting the role government, business, communities, and individuals can all play in addressing California's growing thirst for energy.

INNOVATION

The Search for Solutions

CALIFORNIA IS NOW MORE of a leader on energy than ever before, especially when it comes to developing solutions to sticky energy challenges. At least that is the view of Dan Kammen, a professor with the University of California at Berkeley's Energy and Resources Group (pl. 89). "More of what we do now is being studied, evaluated, copied, and adapted to fit local needs all over the world, including countries such as the United Kingdom and Japan," said Kammen. "The fact that we are willing to develop a framework to address climate change makes the state a vital national and international leader."

AB 32, the Global Warming Solutions Act of 2006, perhaps sums up best how California approaches solutions to the penultimate energy challenge of all time. The law requires California to reduce emissions of carbon dioxide (CO_2) back to 1990 levels by 2025. That equates to approximately 180 million metric tons of CO_2 per year—the amount of carbon spewing from 43 coal-fired power plant stacks—or roughly a 25 to 29 percent reduction from current carbon

Plate 89. Dan Kammen of UC Berkeley's Energy and Resources Group.

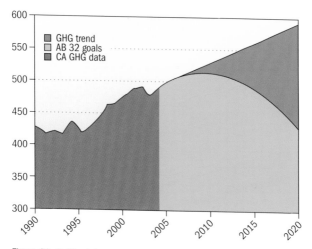

Figure 22. California's recent trends of greenhouse gas emissions (and the aggregate reductions necessary to meet AB 32's 2020 targets).

emission levels (fig. 22). Prior to the passage of AB 32, Governor Schwarzenegger issued a 2005 executive order that set an even more ambitious climate change response program: an 80 percent reduction in CO_2 and other greenhouse gas emissions by 2050. (Other nations and states are now adopting similar aggressive reduction targets in light of recent scientific findings that suggest the world may soon be reaching a tipping point on climate change impacts.) With California's expected population growth, this 2050 reduction target creates great challenges for the state, as it requires a 90 percent per capita reduction in emissions that contribute to global climate change (fig. 23). Meeting this target requires vastly more efficient use of energy and the virtual elimination of all emissions linked to climate change from the state's energy and transportation infrastructure.

California can claim credit for moving ahead of other governments on climate change and other energy issues. However,

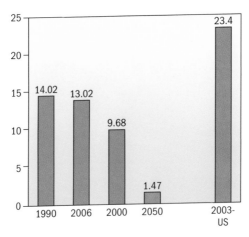

Figure 23. Per capita CO2 reductions necessary to comply with AB 32 near- and long-term goals.

it also needs to be pointed out that it has done so before a full technological and economic plan to reduce greenhouse gas emissions has clearly emerged. This aspect of California's approach to solving energy challenges echoes the past and presents some major risks. "A rush to action led to the energy crisis of 2000–2001, which cost the state severely as a result of the so-called 'deregulation' authorized by AB 1890," acknowledged Kammen. "What came out of the experience, thankfully, was a realization that we must work across disciplines and economic sectors to create an intelligent plan that matches clean energy supply and demand," he added. The interesting thing about California, noted Kammen, is that the energy crisis of 2000–2001 has not seemed to have a lingering negative effect on the state's psyche. "After the debacle of the energy crisis, we've moved on to new stuff. Remember, during the crisis, we were spending $1 billion per day on energy, here in the 8th largest economy in the world. Five years later, we continue to boldly plow forward [with the passage of AB 32 in 2006]. You might think we might be risk averse, but that never happened. I call it the 'California miracle.' We are again leading the world. That argument is more compelling than ever."

Yet Kammen also offered up a contrasting perspective on California's much ballyhooed penchant for moving early on emerging environmental and energy issues:

> One could also argue that we've already wasted 20 years. We've known the climate science good enough to take action on climate change. Sometimes, one has to take calculated risks with new public policies. Of course, the fact is that California's emissions of carbon and other greenhouse gas emissions are still increasing. It is vital that we move from planning to action. The hard part really is still ahead of us: How do we really implement these climate change standards?
>
> We honestly do not know today fully how we are going to achieve a 180-megaton reduction in greenhouse gas emissions.
>
> —Kammen 2007

As John Muir once said, "When we try to pick out anything by itself, we find it hitched to everything else in the universe." California's efforts to address climate change could, if done properly, also solve our traffic congestion woes, shrink our waistlines, and trade digitized isolation for community collaboration. Yet competing egos and state agencies, ivory-tower environmentalists, and ostrich-like corporate CEOs all still sometimes gum up the works. All three state private utilities—PG&E, SCE, and SDG&E—are failing in efforts to meet state mandates to supply 20 percent of the state's total supply portfolio from renewable sources by 2010. In addition, some of the contracts signed by these utilities to meet these same state mandates are with firms that have been unable to secure financing for their untested renewable energy technologies, calling into question their validity.

This disconnection between the image of California portrayed by Kammen and others and reality illustrates a disturbing trend. Progress sometimes stalls when making the transition from bright ideas to on-the-ground success. Today, the state has a reputation for progressive policies on renewable energy sources and global climate change, but it wins low marks from businesses trying to translate good intentions into practical reality. Californians might scoff at Texas and its legacy of rampant energy consumption, but Texas overtook California on wind power in 2006. California has impressive laws and regulations on the books. Yet its eco-consciousness can also frustrate and doom necessary infrastructure to support its still-burgeoning populations. In search of the perfect solution, California sometimes loses its way in the practical implementation of big-vision ideas.

AB 32 might be the most radical climate change policy in the world, but not because it represents a 25–29 percent reduction in CO_2 over the next two decades. Unlike Europe's approach to cooling climate change, AB 32 promises to reduce emissions across all sectors of the economy, which ultimately will include your motor vehicles and home. The European approach focuses strictly on large, centralized sources of pollution, such as power plants and industrial facilities. Of course, the devil is in the details, and a set of related legislative measures will help shape how California translates "cool" visions into everyday actions that can be sustained for years to come.

Kammen and others predict California will benefit from AB 32, since the state can become a net exporter of low-carbon technologies and systems. "We can export these solutions to the rest of the world, who will become buyers." He observed that Spain, Germany, and Denmark already export their wind technologies, Japan does so with its solar technologies, and their industries have waiting lists several years long for orders. "It is the early adopters that get the employment gains," he continued. For every $1 invested in new, clean energy technologies, Kammen's calculations show we get three to five times more jobs created than an equal investment in fossil fuel technologies. "This is not because renewables are better than fossil fuels, but because they are an emerging technological sector where investments drive technology and infrastructure development," he said.

"Sustainable technologies are the next big thing . . . the mother of all markets," said John Doerr, the billionaire who launched Google and who has invested heavily in green technologies. (Google's headquarters sport one of the largest solar PV arrays in the state.) Digging into why Doerr is so supportive of AB 32 underscores why it just might be the best thing to happen not only to our fragile and imperiled planet, but to California's—and the world's—economy. A study released by Kammen's colleague David Roland-Holst at the University of California at Berkeley in August 2006 (Roland-Holst 2006:3) projected that reducing greenhouse gas emissions in California would create 17,000 jobs and add $60 billion to the state's gross domestic product (GDP) by 2020. Given its legacy of clean energy innovation, California is well positioned to attract venture capital investments in companies developing clean energy, transportation, and industrial technologies. In 2007, California led the nation in so-called "cleantech" venture capital with $1.78 billion, representing 48 percent of the total $3.67 billion invested in cleantech nationwide. This represents a 50 percent growth over 2006 in venture investments in California companies.

Despite these impressive statistics, some stubborn economic facts remain. Electricity is a significant cost for many manufacturers operating in the state. At present, businesses operating in California pay roughly 35 percent more for electricity than the national average. Pressures linked to globalization translate into the need for California companies to adopt cost-effective energy efficiency measures to remain competitive. This end-use efficiency, when combined with the high percentage of renewable, hydroelectric, and nuclear power in the state's electricity generation mix, makes California manufactured goods much less carbon intensive than products manufactured elsewhere. If the policies adopted under AB 32 inadvertently encourage industrial production to shift to unregulated regions of the nation and world, AB 32 could actually accelerate global climate change while also decreasing employment, thereby lowering state tax revenues. This scenario is a lose–lose outcome for everybody, including planet Earth.

Andrew Hoffman, a professor at the University of Michigan and author of a study on corporate carbon reduction programs, argues that the key to an industrial renaissance in California—and then the rest of the country—is still more of the same: energy efficiency. "There is such a close link between carbon reductions and increased energy efficiency, the logical first step for any business [to address climate change]. Right now, U.S. companies use twice the energy per GDP as European Union member countries. Where is the world going? Energy efficiency is the future, and if nothing changes, the U.S. industrial sector will be left behind."

While we Californians like to pat ourselves on the back for being 40 percent better than the rest of the country when it comes to energy efficiency, the tiny country of Denmark is 60 percent more efficient than California, highlighting how far we still have to go to be the very best in the world.

California Utilities Go Out on a Limb

Ironically enough, PG&E, the nation's largest combined electric and natural gas utility, is credited with convincing California Governor Arnold Schwarzenegger to sign AB 32 into law. "The threat of greenhouse gas emissions is real and the consequences severe. We start from that place," acknowledged Ray Williams, PG&E's director of long-term energy policy. Decades of investment in energy efficiency

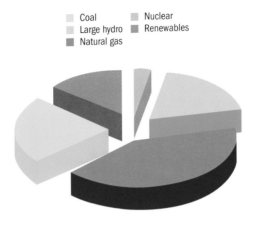

Coal
Large hydro
Natural gas
Nuclear
Renewables

Figure 24. Pacific Gas & Electric supply portfolio.

and renewable energy sources have given it a head start in developing noncarbon energy sources. Though state regulators consider only 12 percent of PG&E's current supply portfolio (fig. 24) as "renewable," over half of its power plants are carbon-free. How is this possible? The utility derives an additional 24 percent from the Diablo Canyon nuclear power plant and roughly 20 percent from hydroelectric facilities that do not meet state criteria as "renewable" supply.

In contrast to the rest of the country, where utilities rely on the most carbon-intensive fuel, coal, to meet half of their supply needs, California utilities derive only 20 percent of supply from coal, imported from nearby states. However, PG&E buys even less than the state's average: just 2 percent. All of these factors add up to giving PG&E a strategic jump-up on its competitors.

No doubt, the most radical initiative launched by PG&E in response to AB 32 is support for plug-in electric–gas hybrid technology (pl. 90). The possibility of fuel switching from petroleum to electricity has California's utility executives

Plate 90. Plug-in hybrid cars could become micro-power plants in the future.

seeing more than one shade of green. In April 2007, PG&E became the first utility in the country to publicly demonstrate vehicle-to-grid charging technology, partnering with Silicon Valley's Google and Japan's Toyota, whose gas–electric hybrids are the hottest cars on the market. Not only is the utility hoping to boost sales by having legions of motor vehicles plugging into its grid at night—when roughly 40 percent of the nation's power plants are turned off as most of us sleep—but PG&E's long-term strategy is to turn our motor vehicles into mini-power plants. The utility is working on technology (dubbed V2G) that allows for the bidirectional flow between vehicles and the electric power grid.

GM is the first major U.S. auto company to announce that it is testing a plug-in hybrid, the Chevy Volt, preparing for a commercial launch as early as 2010. PG&E is also working with Tesla Motors, which is introducing a stylish all-electric vehicle called the Roadster, on a "smart charging" pilot program, whereby motor vehicles' electric charging is controlled remotely by the host utility to help match consumer demand.

"If a customer agrees to allow us, the host utility, to optimize their charging, we would offer them reduced electric rates," said Andrew Tang, with PG&E's clean air transportation group. "The future vision is that vehicles became distributed battery sources," said Tang. "Communication technologies are vital to making this vision real," he added. At present, PG&E cannot really integrate these tiny distributed sources of storage. To show up on the system, storage devices have to reach close to five or ten times the capacity of a typical car. Yet creative aggregation of storage—your car plugged into the wall socket in the garage—via ultra-reactive telecommunications could help create the world's electricity Internet.

Though PG&E saw the immediate opportunity with AB 32, both SCE and SDG&E did not support the legislation. "We were concerned about the costs to our customers," acknowledged Gary Stern, SCE's director of strategy and resource planning. "We opposed AB 32 because climate change is a global issue; it makes more sense to address it at the federal level," said Mike Murray, Sempra Energy's director of policy and legislative analysis.

For its part, SCE can boast that it buys more renewable energy than any other utility in the country, obtaining roughly 16 percent of its power supply from sources deemed "renewable" by the state (fig. 25). (It can also brag that it purchases 90 percent of the nation's solar energy on behalf of its customers.) Furthermore, the utility has recently slashed carbon emissions by a third, having recently abandoned its largest coal-fired source, the Mohave plant located across the state border.

Like PG&E, SCE is touting electricity as a substitute fuel in the transportation sector. "Electricity is cleaner than the internal combustion engine. Most charges will occur during off-peak hours. But this is more than increasing sales on the system," he argued. From his vantage point, plug-in hybrids can harmonize supply and demand between night and day, while still relying on existing infrastructure. "In the future,

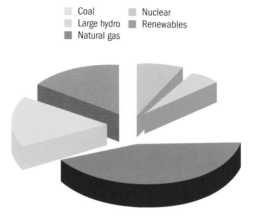

Figure 25. Southern California Edison supply portfolio.

having all of these batteries connected to the grid could introduce operational efficiencies and actually enhance our system," said Stern. SCE is partnering with the Ford Motor Company in the race to bring to market plug-in gas–electric hybrids.

SDG&E has also joined the plug-in hybrid bandwagon. The prime obstacle for SDG&E to meet AB 32's carbon reduction goals is transmission. The utility is located closest to California's best remaining renewable resource basins, but it cannot gain access to these noncarbon sources without construction of new transmission lines. At present, the utility derives only 7 percent of its total portfolio from renewable resources (fig. 26).

A Growing Role for the Private Sector

It is not just electric utilities that are changing their future business strategies in light of global climate change. Oil companies, including Chevron of California, are also shifting gears

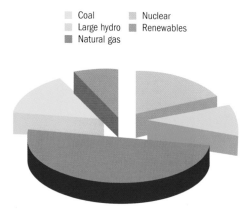

Coal **Nuclear**
Large hydro **Renewables**
Natural gas

Figure 26. San Diego Gas & Electric supply portfolio.

and looking for alternatives to fuel our mobile lifestyles and industrial enterprises.

"Just when the world thinks it is running out of something, science and technology make something else work." These are the words of Don Paul, Chevron's now retired chief technology officer (pl. 91), and they sum up the perspective of many oil industry veterans and other big private sector players in the energy business responding to climate change alarmists. From his perspective, biofuels are a big part of our energy future and a line of business not too dissimilar from oil and natural gas. "Crude oil is biomass that was processed through geologic time spanning millions of years. With biofuels, we are just short-circuiting geologic time. In essence, what we are looking to do in biofuels is cut out that middle step," he said. A huge oil company such as Chevron has to take a long view to develop new kinds of energy, Paul pointed out. "Among the key questions we have are: how much land is needed to grow the necessary biomass? We need to get a whole infrastructure in place to collect, gather, and process biomass into fuel," he said.

Plate 91. Don Paul, former chief technology officer for Chevron.

Responding to criticisms about relying upon former food crops such corn (pl. 92) to serve as the prime feedstock for biofuels, Chevron has partnered with Weyerhaeuser to explore developing biofuels from timber and wood waste. "Our focus is how to develop the next generation of biofuel technologies and go after a large part of our current waste stream as sources for these cleaner fuels," commented Paul. Noting that corn prices have risen as a result of the ethanol production boom in the Midwest, Paul expressed concern about trading off food for fuel. "Much of our corn has traditionally been given away as humanitarian contributions to poor developing nations. What happens to that program when corn is diverted to fuel?" he asked. Given the size of its operations, Chevron takes a 20-year view on emerging energy technologies. The firm has also created partnerships with key agricultural schools at University of California at Davis, Texas A&M, and Georgia Tech. "Ultimately, we hope

Plate 92. Corn—should it be used for food or for fuel?

to tap 'true' wastes such as sewage, trash, and waste grease to create biofuels," he said.

While Chevron is the largest producer of geothermal energy in the world, it does not see geothermal as a major energy source in California. Instead, Paul was much more bullish on solar energy. "California has a lot of sunlight and a lot of flat land in the deserts and San Joaquin Valley," he noted. However, instead of the solar PV arrays that have become so popular with residents and businesses alike, Chevron is instead exploring solar thermal technologies that concentrate solar energy to create steam. "We think it makes more sense to heat water with the sun to create steam instead of converting sunlight to electricity, where you lose two-thirds of the available energy in the conversion to electricity." Chevron hopes to launch a major large-scale solar thermal concentrated power initiative in the near future, he promised.

Six key factors have made California the nation's energy technology leader and will help California overcome its current energy challenges, according to Paul. The first key development in California's history was the evolution of industrial agriculture, with its emphasis on modern technologies and large-scale production of a large diversity of foods. Then, California became the center of the world's oil industry, and because of its unique geology, it prompted radical innovations in extraction and development of premium products. Next, the defense industry buildup during World War II encouraged further advances. "Standard Oil fueled the entire Pacific Fleet with a special high-performance grade of fuel designed specifically for military purposes," noted Paul. The know-how developed in defense industries spilled over into aerospace, which also had a major presence in California, furthering building up knowledge also relevant to energy development. Then computers and Silicon Valley arrived on the scene. "Chevron purchased the first non–weapons lab version of a computer," he said, noting the firm went so far as to construct an analog computer before the emergence of digital systems. We should not overlook Hollywood, either. The emergence of digital movie-making has spurred advances in computer hardware and software that have crossover applications for the oil and natural gas industries, as finding and extracting these energy sources in an eco-friendly manner becomes increasingly sophisticated and requires ever more capability for representing huge amounts of information with fine attention to detail.

In reality, corporations, including oil companies, and consumers each play critical roles in fostering the kinds of changes in energy supply and consumption patterns that will shape our collective future. Recent surveys show that six of ten CEOs believe the general public expects companies to take just as much responsibility as governments for handling social issues. Unfortunately, most corporate executives still see sociopolitical trends as challenges rather than opportunities that can advance solutions. Still, more than seven of ten consumers say that a sharing of social responsibilities between corporations and government should be the norm. Depending on what part of the world you look at, the level of trust between corporation and consumer features a large gap, as shown, for example, by the results of surveys by the McKinsey group discussed in the following paragraphs.

On the consumer side of things, roughly six out of ten consumers trust electric utilities, while only four of ten trust oil companies. Yet consumers believe that oil companies should be second only to government in tackling vexing social issues such as climate change. When asked about record profits racked up by oil companies, consumers were equally divided between giving price breaks to themselves and reinvesting these profits into clean, renewable energy technologies. In the United Kingdom, Japan, China, and India, majorities of those polled actually preferred renewable energy investments to lower prices.

The financial community has made great strides in underwriting new ways to address the social responsibilities of the private sector. Perhaps one of the best examples of this new paradigm shift is Bank of America's $20 billion initiative to support sustainable business solutions to climate change, announced in the fall of 2007. By providing critical financing tools to nurture green business activity, Bank of America is supporting sustainable growth in a most fundamental way. Three other leaders in finance—Citi, JPMorgan Chase, and Morgan Stanley—announced in February 2008 the establishment of the "Carbon Principles." The firms pledged to use these principles to guide future lending decisions in the electric power industry. Developed in conjunction with environmental groups, these voluntary guidelines will not stop the development of coal plants. But the risks and formerly hidden costs associated with these emissions will now be factored into these investment decisions in facilities that, once on the ground, will continue to generate electricity (and pollution) for decades to come. Energy efficiency, renewable energy, and other low-carbon technologies will be favored over fossil fuel facilities that do not offer clear mitigation steps for CO_2 emissions. "Leading utilities and financial institutions understand that the rules of the road have changed for coal," said Mark Brownstein, managing director of business partnerships for Environmental Defense, one of the NGOs involved in creating the Carbon Principles. "These principles are a first step in facilitating an honest assessment of electric generation options in light of the obvious and pressing need to substantially reduce national greenhouse gas pollution." Critics contended that the Carbon Principles are voluntary and that, given the stakes, more profound, mandatory standards will be needed in the very near future.

Although governments at all levels—federal, state, and local—are often demonized, the fact of the matter is that each level of governance is vital to integrating a systems approach to energy solutions. Though it is also true that the nature of governance in the twenty-first century is much different from what it was when industrial energy development began in the nineteenth century, societal laws and regulations are critical tools to enact widespread changes. Shifting with the political winds and popular opinion, government becomes the arbitrator, vowing to represent us all—a task doomed to frequent failure. And yet, what other choice is there?

What Role for Government?

Because of the free market, antigovernment ideology that has prevailed in Washington, DC, over the past decades, state and local governments have been the prime laboratories of energy reforms in the recent past. Because of California's isolation, its unique energy resource base, and a culture that nurtures risk-taking and entrepreneurship, the Golden State has often moved ahead of the federal government when it comes to promoting a more sustainable energy future.

Of course, we cannot forget that we are all part of a greater global community. The Montreal Protocol, the Kyoto Protocol, the Equator Principles, and other global frameworks brokered by the United Nations or other international platforms are societal agreements representing global consensus. Globalization has made all nations more interdependent. Particularly with climate change, an issue that is so big and that knows no boundaries, international agreements and cooperation are absolutely vital. It is on this international stage that the United States has faltered, in the eyes of environmentalists.

The Kyoto Protocol—negotiated in Japan in 1997—might have failed to turn the tide in the ever-rising amounts of CO_2 and other heat-trapping gases now stuck in our atmosphere, but it was an important first step in establishing a framework of international cooperation on climate change. The United States flatly rejected the Kyoto climate treaty, which called for 38 industrialized nations around the world to make steep cuts in CO_2 and other global warming gases, to return to 1990 levels of greenhouse gas emissions. (Former President Clinton approved Kyoto, but he was never able to muster approval in the U.S. Congress.) An effort to move beyond the Kyoto Protocol, which expires in 2012, was launched in December 2007 in Bali, Indonesia. Here in the largest archipelago in the world, and the part of the world where entire island-nations are already disappearing because of sea level rise, nations gathered to persuade the world's largest unregulated nations—the United States, China, and India—to buy into binding urgent and dramatic action, but they largely failed, as have subsequent efforts.

Along with establishing the ground rules by which company, community, and consumer transact, a key role for government when thinking about solutions is underwriting the risky hit-and-miss venture of R&D. In this regard, California is undoubtedly a global leader.

Evolution of Public-Sector Research and Development

The federal government's investments in energy R&D activities date back to World War II and efforts to develop nuclear weapons. The Atomic Energy Commission was created in 1946 and was charged with finding civilian uses of atomic energy (pl. 93). In 1974—the same year the California Energy Commission was created in California—Congress created the federal Energy Research and Development Authority to broaden federal R&D beyond nuclear research. In 1977, another reorganization of federal energy R&D occurred, leading to the creation of the DOE.

Plate 93. Close-up of a nuclear reactor tower.

Between the 1970s and 1990, much of the technology R&D for electricity was funded primarily by individual private utilities and California's EPRI in Palo Alto. EPRI served as the umbrella organization for utilities all over the country. With the help of EPRI, located in the heart of Silicon Valley, investor-owned utilities could pool their resources in organized groups to investigate technologies. This arrangement worked fairly well until the mid-1990s, when electric industry restructuring disrupted business-as-usual R&D strategies.

With the advent of utility industry restructuring, EPRI's role declined, and private utilities shifted focus from advancing new technologies to cutting costs. The state's three major investor-owned utilities reduced their R&D budgets from a collective $135 million in 1991 to $62 million in 1996. CPUC recognized this important shift by indicating that only those utility R&D activities that supported "regulated functions" could be funded by ratepayers in the competitive world. This decision recognized the majority of new power supply was now being developed by nonutility companies. The CPUC also warned, nonetheless, that R&D activities that serve a "broader public interest . . . should not be lost in the transition to a more competitive environment."

Historically, California has had a vibrant science and technology sector. A preponderance of members of the National Academies of Science and Engineering, perhaps as many as a third of the total membership, call California home. Lawrence Berkeley National Laboratory (LBNL) is considered the world's foremost authority on the science of buildings (pl. 94), a legacy that dates back to the early 1970s and the efforts of Art Rosenfeld and other physicists that questioned a sole focus on supply, when reducing demand was easier and less costly. Researchers at LBNL are working with China to cut its huge carbon footprint through aggressive energy efficiency techniques modeled on California's building and appliance standards. Silicon Valley entrepreneurs are

Plate 94. Lawrence Berkeley National Laboratory.

investigating new thin-film "nanosolar" technologies that would enable windows to be covered with thin films of solar PV sprays that could make all of our buildings small power plants, not just a few large-area projects such as carport roofs (pl. 95). While Stanford University researchers contemplated ways to manipulate the process of photosynthesis in order to make plants create electricity instead of biomass—an advance decades away from commercialization—the University of California became the recipient of $500 million from the BP oil giant in 2007 to develop sustainable biofuels.

Among states, California universities, national laboratories, and high-tech companies receive the largest shares of federal R&D funds. Although the DOE sends California a substantial percentage of R&D funds to the state—typically a fifth of the national total—the priorities of the federal government have been at odds with those of California over the past decade or so: the federal government has been investing in nuclear and coal, while California is more

Plate 95. A solar PV carport at Cal Expo in Sacramento produces not only clean energy from the sun but shade for cars as well.

interested in wind and solar. In addition, most of the DOE R&D funding is associated with longer-term, fundamental research rather than energy technology development. Thus, there is an important role for the California state government in fostering cutting-edge solutions to global climate change and other challenges arising from today's energy infrastructure.

With the passage of AB 1890—California's infamous deregulation law—the Public Interest Energy Research (PIER) program was created. PIER is the largest state energy R&D program in the nation. The only comparable state R&D

effort is the New York State Energy Research and Development Authority (NYSERDA), which was created in 1975.

In the next part of this book is a series of examples of recent public–private partnership R&D success stories. The first few examples address the need to reduce California's peak demands for power on hot summer afternoons with the remarkably simple concept of a "cool roof" and ways to automate techniques that lower use of lighting, cooling, and heating services during times of extreme power shortages. These latter technologies are known as "demand response." The other examples address solutions that upgrade transmission and grid reliability, efforts to convert wastes into clean energy, and the several pieces of a puzzle necessary to develop a fossil fuel power plant that emits absolutely zero pollution. Added to this list of solutions are two related ideas—low carbon transportation standards and a Green Biofuels Labeling program—that have been put forward to the California Air Resources Board as critical components of California's effort to comply with AB 32.

Bringing Community Back into the Picture

One hopeful trend is a shift toward solutions that spring up from the local level instead of being dictated down from higher authorities. Living in Sacramento in the 1980s—when the fate of the Rancho Seco nuclear power plant hung in the balance—opened my eyes to the power of people at the grassroots level. This was, after all, the only nuclear reactor to be shut down by a local ballot initiative in 1989. The local municipal utility with the unfortunate acronym of SMUD (Sacramento Municipal Utility District) then went on to lead California and the nation on solar, wind, and energy efficiency. The experience of witnessing first-hand how a community can take its energy future into its own hands has stuck with me and has forever shaped the way I view energy and the world.

Lately, I push for solar and other renewable energy sources in Stinson Beach and the rest of Marin County. I have been spending considerable time on a unique experiment with community energy planning. Marin County as well as other communities in the Bay Area, the Central Valley, and in the Los Angeles Area are investigating "Community Choice Aggregation" (CCA), a legal term that refers to a new way for cities and counties to purchase electricity.

With the CCA, created by the passage of AB 117 by the California Legislature in 2002, local governments can now represent constituents-at-large by choosing their power supply portfolio and set their own rates to support that portfolio (pl. 96). Before this law was passed, the only way for a local government to have a say in where its power (and those of the residents and businesses residing within its boundaries) came from was to become a municipal utility. This law provides an easier way to change the content of the power supply without taking on the burden of managing the power

Plate 96. California's vast Central Valley is becoming a key testing ground in the state's efforts to improve air quality and foster innovation on energy planning.

lines, collecting bills, and the divisive politics involved with the typically highly contested (and expensive) municipalization process.

The CCA law offers many potential advantages to communities seeking to control their own energy destinies:

- AFFORDABLE RENEWABLE ENERGY. Under this program, homes and businesses can enjoy the benefits of non-polluting renewable energy resources at the most affordable price. Communities can determine how their electricity is generated—from clean and renewable resources rather than polluting and finite fossil fuels.

- GREATER PRICE STABILITY. California's growing demand for electricity is expected to be met by an increasing dependence upon natural gas–fired power plants. California already imports about 84 percent of its natural gas from other regions. Renewable energy sources have no fuel cost and are not subject to the price volatility inherent to natural gas markets.

- PROMOTION OF LOCAL, CLEAN DISTRIBUTED GENERATION. Any local government can create its own rates and incentives with a CCA to promote a greater reliance upon local "distributed generation" facilities such as solar PV panels, small on-site wind turbines, and cogeneration facilities or fuel cells that might help businesses be more efficient with their use of fossil fuel supplies.

- LOCAL ACCOUNTABILITY. Unlike investor-owned utilities, local governments are accountable to their citizens through locally elected officials whose tenure is predicated on performance. The decisions of a local power authority would likely be more transparent and responsive to the desires of the community than the actions of a private utility regulated by the CPUC in San Francisco.

- PUBLIC FINANCING OF GENERATION. Local governments have a substantial financial advantage over investor-owned utilities when investing in new power supply. They can access lower-cost, tax-exempt financing and do not have to pay income tax or any profits to shareholders.

Of course, you could also argue that taking on the responsibility of procuring power is always a risk. Furthermore, private utilities must surely have developed expertise in power supply over the decades of being in the business. It should be pointed out, nevertheless, that most new electricity generation developed today is by an army of independent energy producers that would also be providing the same services to local governments. There is also risk attached to sticking with the status quo.

A focus on renewable energy is quite popular among the local governments investigating the CCA option. However, this is not true for all local governments. A CCA formed by San Joaquin Valley cities with the Kings River Conservation District is planning to build a natural gas–fired power plant and large hydroelectric project, both sources that do not meet the state's definition of renewable energy. For these communities at the end of PG&E's distribution grid, the reliability and price stability of power are the primary drivers, though cleaner energy is also a concern. (By the way, it also announced plans for a new CSP facility that could grow to be as large as 80 megawatts.)

How else might communities collaborate on energy? Perhaps the best example comes from the city of Berkeley (pl. 97). With current state and federal subsidies, the installation of efficiency upgrades and clean distributed generation (such as solar PV and solar thermal systems) is now much more cost effective for many residential and commercial property owners. Nonetheless, many obstacles remain, with the most severe being the high up-front cost of these technologies.

In response to this dilemma, the city of Berkeley has proposed an innovative "Energy Assessment District" that could remedy many of the disincentives to install clean, on-site,

Plate 97. Berkeley Mayor Tom Bates announces a new approach to the financing of solar energy through the property tax system that could become a model for the country.

distributed generation systems. It is a novel approach and has the promise to be tremendously effective if used widely throughout the state and expanded to include energy efficiency upgrades as well.

The Energy Assessment District proposed for Berkeley is modeled after existing Underground Utility Districts, whereby a group of homeowners in a neighborhood work in coordination with the municipality on a plan to place utility distribution poles and wires underground. All property owners in the designated area vote on the proposal. If a sufficient majority votes in favor, the city works with the local utility to contract to have the infrastructure placed underground. The entire cost of the project is paid for with a non-tax-exempt municipal bond. Homeowners repay the bond as an assessment on their property tax bills over a fixed period, typically 20 years or so. The assessment is officially in "second position" as a lien on the property—behind property tax and in front of the mortgage—giving excellent security and a corresponding low interest rate. A 20-year period fits well with the expected minimum lifetime of solar PV panels too.

The city of Berkeley is creating a citywide voluntary Energy Assessment District. Under this new program, property owners (residential and commercial) can install solar PV systems (and ultimately make energy efficiency improvements) to their buildings and then pay for the cost as a 20-year assessment on their property tax bills. No property owners would pay an assessment unless they chose to include their property in the program. Those who do have work done on their property would pay only for the cost of their project and fees necessary to administer the program.

This approach solves many of the financial hurdles facing property owners. First, it significantly reduces the up-front cost to the property owner. Second, the total cost of the system might be less than a traditional equity line or mortgage refinancing. This is because the well-secured bond should provide lower interest rates than are commercially available. (Another factor is that the city would require multiple projects to be aggregated to reduce construction costs.) Third, the tax assessment is transferable between owners. If the property is sold prior to the repayment of the assessment, the next owner would take over the assessment as part of their property tax bill.

Another way to broaden the market for decentralized renewable energy sources is based on the notion of "community solar." Today, the term means different things to different people. In essence, the term of "community solar" or "solar shares" refers to the fact that multiple users can draw from a single solar PV array, or a series of arrays on different buildings, but operated as a single system, supplying clean electricity to community institutions (e.g., fire station and community centers) as well as residents that lacked good solar exposure on their own rooftops or are renters. Under this community solar model, participants, in essence, purchase shares of the total output from solar systems. To date, the few community solar projects being developed in the nation have been in Sacramento, California; Ashland, Oregon; Ellensburg, Washington; and on Washington's Orcas Islands. In each of these examples, the systems were developed by a municipal utility or a rural cooperative.

The concept of "community wind," which is more advanced than the notion of "community solar" both here in the United States as well as Europe, connotes direct ownership of renewable energy resources, often through the Limited Liability Corporation (LLC) model. In Minnesota, for example, farmers own shares of a single commercial-scale wind turbine through this model, thereby benefiting from not only the power generated, but direct local ownership of the assets.

Yet another radically new idea for community collaboration on energy is the concept of a "Solar Safety Net," which could help integrate solar energy into emergency backup systems throughout California's rural communities most vulnerable to blackouts. This sort of emergency planning can help build the case for accessing new federal and state funding currently earmarked for national security or emergency preparedness. The "Solar Safety Net" concept is designed to build new constituencies for solar energy: local fire departments, community centers, and state and federal agencies dedicated to homeland security and disaster preparedness. Under the model currently under development by the Solar Economy Institute, these solar systems could be installed at key community institutions, such as the local fire station, or on the best residential sites on a neighborhood-by-neighborhood basis (pl. 98). Each transformer on the distribution grid could host an emergency solar backup system. They could supply clean electricity feeding into the grid under normal conditions. They could switch to batteries for storage in the event of a power outage, thereby providing power to maintain key telecommunications, refrigeration, and other services in rural areas that frequently suffer from long-term disruptions in electricity service.

Plate 98. Jerry Lunsford (who lives off-grid with solar power) points to the roof of the Dance Palace community center in Point Reyes Station, site of the nation's first "Solar Safety Net" installation.

While concepts such as "community choice aggregation," "community solar," "community wind," and the "solar safety net" continue to be tested and perfected, there are plenty of examples of present-day community efforts to address energy challenges in California. Among the most noteworthy is the localization effort underway in Willits in Mendocino County. Called WELL (Willits Economic Localization), the effort is a broad program tying together energy, transportation, housing, and food supply concerns with an overall goal of generating as many of the services as possible from within the local community, hence a focus on local solar, wind, and other renewable resources as the communities' first choices for power supply. Partnering with organizations such as the Post Carbon Institute and the Renewable Energy Development Institute, the 13,500 people residing within the 322 square miles that are comprised in the 95490 zip code are creating an antidote to globalization. They hope to shift much of the $30 million they spend on imported energy sources to local purveyors of green forms of energy.

In My Own Backyard

Driving up the steep gravel road leading up to the Stubbs Vineyard on the northern fringes of Marin County near Marshall, I squinted to see a tiny wind turbine spinning furiously way up at the top of hill, virtually invisible from the nearest road. Along with the 1-kilowatt Southwest Windpower wind turbine, the Stubbs Vineyard relies upon less than 1 kilowatt of solar PVs (pl. 99) and a biodiesel backup generator for all of its electricity needs. Because the PG&E grid is a mile away from either side of their property, the Stubbs Vineyard lives "off-the-grid" and is likely the greenest vineyard in all of California.

"We probably use 5 to 10 percent of the energy of your average American household," said Tom Stubbs, who freely acknowledged that life on his specially designated "alternative energy home" was not easy. "Our best time for wind power production is spring," he said. "Our energy supplies are at

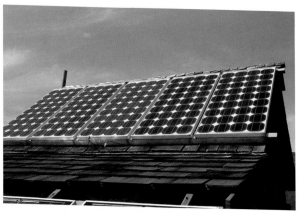

Plate 99. Five of the eight solar panels that help the Stubbs Winery, producer of premium organic Chardonnay and Pinot Noir, to be off-grid and rely completely on renewable energy systems.

their lowest in winter, and I become a bit of a tyrant with our children, following behind them turning off lights," he said.

Mary and Tom Stubbs moved to this property in 1992 and then planted Pinot Noir and Chardonnay grapes in 1996. At present, they are the only certified organic vineyard in Marin County. Plans for a new vineyard and tasting room might require them to add another wind turbine and more solar panels. In addition, they might finally connect to the PG&E grid, though Stubbs agonizes over that prospect. "I like the independent aspect of not being beholden to anybody." Just the same, if he were connected to the grid, he could take advantage of a program called "net metering," which would allow him to sell the energy he did not use back to the grid and draw from the grid when his on-site power sources stopped producing because of a lack of wind or sun.

Stubbs is keenly aware of the pros and cons of both wind and sun. "At good sites, there is plenty of wind, but I think Marin County lends itself better to solar energy. It doesn't offend anybody." Stubbs' comments were a reference to the nearby McEvoy organic olive farm, whose proposal for a 660-kilowatt wind turbine was shot down by the County Planning Commission in 2006. The rejection of this wind turbine in Marin County, a part of California well-known for its environmental ethic, highlights the role individuals and community play in moving toward a local green energy economy. If California really wants to move toward a local and regional approach to energy solutions, then it is incumbent upon individuals to become informed about on-site clean power sources, such as wind turbines, and the trade-offs involved between local visual impacts and the consequences of deriving power from distant, polluting sources.

A revised proposal for the organic olive farm put together by Tom Williard, principal with Sustainergy Systems, now features a 225-kilowatt wind turbine and was unanimously approved by the County Board of Supervisors in January 2007. Willard expects the turbine to be in the ground in early 2009.

Luckily, a state rebate of $350,000 will help cover about half of the wind project's total costs. "We have had five years of legal wrangling, with many lawyers knocking over hurdle after hurdle to this project," he explained, noting that pioneering green energy projects often cost more than expected. "Unless you are a geek, and want to tinker with your turbine two or three times a year, small wind is not too appealing of an option for the vast majority of people," concluded Williard, expressing a sentiment shared by most, but not all, renewable energy advocates.

Mark Pasternak of Devil's Gulch Ranch in Marin County's town of Nicasio disagrees with Williard and is bullish on wind power, whether large-scale wind farms or small-scale, on-site machines. In 2006 he purchased a used 35-kilowatt Vestas V-15 wind turbine (pl. 100). Like Stubbs, Pasternak first lived "off-the-grid" and relied upon a 2-kilowatt wind turbine between 1971 and 1982. When he planted his vineyard in

Plate 100. A recycled Vestas wind turbine, yanked out from the Altamont Pass, now provides clean electricity for Devil's Gulch Ranch in Nicasio.

1980, however, he connected to the grid because of increased water pumping. Pasternak was initially frustrated by technical glitches related to adjustments necessary to integrate the "new" machine into the more primitive local grid. Yet, he quickly points out, the turbine has required zero maintenance since it began operating in May 2006.

Pasternak's wind turbine supplies all of the energy for his home and about half of his ranch's needs. From his vantage point, small wind turbines make a lot of sense in Marin and other parts of rural California, particularly the used Vestas turbines that he has. (Even Williard acknowledged the superiority of this technology. "They are like the Volkswagen Beetle cars, they just go and go and go.") It is estimated that there are over 800 used Vestas turbines now available on the market, as they are being replaced by newer, larger turbines in California's Altamont Pass and other existing wind farms, as described in the preceding section of this book, The Risks of the Status Quo and Systems Overhaul. (The bird kill problems described in that section have not occurred on Pasternak's ranch.) Pasternak summed up his views in this way: "I think wind turbines look really cool. I don't see them as detraction, but rather as an enhancement to the environment."

While Marin County may have a reputation for being environmentally advanced, San Bernardino County is the state's clear leader in small, on-site renewable energy systems. All wind (as well as solar energy) applications are exempt from local government fees. Applications for new homes that feature green building designs will get their county applications expedited too. The largest county in terms of acreage in the lower 48 states, San Bernardino County already boasts the largest population of small wind turbines in the nation.

Reducing Our Collective Eco-Footprints

One dramatic way to visualize each of our respective environmental impacts upon the world—whether from our cars or our homes and lifestyle—is the concept of the ecological footprint, a technique that attempts to measure the amount of productive land required to provide all of the resources (food, energy, and materials) for a person from a specific region and income level. Key components in the calculation of an ecological footprint include gasoline, diesel, and natural gas use as well as electricity. Types of vehicles and average miles traveled are included, as are acreage of residence, characteristics of the lodging structure itself, and waste and recycling rates. (Levels of toxic waste are not included in the computation.)

Energy is the largest single component of this exercise, and it is the CO_2 released into the atmosphere from the burning of fossil fuels that makes up the largest share of the energy contribution (hence the ecological footprint is often referred to as the "carbon footprint"). To illustrate this footprint concept, consider that two-and-a-half acres of forest are required to absorb one metric ton of CO_2. For every metric ton of CO_2 released by your activities over the course of a single year, 2.5 acres are added to your ecological footprint.

On a global scale, fossil fuel combustion accounts for the largest share of the ecological footprint. This is due to the high consumption rates of coal, oil, and natural gas in the developed, industrialized world. (For lower-income, developing countries, agriculture is the largest contributor to their ecological footprints.)

Let us repeat this embarrassing statistic. The United States represents less than 5 percent of the world's population, yet consumes nearly 25 percent of the world's energy. To be sustainable, each citizen on the planet would limit its ecological footprint to less than 5.4 acres.

I went to the "Yahoo! Green" website to see where I stood in terms of my own carbon footprint. In less than a minute, and after answering less than a dozen questions, I discovered my carbon emissions were more than twice the U.S. average—and I consider myself an environmentalist! According to Environmental Defense, the average American emits 9.44 metric tons of CO_2 annually, while my total was 25.1 metric tons. Because I am a renter in a rural part of California that lacks decent mass transit systems, my options for reducing emissions from my home and local travel were limited. Interestingly enough, my home—an apartment of modest size—was the least part of my problem. Because I regularly drive to a city two hours away and back on a biweekly basis, my truck alone contributed as much carbon as the national average for home, motor vehicle travel, and air fare combined!

Yet, it was my one average trip to Europe to visit family, one average trip across country (conference), and one average short trip elsewhere that put me way over the top. (Some years, I have traveled much more than that, but have actually cut back in recent times because of fiscal concerns and, yes, some concerns about our climate.) When I went through the program to develop a plan to reduce my emissions, I could only find steps—over 20 in total—that would trim roughly 5 metric tons from my 25-metric-ton carbon footprint.

Luckily, Yahoo! Green offered an easy way not only to buy light bulbs and other efficiency devices, but to offset the rest of my carbon by contracting with Terra Pass, a firm that develops renewable energy projects to make up for my carbon sins. For example, I discovered that I could offset my truck's carbon emissions at a cost of $79.95 for one year. That is enough cash to clean up 20,000 miles' worth of annual driving.

Upon further investigation, I discovered that West Marin, my home and a place of extreme beauty preserved for future generations, has one of the largest ecological footprints in the nation. According to the Marin Countywide Plan, I would need an average of 27 acres to support my lifestyle. According to the county's methodology, the U.S. average is 24 acres, while the world average is just 5.5 acres. Given the current global population, there are actually only 4.5 acres actually available to support each of us sustainably, a statistic that speaks volumes about what needs to be done in the very, very near future.

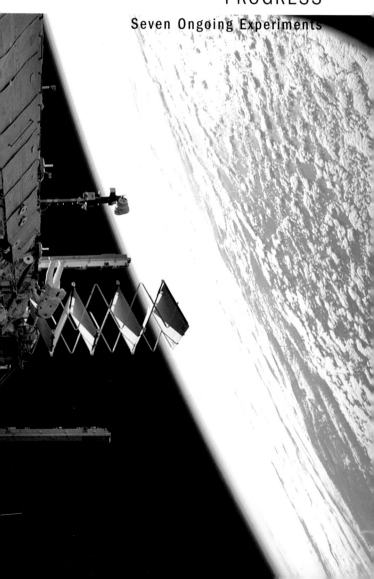

Cool Roofs

Hot summer afternoons place phenomenal stress on California's electricity grid, particularly when consumers boost electricity demand by switching on their air conditioners. A spike in electricity demand not only leads to higher energy costs but can, in severe cases, result in equipment failure and corresponding rolling blackouts. This increased demand for energy is an economic issue, because constructing electricity generators that might be used for only a few days or even hours during demand peaks represent a large sunk investment. It is also an environmental issue, because the generators used to meet emergency power needs are often among the most polluting fossil fuel sources of electricity and operate just at the time when air quality is most vulnerable, contributing to the global climate change threat.

According to the federal Energy Information Administration, commercial buildings account for 35 percent of total electricity demand. On top of that, these same commercial buildings represent 45 percent of summer peak demand, more than any other sector of the economy.

A good first step in addressing this challenge is based on the science of color. Generally speaking, dark colors absorb more solar radiation than light or reflective materials. A traditional asphalt roof is dark colored rather than reflective and therefore absorbs over 90 percent of the energy radiating down from the sun. In sunny California, that absorption translates into peak roof temperatures ranging from 150 to 190 degrees F on hot summer days and contributes to peak demands for electricity. In comparison, reflective, light-colored "cool roofs" are 50 to 60 degrees cooler on average. The dramatic drops in rooftop temperatures created when a cool roof reflects and radiates away the sun's heat translates into even greater savings in very hot climates, such as the San Joaquin Valley, Imperial County, and the Inland Empire. A cool roof can reduce a building's cooling electricity consumption from 10 to 40 percent. Though cool roof technologies have been around for at least four decades, the technology was largely unknown to the majority of building owners and comprised a very small percentage of the total roofing market.

According to Hashem Akbari, the lead principal investigator for development of cool-colored roofing materials at LBNL, cool roofs offer the opportunity for tremendous energy savings, not only in California, but across the nation. "Our research in 1997 showed that the potential net energy savings in the United States achievable by applying white roofs to commercial buildings and cool-colored roofs to houses was valued at more than $750 million per year," he said. With today's energy prices, Akbari estimated these savings could "easily surpass $1 billion per year." Beyond the enormous energy efficiency savings generated by widespread adoption of cool roof technology, there is a long list of ancillary benefits. For example, cool roofs also reduce the "urban heat island" effect, a phenomenon caused by large areas of dark surfaces found in cities (i.e., roofs and pavements) that absorb and hold solar energy. Heat islands also can accelerate the rate of smog production through photochemical reactions between pollutants in the air. These reactions increase as temperatures rise.

Because of their reflective properties, cool roof systems may slow down the deterioration of the roofing materials and therefore may reduce roof maintenance costs. In many cases, roof tear-off wastes can be avoided altogether when installing a cool roof. This translates into less ground, water, and air pollution originating from landfills. Because of state R&D investments, cool roof technologies that now include darker-colored, but still reflective, roofing materials are widely available (pl. 101) and are being incorporated as standard equipment in all new homes being built in California. This is a great example of how government can force widespread adoption of beneficial technologies that lock in energy savings for decades to come. These

Plate 101. Cool roof materials now come in a variety of colors, not just white.

same pigments can be incorporated into motor vehicles, cutting the need for air-conditioning (and thereby gasoline consumption) in the transportation sector as well.

Demand Response Technologies

"Demand response" technologies are designed to provide immediate, short-interval reductions in energy use to respond to weather patterns, stress on the electricity grid, and real-time market energy prices. Today's manual demand response systems are expensive, labor intensive, and ultimately unreliable. Automated Demand Response (AutoDR) technology takes human error out of the equation and relies upon telecommunication advances to turn noncritical energy uses off when given the right computer signal during critical peaks in demand. Results from four years of R&D involving over 40 different facilities (for example, office buildings, a high school, a museum, data centers, a postal facility, a library, retail chains, and a supermarket) revealed average demand reductions of about 10–15 percent during the three- to six-hour-long demand response events.

Because of the success of this AutoDR testing, each of the state's three private utilities implemented these control technologies in their service territories in 2007. "I think this is as good of a success story as there can be in the R&D arena," acknowledged Wayne Krill, senior project manager for PG&E. "PIER funding underwrote the development work, and now utilities such as PG&E are taking it through the next critical step of market introduction and into widespread use, highlighting the synergy of public–private partnerships." It is estimated that employing strategies and technologies such as AutoDR can save the equivalent of 1,000 megawatts of electricity capacity, or roughly enough electricity to provide power for more than approximately one million homes.

State ratepayers have also invested in a Demand Response Business Network (DRBizNet) that allows businesses to coordinate their own internal demand response programs with regional and statewide efforts to manage the state's demand response capacity better. While the AutoDR project is designed to automate key demand response activities at individual commercial facilities, DRBizNet takes a broader systems approach to managing these resources on a statewide basis. Another way to look at it is this: AutoDR technology is the physical hardware for automating demand reductions on a site-by-site basis, while DRBizNet provides the enabling technology for back-end systems to automate and streamline demand response-related processes, such as customer enrollment, verification of program participation, and financial settlements.

At present, California utilities, businesses, and other large energy consumers are moving forward with new and substantial investments in information technology (IT) infrastructure, but they lack a unifying architecture that will enable them to speak the same language when engaged in demand response activities. Current processes to manage demand response programs are cumbersome and often depend upon manual phone calls as well as multiple channels, hindering the reliability and efficiency of these demand response resources. Deploying a real-time demand response network as envisioned with DRBizNet has the potential to boost the benefits of demand response by a factor of 10 at one-tenth the cost of today's uncoordinated system. Furthermore, DRBizNet lays the foundation for a dynamic marketplace for demand response that could ultimately count on the state's 11 million residential customers to also engage in demand response activities on a daily basis, involving all ratepayers in the effort to maintain electricity system reliability while minimizing costs.

Transmission and Reliability Upgrades

Managing California's electricity transmission system used to be a simple task: move electricity from centralized power

Plate 102. Transmission infrastructure may not always be pretty, but it is critical to making tomorrow's energy system more nimble.

plants to consumers via progressively smaller distribution lines. Over the past few decades, however, new transmission capacity has failed to keep up with growth in electricity consumption. New demands being placed on an increasingly interactive power grid have increased both the risk and consequence of blackouts. California's aggressive RPS goals require additional transmission lines, but environmental and social concerns often stifle development, frustrating goals to reduce greenhouse gas emissions (pl. 102).

If California fails to modernize its transmission capabilities with emerging technologies, the state will need to site thousands of miles of new high-voltage lines (pl. 103), fail

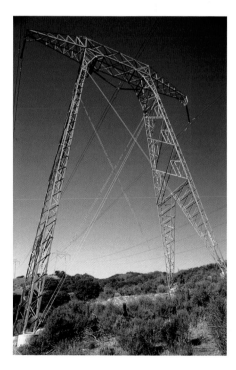

Plate 103. Transmission tower carrying high-voltage lines, with leg lengths and footing placements uniquely designed for its location to keep the tower vertical and the lines on the level across sloping ground.

to meet its legislative mandates on renewable energy, and increase risks of blackouts and costly disruptions. At present, these costs total roughly $8 billion annually.

Here is part of the problem: The stated capacity of most existing transmission lines in California is static. Based on very conservative assumptions about weather conditions to maintain minimum ground clearances to ensure public safety, this approach does not maximize efficiency. What if the California utilities that own transmission systems could rely on sensors that provided real-time data on the condition of these lines?

California is now introducing more of this kind of intelligence into the grid, making it more interactive like the Internet. Real-time monitoring and dynamic rating technologies—one using a "smart" camera—are being field tested by California utilities, which will allow greater amounts of power to pass through existing lines, because it can sense the actual real-time conditions of the transmission grid. Transmission infrastructure is complicated and requires constant adjustments to balance customer demand and generator supply, as well as to ensure that electrical attributes, such as voltage, are maintained within safe operating ranges. Transmission systems also become vulnerable during extreme heat waves as peaks in electricity demand push the system to its limit, conditions expected to increase in the near-term as a result of global climate change. The extra flow of electricity heats the wires, sometimes causing excessive line sag, which was the cause of the major power outage that hit California and the western United States in August 1996.

A technology with the name of SLiM (for Sagging Line Mitigator) is designed to address this sag problem directly. As temperatures spike and transmission lines expand, a special bar in the SLiM device also expands and pushes on a lever, which pulls the transmission lines taut again. Although it relies upon state-of-the-art materials science, SLiM is a low-cost technology that can increase electricity throughput and improve public safety at the same time.

Another technology developed with state funding to improve reliability while decreasing wear and tear on some of the state's oldest and most polluting electricity generators (while promoting on-site clean distributed power options) is the flywheel energy storage system. A new flywheel energy storage system from Beacon Power of Wilmington, Massachusetts, can provide reliability more efficiently without burning fossil fuel. In fact, it would take a 400-megawatt fossil fuel plant to provide the same level of storage and reliability support as a 20-megawatt flywheel energy storage system. Beacon's system works by accelerating a carbon-fiber composite flywheel to a very high speed to store electricity in the form of kinetic energy. The beauty of this technology is that it can absorb energy instantaneously when supply exceeds demand and discharge that energy when demand exceeds supply. Whereas it takes conventional power plants up to five minutes to ramp up or down, the flywheel storage energy system takes only four seconds to respond.

Electricity storage has the potential to enable higher percentages of intermittent renewable energy to penetrate California's power supply portfolio, allowing the state to take better advantage of its abundant renewable resource endowments. Along with flywheels, storage options include pumped hydro storage, compressed air storage, thermal storage, or batteries. Advances in each of these technologies can potentially transform intermittent power sources such as wind and solar power into resources capable of offering firm electricity supply to the grid, thereby reducing reliance on polluting gas-fired facilities turned on during spikes in electricity demand. Moreover, electricity storage in the form of plug-in electric vehicles has the potential to reduce reliance on fossil fuels in the transportation sector.

With the appropriate strategies, policies and incentives, these energy technologies will spur monumental reductions in carbon while altering the way that electricity is traditionally generated and consumed.

Transforming Our Wastes into Clean Energy

The annual production of municipal solid waste has more than doubled since 1960. When solid waste is placed in a landfill, microbes decompose matter, and gas composed primarily of methane—a fuel, but also a potent greenhouse gas—is released. Nationally, only 25 percent of this potential fuel is captured and combusted for electricity generation.

Our waste streams might seem like odd places to find clean, renewable energy sources of electricity. Yet if we truly want to find solutions to our energy supply needs—and are committed to a systems view of our economy and environment—generating energy from wastes must be a top priority. A promising technology currently being tested in California can derive clean electricity from municipal landfills.

The primary technical barrier to widespread reliance upon landfill gas as a substitute fuel for natural gas has been slow rates of composition, limiting the size of electricity generators, and corresponding economic feasibility. A grant from the state helped Yolo County investigate an accelerated anaerobic composting process that creates a landfill bioreactor (pl. 104). Interest in bioreactor technology dates back to the 1970s, but the technology has, for the most part, been delegated to lab research with few large-scale demonstration projects. By accelerating methane production in an environmentally sound manner, generating electricity from landfill gas suddenly looks more cost effective and emerges as a key climate change response technology.

Plate 104. Worker checking methane levels and leaks at the Yolo
Bioreactor.

In this project, three methane-enhanced bioreactor
cells were designed and constructed. Controlled quantities of liquid were added and recirculated to increase the
moisture content of the solid wastes. This landfill bioreactor process speeds up the biodegradation rate of waste,
thereby dramatically reducing the amount of time for
wastes to decompose and generate methane gas, an alternative electricity fuel. It also offers the opportunity for making these landfills truly renewable resources by managing
them for long-term methane production. The full-scale
bioreactor landfill at Yolo County is expected to produce
over 57,000 megawatt-hours of electricity, equivalent to
about 90,000 barrels of oil, over the expected 10-year life of
this landfill. "The state grant allowed us to build to a larger
scale, to test this full-scale system, and collect extensive
data," observed Ramin Yazdani, project manager for the
Yolo County Planning and Public Works. "Our plan is to
use this data to persuade the federal EPA to revise current

rules prohibiting widespread adoption of this advanced landfill bioreactor system."

Bioreactor landfills can help California meet its aggressive renewable energy procurement goals by increasing methane gas production for faster and more efficient energy recovery, resulting in a reduced dependency on nonrenewable fossil energy sources. Other environmental benefits include less discharge to the local wastewater treatment plant, reduced long-term environmental liability, a reduction in postclosure care and maintenance, and an increase in life expectancy of the landfill itself.

Another method to generate clean power from wastes involves anaerobic digesters, which are, in essence, covered lagoons. Dating back centuries ago to ancient China, this simple technology still lacks technical maturity. Although California is the largest agricultural state in the nation, the food-processing industry has few anaerobic digesters in commercial operation, leading to extremely high municipal wastewater discharge costs.

In the case of Valley Fig Growers, high wastewater volumes have been an ongoing issue with the city of Fresno. Because of population growth, sewer rates went up 18 percent in 2007, another 18 percent in 2008, and 21 percent in 2009. The fig

Plate 105. The covered digester lagoon at the Valley Fig Growers facility in Fresno puffs up, capturing fuel from fig waste for electricity generation.

Plate 106. This microturbine burns gas from the Valley Fig Growers anaerobic digester to produce 70 kilowatts of electricity.

growers received a state grant to figure out a way to turn the sugars washed off of figs into a methane gas, which would then reduce demands on the local sewer system (pl. 105). By pretreating its wastewater in this way, the local municipality wins, but so does Valley Fig Growers.

The organic biogas was used to fuel a 70- kilowatt electricity generator through a microturbine, a scaled-down jet engine about the size of two refrigerators (pl. 106), which can supply the minimum electricity requirements for the entire facility. A two-year demonstration project yielded impressive results. Valley Fig Growers generated the vast majority of its own electricity supply from previously discharged wastewater that had been converted into biogas. It was able to recycle 50 to 100 percent of the waste heat from the microturbine to the anaerobic digester itself or to heat water and the dehydrator. Finally, solid wastes shipped off-site were reduced from two to one truckload per day. All in all, it trimmed $100,000 from its annual waste management costs. This digester freed up sewer service for the equivalent of 2,500 homes.

Zero-Emissions Fossil Fuel Power Plants?

Generating electricity is responsible for 20 percent of California's greenhouse gas emissions. Renewable energy technologies such as solar and wind power are extremely clean and emit no carbon into the atmosphere, but they can offer only fluctuating amounts of power and only when the sun shines or the wind blows if storage options are not available. California could benefit from low-carbon/no-carbon clean power technologies that can operate around the clock or that can be called upon quickly during sudden peaks in demand, when electricity is the most expensive and air quality is most threatened.

Enter the concept of a zero-emissions fossil fuel plant. The concept of a "zero-emissions, climate-neutral power plant" might seem counterintuitive, but here is how this configuration works (fig. 27). Natural gas is combusted in the gas generator with pure oxygen rather than air. Because no nitrogen is present, no nitrogen oxides (NO_x) are released

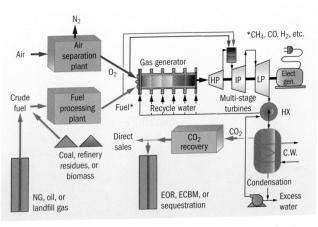

Figure 27. Several steps are necessary to create a zero-emission fossil fuel plant. First, a gaseous fuel is combusted with oxygen in a gas generator. The residual gas, consisting of steam and CO_2, powers a multi-stage turbine and generator to produce electricity and condensation and to recycle the steam. The CO_2 can then be recovered and sequestered or used for enhanced oil recovery (EOR) or coal bed methane (ECBM) recovery. Water condensed in the cooling water (CW) tank is recycled into the heat exchanger (HX). Water from the heat exchanger is recycled into the gas generator as a coolant at each bolt ring.

Plate 107. Clean Energy Systems, Inc., technology installed at the 20 megawatt Kimberlina pilot project site. Gaseous fuel, oxygen, and water are delivered to the injector face from the tubes in the foreground. Combustion occurs at this end of the barrel, with cooling water injected at each bolt ring. Drive gas, a mixture of steam and CO_2, exits through the large pipe at the far end and goes to power the turbo-generator on the floor above.

into the surrounding environment. (NO_x is a major contributor to urban smog.) The resulting exhaust is composed of nearly pure steam and CO_2, which powers a steam turbine and generator (pl. 107). The steam is condensed and recycled through the system for cooling. The CO_2 can be sequestered and stored or sold for commercial use.

One commercial application for the captured CO_2 is enhanced oil recovery. If pumped underground, the CO_2 loosens deposits of oil, which then can be recovered in an economical manner. By allowing for the economic recovery of more domestic oil supplies from existing sites, the sequestration process could lessen U.S. dependence on imported supplies. Up to 5 billion barrels of oil could be extracted under California alone with this technology, according to some estimates. The firm responsible for the design of such a counter-intuitive solution to energy supply was founded by a group of engineers and scientists—many from the NASA space program—who decided in the mid-1990s to address the issues of global climate change. They pooled their expertise to adapt rocket propulsion technology to a pollution-free power plant. "Rockets use oxy-combustion to achieve instantaneous power," recalled Keith Pronske, president and CEO of Rancho Cordova–based Clean Energy Systems, Inc. (CES), referring to the process of burning fuel in pure oxygen instead of in air. "The same combustion process can also make zero-emission electricity." Southern California Gas Company purchased CES stock in 2006 and announced in January 2007 it was seeking DOE funding to build the nation's first zero-emissions power plant in southern California. Under this proposed project, to be developed in conjunction with CES, the CO_2 would be permanently sequestered and used for enhanced oil recovery.

To be clear, the only way this technology can truly be called a "zero-emission power plant" today, because of new state controls on carbon dioxide, is for the successful demonstration of the compelling idea of storing these emissions in giant underground caverns. California is currently involved in one of seven partnerships established by the DOE to evaluate the feasibility of capturing CO_2 and storing it in appropriate geological reservoirs, as well as in terrestrial ecosystems such as forests. Known as the West Coast Regional Carbon Sequestration Partnership (WESTCARB), members beyond California include the states of Alaska, Arizona, Nevada, Oregon, and Washington, as well as the province of British Columbia. To date, WESTCARB researchers have discovered that California offers outstanding geologic sequestration opportunities, though in the case of California, the focus of research is on the potential for value-added benefits from enhanced oil and natural gas recovery, not coal. Research shows that saline formations in the 10 largest sedimentary basins in California could potentially store up to 5,000 years' worth of the state's current power plant and industrial-sector carbon emissions. California would require approximately 40 million metric tons of CO_2 of sequestration to offset greenhouse gas emissions from the state's existing fleet of fossil fuel power plants.

Lower-Carbon Transportation Fuels

CARB has implemented a Low-Carbon Fuel Standard (LCFS) for future transportation fuels, but much more will need to be done to address the massive amounts of carbon emitted into the atmosphere from our transportation system. The LCFS establishes a statewide goal of reducing the carbon intensity of California's transportation fuels by at least 10 percent by 2020, a modest but important first step in driving our transportation fuel carbon content toward zero.

To complicate matters, biofuels and other new alternative fuel products can have either a positive or negative effect on global climate change depending on production methods and other factors. Current corn-based ethanol production often releases GHG emissions similar to, and sometimes higher than, those of traditional fossil fuel transportation fuels once all of the air emissions effects are accounted for. International, federal, and state standards for sustainable low-carbon biofuels are currently being developed. So far, however, they do not offer any environmental performance information to consumers. With additional tracking standards, these systems could be used to engage consumer demand through a "Green Fuels Labeling Standard" in California.

Such a biofuels program could also have an impact on forest fuel management projects. A green fuels labeling program can provide a three-way climate gain by restoring forest ecosystems to more resilient conditions, directing excess fuels to biomass energy production to help meet the LCFS, and reducing wildfire emissions from intense crown fires. Decades of fire exclusion have left many forest stands in unnatural conditions, and sensible projects can be designed to utilize excess forest materials in ways that benefit both the forest and the climate. However, recognizing the strong public concerns regarding potential over-exploitation of forests for biomass fuels, confidence in the ecological basis for fuel projects needs to be bolstered if such efforts are to play any role in California's future energy strategies.

A voluntary or mandatory Green Fuels Labeling Standard could be created to guide consumer purchasing preferences. This is especially important for biofuels because of the potential negative environmental and social implications of different feed stocks and cropping methods. Once waste-derived biofuels are fully commercial, new incentives could be used to expand the blending of biomass-derived fuels with conventional fuels beyond LCFS requirements. This information could be included on fuel content labels.

Many technology-based opportunities also exist for developing cleaner fuels and vehicles. An overlap between electricity generation and transportation fuels is inevitable. Electricity supply infrastructure in the planning stage today will need to accommodate near-term deployment of plug-in hybrids or electric-powered transportation systems. In addition, full performance battery electric and fuel cell vehicles, which could be powered by hydrogen derived via the hydrolysis process, are expected to be fully commercialized by 2030. These projections are well within the expected lifetime of electric generation, transmission, and distribution systems being planned today. Forward-looking planning will be necessary to capture the potential synergies between energy sources employed for traditional electricity use and new vehicle fuels.

Luckily, there are those individuals working on personal, locally based solutions to our stubborn and lingering addiction to the comforts and familiarity of today's petroleum-based lifestyle. Alternative transportation fuels such as biodiesel seem to be emerging sustainable alternatives, but for perfectionists such as Andy Cooper of Footprint Recycling, the industry has a long ways to go if it wants to become a legitimate answer to our transportation challenges. Cooper is based in Humboldt County along the North Coast, a place where lofty ideals about each of our relationships to community are the norm.

"We need to educate the consumer, because most of the biodiesel I've sampled throughout the state is pure !##!+^!" Cooper went on a rant, claiming that 19 of the 20 samples of biodiesel brought to him by loyal customers on long road trips up and down the state all flunked his own quality control tests (pl. 108). "There's a

Plate 108. Samples of biodiesel reveal a large quality control gap.

Plate 109. Footprint Recycling's humble biodiesel truck.

very simple test. When you mix your biodiesel with water, the fuel should rise to the top, and the water should remain clear on the bottom," said Cooper. There should be no cloudiness. Furthermore, when things turn cold, there should be no waxy fallout in the fuel. "Mixing real diesel with inferior biodiesel is like putting on a Band-Aid that just won't stay on," he said, warning that motor vehicles relying upon inferior biodiesel fuels will feel the impact after 60,000 to 100,000 miles. "Buyer beware" apparently applies to "green" products too!

Cooper takes sustainability seriously. More than 70 percent of his company's equipment is salvage from scrap yards and dumps (pl. 109). "My supply of fuel will always be finite since my sources are local restaurants," he added. "Biodiesel brought here from America's heartland is a net energy loss because five to seven gallons were burned to get it here. The only way biodiesel makes sense is down at the regional and community level," Cooper said. "It is important to see the impacts right at home. When done right, biodiesel re-values the commodity of waste grease and recycles dollars three or four times before leaving Humboldt County."

Smart Growth Land Use Planning

California drivers used an estimated 18.1 billion gallons of motor fuel to travel 330 billion miles in 2005—a 15 percent increase since 1990—at an estimated cost of $44 billion. If current growth trends continue, gasoline use and related CO_2 emissions in the transportation sector will grow by approximately 30 percent over the next 20 years. This increase carries a substantial environmental price tag as well as the economic penalty of a $22 billion increase in the annual cost of fueling the transportation system (assuming a cost of $4.00 per gallon of gasoline). Considering that over 50 percent of the petroleum consumed in California is imported, the near-total reliance of the transportation sector on this fuel exposes the state's economy to price spikes created by the dynamics of national or international markets. The corresponding outflow of capital from California to countries and regions supplying petroleum reduces the purchasing power and living standard of growing numbers of state citizens.

It is notable that each one percent reduction in transportation energy consumption (or rate of consumption growth) could add up to more than $400 million in annual savings. The California Department of Transportation calculates that every one percent reduction in greenhouse gas emissions from the transportation sector stops 1.81 million metric tons of these emissions from being released into the atmosphere or half of one percent of California's total contribution to global climate change. The decreased cost of purchasing fuels will also result in macroeconomic benefits because of a shift of consumers' dollars from purchasing imported oil to purchasing more in-state goods and services, giving a boost to the state economy.

One of the most promising solutions to our transportation carbon footprint is the concept of "smart growth." This is an urban planning and transportation strategy that emphasizes growth near city centers and transit corridors to prevent urban sprawl. This approach promotes mixed-use, infill and transit-oriented development; transit, bicycle, and pedestrian-friendly infrastructure; preservation of open space; affordable housing; and other strategies to reduce traffic injuries and improve the livability of urban neighborhoods. Among the tools being promoted by smart growth advocates are nonresidential speed limits, roundabouts, and shared parking arrangements. In order to implement such smart growth plans, local governments need to embrace flexible zoning programs that encourage increased densities and mixed uses as well as innovative strategies for land acquisition and development. In the end, this solution to energy and climate change also can help reconnect state citizens to neighborhoods designed to emphasize a sense of place.

Land-use planning decisions by local agencies are critical to efforts seeking to reduce California's current 3 percent annual increase in vehicle miles traveled (VMT) by state residents. While increasing urban density might reduce VMT, it could also contribute to the heat island effect. Planting more trees could reduce air-conditioning demand, but if not implemented in a strategic manner, it could limit solar PV installations on rooftops. Working with the Gas Technology Institute, San Diego State University, the DOE and the City of Chula Vista, the CEC has helped establish the National Energy Center for Sustainable Communities. This Center is comparing business-as-usual development plans for three new communities planned on 1,500 acres of land that is part of Otay Ranch. The city of Chula Vista hopes this research on developing a model land use plan that reduces energy consumption will guide all future development within its municipal boundaries. Hopefully, such efforts can be copied and implemented throughout the state, in the process improving tools to integrate energy considerations into future planning and development efforts. Smart Growth blueprints have also been completed for Sacramento, the San Francisco Bay Area, and southern California and are under development in other areas, including the San Joaquin Valley.

CONCLUSION

Clearly, the only way to succeed on climate change and other energy challenges is to take a systems approach—a comprehensive and integrated plan that involves not only utilities, oil companies, and banks but also federal, state, and local governments and *you*. An event hosted by Congresswoman Lynn Woolsey (D-Santa Rosa) at the Marin County Civic Center in early August 2007 specifically addressed this sort of cooperation. Marin County Supervisor Charles McGlashan summed up the challenge this way: "We have to do everything, everywhere, yesterday. We need a level of mobilization equal to what the U.S. did during World War II."

He went on to note that simple steps, literally, can make a difference. In the Netherlands, for example, he pointed to statistics showing that half of all transportation activities there involved bikes and feet, and another third relied upon public transportation. Here in the state that glamorized "freeways" and helped the nation become hooked on oil by dismantling the nation's largest electric trolley systems, making that kind of cultural shift seems iffy. In McGlashan's view, issues such as affordable housing also suddenly become climate change issues, since one of the prime reasons we still waste too much energy is our suburban sprawl. "Dumb growth could swamp everything else we do on climate change," added State Assemblyman Jared Huffman (D-San Rafael), who also participated in the same governmental forum.

There is no doubt that change is in the air. Consider the fate of the incandescent light bulb, the symbol of Thomas Edison's triumph of invention and ingenuity. Until recently, 95 percent of all light bulb sales were the traditional incandescent bulbs. If we as a society could change out all of these light bulbs, that single act could slash electricity consumption by 75 percent. Legislation to phase out future sales of Edison's signature invention in California failed in 2007, but corporations such as Wal-Mart and Yahoo! launched voluntary campaigns to make it easy to switch with a simple click on the Internet. Called "18 seconds. . ." (because that is the amount of time it takes to substitute a super-efficient compact fluorescent for an incandescent bulb), the campaign has been a hit. Wal-Mart estimates that if each of its 100 million customers makes the switch, they could collectively save $3 billion in energy costs over the life of each light bulb!

As of early 2008, CARB had adopted rules and regulations to implement AB 32 that impacted refrigerators, docked ships, cement kilns, semiconductors, the trucking industry, and auto tune-up and oil change shops. There are many more rules and regulations to come. Perhaps the most contentious issue for CARB is "carbon offsets." Providers of "carbon offsets" create a commodity by selling the reductions in greenhouse gas emissions created when fossil fuel sources are displaced by a wind farm or other type of renewable energy generation. A variety of banks and other companies now allow consumers to offset the carbon created by your flight across the country, as was noted previously.

In the end, it is safe to say that our energy consumption, whether provided by electricity or fossil-fueled transport, is our greatest imprint on the world. Despite California's addiction to the convenience of roads and cars, it still might be advances in production and delivery of electricity that offer the brightest hope for reducing ecological footprints. We need integrated energy systems that become intelligent displays of interactivity and efficiency and equity. We need new technology as well as old common sense. We need to go forward and backward—at the same time.

That is the vision. What has to happen is something that Malcom Gladwell described in his seminal book *The Tipping Point* (Gladwell 2002:9). Contagiousness—a term Gladwell describes as how little causes can have big effects—is a key factor to the success of any mass movement. You also have to understand that change does not always happen gradually, but can leap forward in one dramatic moment in time. These principles are what Gladwell has identified as elements that contribute to a tipping point that leads to widespread revolutions. Reaching a tipping point on energy issues is our greatest hope in addressing climate change, world poverty, and the ever-present search for a better life.

The sudden jump in awareness of global climate change in 2006, culminating with the passage of AB 32 in California, could be the beginning of something grand. California is the great hope, on the unstable tectonic fringes of Western civilization, a place where risk-taking and great leaps into the unknown are an everyday way of life. As I gaze out at the Pacific, the ocean's waves seem to tell me there is more to the story, yet we are on the right track (pl. 110).

A visit to wind farm developments in the Montezuma Hills during the summer of 2007 helped fill me with optimism. To me, wind farms have always been a magical reminder of how nature and technology can coexist. The fact that these giant moving sculptures can harness the kinetic and wild energy flowing in the wind never ceases to amaze me. I was literally blown away by the size and majesty of the machines now going in the ground on these bare, dry rolling hills populated with sheep, cows, and other animals. So few Californians come to this little corner of the world, but this visit filled me with awe.

Opposition to wind farms based on aesthetics and wildlife impacts might represent credible concerns. Being a

Plate 110. Sunset at Stinson Beach in Marin County.

bird watcher, I am particularly interested in how new wind farm operators are redesigning their machines and farms to lessen impacts on birds (as well as bats and other creatures). If California indeed is going to cut our collective per capita carbon habit by 90 percent by 2050, then wind farms such as these, solar panels on rooftops, and the immense energy of the pounding surf will all have to be tapped in ways that harmonize and sustain our environment and economy. Of course, these gadgets grab our attention, but a lot of the difficult work ahead involves much more mundane matters, such as cutting our obscene energy budgets in our current homes, cars, and toys. As Art Rosenfeld noted in this book's Foreword, there is no cleaner and greener energy source than the energy we do not have to produce in the first place.

Multinational corporations, all levels of government, communities, and individuals all need to become part of the solution. If the past is any guide, California will be in the lead, forging ahead, making its fair share of mistakes, but also pushing the envelope on answers and helping to make the world a better place to live for all.

CALIFORNIA'S ENERGY INNOVATIONS BEYOND POWER ROAD

Arthur O'Donnell, *The Energy Overseer*

Twenty years ago, when I first began reporting about California's energy and electric utility industry, a revolution of innovation was taking place. Long structured as a business based on government-sanctioned territorial monopolies, the stodgy and stagnant power marketplace was slowly being pried open by advocates of competition.

This was first experienced via the federal deregulation of markets for natural gas. Driven by air quality concerns in smoggy Los Angeles and propelled by lawmakers' desire for "energy independence" from costly Middle East petroleum sources, cleaner-burning natural gas was beginning to displace dirty oil as the fuel of choice for power generation in the state. New companies sprang up to tap the gas wells, and previously closed pipelines were forced open as "common carriers" for anyone willing to pay the toll. Soon, the clamor for more open markets rattled the golden cages of the electric utility monopolists as well.

I was part of a small band of energy journalists—Peter Asmus, the author of this book, was another—who specialized in covering a similarly small band of "independent power producers" (IPPs) who were taking advantage of the provisions of a 1979 federal law called the Public Utility Regulatory Policies Act (PURPA) to sell electric energy to utilities.

These IPPs promoted a new generation of gas-fired combustion turbines that far outstripped the existing utility plant in terms of efficiency of production and cleanliness of emissions output. And, increasingly, they were bringing into the market "alternative" resources that utilities had long held could never work: solar collectors, wind turbines, geothermal power, and small-scale hydroelectric facilities. Under federal parlance, these generators were also called "qualifying facilities" (QFs), defined by the language of PURPA.

The rules of this marketplace, as devised by state regulatory agencies whose main clients had always been the utilities, were arcane and the barriers to entry many. The utilities complained that they were being forced into these QF power-purchase contracts against their will, at prices that far exceeded their own built-in costs. The reality was that the IPPs and QFs had to meet rather strict standards for selling energy at an "avoided cost" rate—equal to or better than the cost the utility would incur to build its next needed generation resource, or even expand or modernize its existing fleet.

New, large gas-fired turbines with favorable economic profiles (compared to, say, a costly and risky investment in a nuclear power project) managed to establish footholds in several states. California was the place where lawmakers and regulators allowed IPPs and alternative QFs to thrive (relatively, as it was never a simple matter to win a contract, license a site, secure financing, and bring a new project into operation), and by the early 1990s, there were hundreds of these new projects in the works or already operating.

My forum for documenting this evolving energy marketplace was a weekly newsletter I started in 1989 called *California Energy Markets*—staffed not by professional industry analysts with a built-in bias against change, but by independent journalists who served as outside observers to these intriguing new developments.

Some of my crew—admittedly, proudly—came from the ranks of activists who had protested against utility rate hikes or marched against nuclear power construction. Others were engineers or legal professionals who found in journalism a more fulfilling, if not financially rewarding, calling than in corporate jobs.

Mostly, though, we were young, dedicated reporters who just happened to find the whole energy business in transition a fascinating field of inquiry (pl. 111).

Asmus, who was living in Sacramento at the time, became our field correspondent at the State Capitol and eye witness to the pains and tribulations of the local municipal utility, which was about to put its failing Rancho Seco nuclear power plant out of its misery (pl. 112).

While considered specialists—certainly compared to our colleagues at newspapers and other mainstream media, who had to argue with ignorant or skeptical editors over adding utility reporting to their other business-news beats—we were still learning how this industry had come to be and

Plate 111. Transmission lines spread out in intricate webs across the landscape.

Plate 112. The American flag still waves at the Rancho Seco nuclear power plant, the facility that prompted the author to examine our energy system.

struggling to understand how it was changing before our eyes. That meant we found ourselves spending long hours in regulatory hearings and public forums; poring over filings, contracts, and obscure documents in claustrophobic libraries; and attending as many industry-oriented conferences as possible where we could ask hard questions of utility executives, regulators, and other decision makers who would rather we did not exist.

Achieving such understanding usually involved piecing together small bits of information from disparate sources into a larger context that sometimes gelled into a useful insight.

That is how I developed the idea for "Power Road."

Reading through dozens of site license applications and power-sales contracts, I discovered a trend. Many of the new IPPs and QFs were being located on or near California's Hwy. 58—a 350-mile stretch of two-lane asphalt running eastward from near San Luis Obispo out past Barstow and into the Mojave Desert. There the road splits into I-15 heading to Las

Plate 113. These dramatic early-generation solar PV arrays have come and gone, but their home, the Carrizo Plains, is now being considered for a new generation of concentrated solar power technologies.

Vegas and I-40 going eastward through Arizona along the path of old Route 66.

All of the newest technologies for electricity generation were represented on Power Road and appeared to be breaking down the traditional industry lines: Oil giant ARCO had built a field of solar photovoltaic collectors in the Carrizo Plains (pl. 113); gas-fired cogenerators by the dozens were reviving the dormant oil drilling industry in Bakersfield and providing inexpensive steam for the Central Valley's huge agriculture and food-processing businesses; wind turbines dotted the hills of the Tehachapi Mountains; rows and rows of solar power collectors of an innovative "rotating trough" design were being installed at Kramer Junction and Daggett. There was even an experimental synthetic fuel processing plant, being developed by Texaco, that turned black coal into a liquid synfuel, which boasted of being "the world's cleanest coal power plant."

A little bit off the main road, you could find several of the more traditional utility facilities—river-run hydroelectric

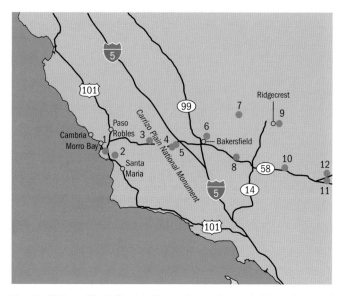

Map 12. Highway 58, California's "Power Road." A remarkable confluence of energy history and innovation occurs along California's Highway 58.

1. Diablo Canyon Nuclear Reactors: This twin-reactor complex is currently the cornerstone of PG&E's power generation system, but was the focus of intense large-scale demonstrations in the late '60s through the early '80s.

2. Pismo Beach: Native Chumash tribes found many uses for the petroleum—known as "pismo"— that would float up from underwater fissures, proof of substantial oil deposits off of California's shoreline.

stations that dated back to the beginning of the twentieth century, fossil-fueled generators built in the 1950s, and a hub of transmission substations at Midway that tied together the state's network of high-voltage power lines and anchored the entire western North American electricity grid from British Columbia to New Mexico.

This region was also the terminal point for a half-dozen natural gas pipelines being built to transport the new "fuel of choice" from producing basins throughout the southwest.

3. Carrizo Plains: This is one of the sunniest spots in all of California and the site of what was once the largest solar PV array in the world, operated by ARCO Solar between 1984 and 1993.

4. McKittrick: Now a desolate town, McKittrick was once bustling with hustlers as it was one of California's earliest oil boom cities.

5. Midway Substation: Located in Buttonwillow on Kilowatt Way, the Midway Substation is where the high-voltage transmission towers of PG&E and SCE meet.

6. Kern County Oil Fields: Oil defined Kern County since the 1920s, but in the '80s, the focus shifted to natural gas and the development of cogeneration plants that serve enhanced oil recovery operations as well as food processing and other manufacturing facilities.

7. Kern River Hydroelectric Plants: North of Bakersfield, one can find some of the state's pioneering hydro plants at Lake Isabella.

8. Tehachapi Wind Farms: Tehachapi Pass is one of California's best wind resource areas and the focus of current efforts to build-out more wind capacity to fight global climate change and to meet state renewable energy deployment goals.

9. Ridgecrest and Coso Geothermal: Take a small road trip north of Highway 58 to Ridgecrest, where one can find geothermal power plants located near the U.S. Navy's weapons testing facility.

10. Kramer Junction Concentrated Solar Power: The world's largest solar power generating stations can be found where Highway 58 intersects with Highway 395

11. Daggett: Hosting some of the earliest solar generation facilities in California, Daggett was also the site of an experimental clean coal plant that was abandoned, but which could be revived with renewed interest in low-carbon technologies.

12. Calico: Power Road ends here, site where remains of some of the earliest human beings were found. This not only raises the question of how humans got here, but also where they are going.

Extending the lines a bit further west of Hwy. 58 brought the controversial Diablo Canyon nuclear plant into the Power Road construct, and a northern jaunt from Mojave led to the Coso geothermal fields being developed at a U.S. Navy weapons testing site at China Lake near Ridgecrest.

"A Route 66 for energy" is how I described Power Road (map 12).

There were certainly other locations in California where wind, solar, geothermal, cogeneration, and other technologies were being installed—but no place where they all came together to illustrate how the deconstruction of monopoly energy markets could spur technological innovations along many fronts.

Flash forward a decade or two, and Power Road still appears a remarkably viable concept. No longer "alternative" tech, the cogenerator, wind, and geothermal power plants have proven themselves through day-after-day operations as mainstream resources and long-term investments.

Some technology experiments failed—of course they would; the ARCO solar fields have long gone fallow, and the Texaco synfuel plant never proved viable. It still stands like a ghost town of steel towers and unfulfilled dreams.

However, in the sense that "everything old is new again," there has been a revival of interest in coal-to-liquid technologies, and just recently another hopeful solar power developer has inked a contract to sell power to Pacific Gas & Electric from a proposed facility on the Carrizo Plains.

Sometimes, the original IPP/QF company went bankrupt, as at the Luz desert solar collector sites, and new owners or financial investors took over. Through it all, the solar troughs kept collecting sunlight and launching electrons. Now, another generation of concentrated solar troughs is updating the Luz designs, building on past foundations with somewhat better financial models.

Market restructuring a decade ago forced the divestiture of some of the utility power plants to nonutility companies, while a great many of the independent plants changed hands for a variety of other reasons. Hundreds of wind turbines were retired and replaced with better designs (pl. 114).

Still, the major features of Power Road remain intact (including Diablo Canyon), and some are now recognized as the "future" of the industry. Tehachapi Pass is slated for a major expansion of wind energy to meet California's low-carbon, high-renewables-content laws. This requires a multibillion dollar investment in new transmission lines and substations along Power Road. These transmission hubs and

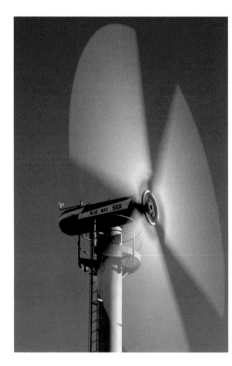

Plate 114. Blades rotating on an early wind turbine design conjure up the endless optimism of California and its pioneering approach to solving our energy supply challenges.

gas pipelines are also the conduits for an entire financial and energy-trading marketplace that did not exist 20 years ago.

There is a renewed interest in the solar trough collectors at Daggett and a metastasizing of technology innovations derived from facilities all along this route to other parts of the state, nation, and world.

The New Power Road

However, if the identifying characteristic of Power Road was as a physical location where innovation could be seen and explored in multiple variations, the future of energy markets might well be more diffuse and less geographically defined.

The vestiges of utility territorial monopolies remain, to be sure, and might have been permanently cemented by the catastrophic failure of California's experiment in electric restructuring in 2000–2001. However, innovation cannot be contained or confined.

In the 1970s, the need for cleaner air and a push for energy independence—along with an influx of talented entrepreneurs eager to break down traditional barriers and find new solutions to old problems—set the stage for the innovations that I found along Power Road. Concurrent innovations in energy efficiency, building codes, and appliance standards that have been part and parcel of California's energy business and regulatory policies for decades (well documented in other sections of this book) are now being recognized as essential strategies throughout the world.

Now, containing greenhouse gas emissions has become the single filter through which all of California's energy and environmental policies flow. The passage in 2006 of the landmark legislation AB 32 will dictate utility resource procurement, land use, and investment patterns for decades to come. It will determine what new technologies are allowed to enter the market, and it is already causing developers and utilities outside the state to rethink their plans to build conventional coal plants.

As other regions—and maybe even the federal government—come to terms with the global warming issue and play catch-up with California's leadership, we could see profound changes in how we produce and use electricity.

We have long talked about decentralized or "distributed" generation that reduces the need for building big power plants and stringing transmission lines to reach remote locations where wind, solar, geothermal, and other resources lie. We are not there yet, and probably will not be for several more years, but California's innovators continue to work on and improve fuel cells, roof-top solar, and wind generators. Just two houses down the street from where I live, you can see in action a brand new, innovative wind turbine design that someday could be as ubiquitous as plasma TVs or laptop computers.

Even the utilities are finally realizing ways to employ innovations in energy distribution—as long as regulators allow them into rate base—and "smart grid" advances, interactive energy management, automated meters, and other new tools are moving into the mainstream in millions of homes and business locations.

An influx of new money and ideas into the energy sector has the potential to completely change the rules of the game for investors, producers, and consumers. I can easily imagine how a breakthrough in battery technologies meant to improve cell phones and laptops could translate into improvements in electric automobiles and maybe even energy storage—the plug-in car is not a science fiction concept but a working prototype.

There are entrepreneurs who readily see how ethanol will give way to biodiesel and how the same cellulosic feedstock being developed for transportation fuels could also be cracked, manipulated, or genetically engineered into a whole range of products that will alleviate our petroleum dependence.

These are people who (as in the computer industry) simply will not accept old ways of thinking or be deterred by the kinds of barriers that utilities and regulators tried to put in the way of the old IPPs/QFs.

In fact, I have met several new "clean tech" executives who began their careers as California independent power producers, but who now are trying to train algae to consume carbon emissions, for example, or apply the biochemical principles of deep-sea photosynthesis to achieve much higher levels of production efficiency for rooftop solar cells.

As I said earlier, innovation cannot be contained.

However, the most positive aspect, I think, is that we are seeing a new level of interest in energy and the environment among college students and those even younger. Where five years ago, universities were closing down their electrical engineering programs for lack of interest, there is demonstrable a move back into the sciences that can be applied to understanding and solving the climate change dilemma—and energy will be a major part of that.

Somewhat as a previous generation whose imagination was captured by ecology, alternative energy, and a desire to change the world, this new blood represents the future. They will be involved for the long haul, and they are the real drivers of whatever energy market we will create.

California's New Power Road is where we will be test-driving the future.

GLOSSARY

AB 32: The Global Warming Solutions Act of 2006, which requires California to cut its greenhouse gas emissions back down to 1990 levels by 2020. That equates to roughly 180 million metric tons of carbon per year, or a 25 to 29 percent reduction compared to business-as-usual economic activity.

AB 1890: Assembly Bill 1890, which was signed into law in 1996 after passing unanimously by the California Legislature. This legislation restructured California's electricity market, separating former utility electric monopolies into the following separate business lines: generation; transmission, and distribution. The end result was that utilities such as Pacific Gas & Electric (PG&E) became distribution utilities. Transmission service was handed off to the California Independent System Operator (Cal-ISO), and power generation services were to be handled by independent power producers and marketers. Municipal utilities such as the Sacramento Municipal Utility District (SMUD) were granted the right to maintain their own generation and transmission services.

Alternating Current: The flow of electricity that constantly changes direction between positive and negative side. Almost all power produced by U.S. electric utilities shifts directions at a rate of 60 times per second.

Ampere: A standard unit of measurement of the strength of electric current or the rate of flow of electric charge through a conductor, similar to the practice of using gallons per minute to measure the flow of water. A 1,200-watt, 120-volt hair dryer pulls 10 amperes of electric current (watts divided by volts). The unit was named after French physicist Andre Marie Ampère.

Appraisal Well: A well drilled as part of prospecting to determine the physical extent of any oil or natural gas reserve and the likely production rate of the same reservoir.

Atom: The smallest unit of an element, containing electrons, protons, and neutrons.

Avoided Costs: A regulatory term used throughout the country that refers to the investment necessary for an electric utility or other provider to provide the next increment of electrical energy. This figure is used to calculate the value of power purchased from an independent power producer. Federal law establishes guidelines for determining these "avoided costs" that determine how much "Qualified Facilities" (QF) get paid for power sold to a utility under the Public Utility Regulatory Policy Act (PURPA).

Barrel: A unit of volume to measure petroleum, equal to 42 U.S. gallons. One ton in weight equates to 7.3 barrels. One cubic meter equates to 6.29 barrels.

Base Load: The lowest level of power needs required to serve customers during a season or day (compare to "peak load").

Base Load Power Plant: A power plant that is intended to run constantly near its full capacity.

Bcf: Billion cubic feet. One bcf of natural gas equals approximately 24,000 tons of oil.

Bcm: Billion cubic meters. One bcm equals 35.3 billion cubic feet.

Biomass: Plants, trees, crops, and agricultural and forestry wastes that serve as fuel for traditional combustion power plants to generate electricity and that serve other public purposes such as waste management and forest fire prevention. Biomass also sometimes refers to algae, sewage, and other organic matter that can be converted through chemical processes into fuels to produce electricity.

Blowout: Failure of a wellhead valve to contain oil because of pressure build-up from reserves down below.

Breeder Reactor: A nuclear reactor that generates more fissionable fuel than it consumes in the power production process.

Btu: British thermal unit; the amount of energy required to raise the temperature of one pound of water one degree Fahrenheit at 60 degrees F, equal to 1,055 joules or 252.1 calories.

Bulk Power: Large amounts of electrical energy transmitted over transmission lines at high voltage. These transactions are typically measured in megawatt-hours (MWh).

California Independent System Operator (Cal-ISO): A not-for-profit corporation established by AB 1890 that is responsible for the operation and control of the statewide transmission grid.

Capacity: The maximum amount of electricity that a power plant can produce under the most favorable conditions. Power plant capacity is measured in megawatts (MW) and is often referred to as "nameplate capacity."

Capacity Factor: A percentage that specifies how much of a power plant's capacity is being used over time, often calculated on an annual basis. For example, contemporary typical power plant capacity factors range from 90 percent for geothermal steam electricity generators to 40 percent for wind farms located in the best wind sites.

Circuit: One complete run of a set of electric conductors from a power source to one or more electrical devices such as appliances or lights and back to the same power sources.

CO_2: Carbon dioxide, a colorless, odorless, nonpoisonous gas produced by burning of fuels containing carbon and by the metabolism of living organisms such as humans and animals. CO_2 is the best-known greenhouse gas, and recent rising CO_2 levels due to the burning of fossil fuels (releasing millions of years' accumulation of carbon in a few decades) have been linked to escalating worldwide temperatures. CO_2 is absorbed by growing green plants and the ocean. Renewable sources of electricity typically do not release CO_2 and other air pollutants.

Cogeneration: Production of heat energy and electrical or mechanical power from the same fuel source in the same facility. A typical modern cogeneration facility burns natural gas fuel to produce electricity *and* steam for industrial process use simultaneously.

Combined-Cycle Plant: A power-generating technology that utilizes waste heat from natural gas turbines to generate steam to power conventional steam turbines.

Coulomb: A unit of electrical charge, equal to the amount of charge passing in one second through a point in a circuit through which a current of one ampere is flowing, named after Charles-Augustin de Coulomb, who discovered the law of static electric attraction and repulsion.

Critical Mass: The amount of uranium or other fissionable material required to generate a self-sustaining nuclear chain reaction.

Crude Oil: Untreated liquid petroleum as it comes out of the ground.

CSP: Concentrated solar power, also known as solar thermal power, in which sunlight is concentrated on a relatively small area to capture its energy by heating a fluid. The largest solar power plant in the world, located near the Mojave Desert near Barstow, uses parabolic trough-shaped reflectors to focus sunlight on pipes full of oil, which then goes through a heat exchanger to produce steam that drives a generator through a turbine. Other solar thermal technologies include the Solar Tower Central Receiver and Stirling solar dishes.

Cubic Foot: A unit of volume equal to 0.0283 cubic meters, used as a standard unit of measurement for natural gas based on a temperature of 60 degrees F and a pressure of 14.73 pounds per square inch. Burning one cubic foot of natural gas produces approximately 1,000 Btu of heat.

Demand: The rate at which a product such as electricity is delivered to consumers at a given point in time. Electric energy demand is measured in watts, kilowatts, megawatts, or gigawatts, and it fluctuates from moment to moment as many different end users turn lights, appliances, electronics, or car battery chargers on and off.

Demand-Side Management: Methods used to manage and shift demand for energy, most often to times of the day when the cost of energy is less. Demand-side management activities include energy efficiency programs, electricity load-shifting activities and devices, and fuel substitutions.

Derrick: The tower-like structure that houses most of the equipment for drilling an oil well on land.

Direct Access: The right of an energy customer to choose the producer for the customer's electricity or natural gas, regardless of whether the supplier is controlled or owned by the company providing the customer's distribution and billing services.

Direct Current: Electricity that flows continuously in one direction.

Distributed Generation: Small, modular power sources sited at the point of power consumption. These systems can operate as a stand-alone system or can be connected to the electricity grid. Residential homeowners might install a solar photovoltaic system on their rooftop. For commercial customers, distributed generation might come in the form of on-site gas-fired cogeneration, a fuel cell, or an array of diesel generators.

Distribution System: The equipment (such as substations, transformers, and distribution lines) that conveys electricity from high-power wholesale transmission lines to the ultimate retail customers.

Drilling Rig: A machine for drilling oil wells, not secured permanently to the sea floor; this term can also refer to an oil derrick and all related machinery.

Dry Gas: A form of natural gas composed primarily of methane that also lacks the heavier hydrocarbons associated with fuels such as gasoline.

Electricity: A basic property of matter, consisting of positive and negative charged particles that can exert forces on each other; the use of currents of these charges to carry energy to do useful work. Such currents are typically produced at a power plant and then distributed to end users by way of the wholesale transmission system and the retail utility distribution system.

Energy: In its most basic sense, the amount of change in a physical system (e.g., a certain change in a certain object's speed, a certain weight lifted a certain distance, a certain increase in the temperature of a certain amount of water) or the capability of making such a change. In the natural gas business, energy is conceived of as heat and is measured in Btu, whereas in the electricity business energy is conceived of as power supplied to equipment over time and is measured in kilowatt-hours.

Energy Efficiency: The amount of useful work a piece of equipment can do given a unit of energy. Improvement in energy efficiency, using less energy or electricity to perform the same function, is considered the resource of first choice, because a unit of energy that does not have to be produced in the first place is the cheapest and cleanest of all.

Enhanced Oil Recovery: A process to boost production from existing oil wells when natural pressure no longer brings the oil up to the surface.

Externalities: Any costs or benefits not accounted for in the price of goods or services. In the electricity market, these externalities include the costs associated with damage to the environment or public health caused by air pollutants.

Firm Energy: Power supplies that are guaranteed to be delivered from producer to consumer under terms defined in a power purchase contract.

Fission: The process by which a nucleus of an atom is split to release energy in the form of heat.

Fixed Costs: Costs associated with power plants that must be paid regardless of the amount of electrical energy produced. These costs often include items such as up-front capital investments, interest, insurance, and taxes.

Fossil Fuels: Oil, coal, and natural gas; fuels that were formed in the Earth in prehistoric times from the remains of living organisms.

Fuel Cell: A device that converts the chemical energy of fuel such as hydrogen or natural gas directly into electricity without burning. Hydrogen atoms give up their electrons, thereby creating electrical current that goes out into the circuit. The return current donates electrons to oxygen, which unites with the hydrogen ions to form water.

Fusion: A form of nuclear power whereby atoms are joined to make heavier elements, releasing energy.

Gas Injection: Pumping gases back into an oil reservoir to maintain pressure or for long-term conservation purposes.

Gas Well: A well designed to extract natural gas from one or more reservoirs.

Geothermal Energy: Natural heat within the Earth. In regions with previous and current volcanic activity, this heat can be captured (usually in the form of steam) for production of electricity, space heating, or industrial processes.

GHG: Greenhouse gas, a gas in the atmosphere that traps heat that would otherwise be radiated from the Earth into space, thus raising the temperature just as the glass windows do in a greenhouse. Gas molecules containing more than two atoms or more than one element, such as methane or carbon dioxide, can be GHGs, trapping heat in the form of vibrating chemical bonds. Some greenhouse effect is necessary for life on Earth, but rising temperatures due to increased amounts of GHGs released by human activities are a cause for concern.

Gigawatt: One thousand megawatts (1,000 MW), or one million kilowatts (1,000,000 kW), or one billion watts (1,000,000,000 watts). One gigawatt of electricity would supply roughly one million average California homes.

Heat Rate: A number that indicates the efficiency of a thermal power plant. Specific heat rates for power plants are calculated by dividing the Btu content of the fuel by the kilowatt-hours of electricity output.

Hertz: An international measurement of frequency equal to one cycle per second; named after Heinrich Hertz, who discovered that information and energy can be propagated through space by electromagnetic waves.

Hybrid System: An electricity generator that does not rely upon one exclusive fuel source. For example, some solar photovoltaic systems can rely upon diesel, gasoline, or wind generators as backups when solar radiation is insufficient because of heavy clouds. Utility-scale solar thermal facilities in southeastern California use sunlight to boil water, but they are allowed to rely upon natural gas when there is insufficient sunlight supply 25 percent of the time.

Hydrocarbon: A gas, liquid, or solid compound containing only the elements hydrogen and carbon.

Hydroelectric Power: Electricity produced by falling water that turns a turbine generator; often referred to as "hydro" power.

Interconnection: The linkage of either transmission utility line systems or a customer's on-site distributed generation system to the host utility's distribution lines. In either case, agreements on interconnection enhance system reliability and define the terms by which electricity is sent back and forth.

Investor-Owned Utility: A private company providing electricity or water to a monopoly service area and governed by the California Public Utilities Commission.

IPP: Independent power producer, a generator of electric power, other than a utility or government agency, that sells its energy to electric utilities at wholesale prices. The utility then sells this power to end-use customers. IPPs may or may not be qualified facilities (QFs). Reliance upon IPPs has grown over recent years as utilities focus more on transmission and distribution, while power generation increasingly is being provided by the private sector.

Isotope: Any of the different forms of any element distinguished by the number of neutrons in its nucleus. Uranium-238 and uranium-235 are the most common isotopes of uranium. The most common isotope of hydrogen has no neutrons, whereas deuterium is an isotope of hydrogen containing one neutron.

Joule: A unit of energy, equal to the amount of work done by a force of one newton acting through a distance of one meter, or by one watt of power supplied for one second. It takes 1,055 joules to equal one Btu. The unit is named after English physicist James Prescott Joule, who discovered that heat was a form of energy.

Kilowatt: A unit of electrical power equal to 1,000 watts.

Kilowatt-Hour: A unit of electrical energy or work equal to that done by one kilowatt of power acting for one hour. A toaster running for one hour will use about this much energy.

Landfill Gas: Gas generated by the natural decomposition of municipal solid waste by anaerobic microorganisms in landfills.

The gases produced—carbon dioxide and methane—can be collected and processed into a medium-Btu gas that can be burned to generate electricity or steam.

Levelized Life-Cycle Costs: The present value of an electricity resource's cost converted to a stream of equal payment amounts. This stream of payments can then be converted to a unit of energy cost by dividing the total by the number of kilowatt-hours produced or saved by the resource. By levelizing costs, resources with different lifetimes and generating capabilities can be compared to each other.

Light-Water Reactor: The most common type of nuclear power–generating facility. It relies on ordinary water (not containing deuterium) to cool the reactor core and create steam, which then turns a turbine to produce electricity.

Line Losses: Electricity that is wasted in the normal transfer of electricity from a power plant along the transmission system down through distribution lines and then to the end-user.

LNG: Liquefied natural gas, natural gas that has been condensed down to a liquid by cooling to minus 260 degrees F for long-distance transportation in ships. LNG has been a controversy in California because of the state's growing dependence upon natural gas. Critics contend that LNG development might jeopardize the state's energy independence and increase possibility of terrorist attacks at LNG terminals located along California's coast.

Load: The amount of electrical power supplied to meet one or more end-users' needs.

Load Factor: A percentage specifying the amount of electricity a consumer used during a given time span in terms of the amount that would have been used if the usage had stayed at the consumer's higher (peak) demand level during the entire period of time.

Marginal Cost: A figure used to represent the investment required to procure the next increment of a product or service of a particular utility or region. The marginal cost of electricity is the price to be paid for kilowatt-hours beyond those supplied by the current system's production capacity. Recently, the marginal cost of new power supply has been based on the cost of adding new power plants that burn natural gas, today's dominant fuel for new power plants.

Megawatt: A unit of energy equal to 1,000 kilowatts or 1,000,000 watts.

Megawatt-Hour: A unit of energy equal to the transmission of 1,000,000 watts of electricity over the course of a one-hour period of time.

Methane: A light hydrocarbon that is the primary component of natural gas. If released into the atmosphere, methane is a greenhouse gas, even more so than carbon dioxide.

Metric Ton: 1,000 kilograms, equivalent to 2,204.61 pounds. A metric ton contains 7.3 barrels of oil.

Municipal Electric Utility: An electric utility owned and operated by a local jurisdiction. At present, roughly 25 percent of Californians are served by municipal utilities, with the Los Angeles Department of Water and Power being the largest municipal utility in the country.

Municipal Solid Waste: Garbage collected by local governments that can be burned as fuel and is often considered a "renewable" source of electricity.

Natural Gas: Hydrocarbon gas found in the Earth consisting of methane, ethane, butane, propane, and other gases. Natural gas is currently the most popular electricity fuel, though recent price increases are giving a boost to coal, nuclear, and wind power.

Newton: A unit of force sufficient to accelerate a mass of one kilogram by one meter per second in a time of one second. One newton is equal to a weight of 0.225 pounds. The unit is named for Sir Isaac Newton, discoverer of the laws of motion.

Nonfirm Energy: Electricity energy not committed to power purchase contracts and often sold on the wholesale open market.

NO_x: Oxides of nitrogen, a chief component of air pollution created by the burning of fossil fuels. NO_x contribute to urban smog and respiratory disease. A dilemma in air pollution control is that if combustion in air is complete enough to eliminate unburned fuel, particulates, and carbon monoxide, it increases the emissions of NO_x.

Nuclear Power: Electricity obtained by splitting heavy atoms (fission) or joining light atoms (fusion). A nuclear reactor uses a controlled atomic chain reaction to produce heat. The heat is then used to make steam to drive conventional turbine generators.

Offshore Reserves: Oil and natural gas deposits that are located in federal or state boundaries off the coast.

Ozone: A kind of oxygen that has three atoms per molecule instead of the usual two. On the ground, ozone is a poisonous gas formed by reactions between the pollutants from some fossil fuel plants, but a layer of ozone in the upper atmosphere shields life on Earth from damaging ultraviolet radiation from the sun.

Particulate Matter: Solid particulates that are released from combustion processes in exhaust gases at fossil fuel plants. These fine emissions are among the pollutants emitted by coal-burning plants. These emissions stick to lung tissues and have been linked to alarming increases in urban asthma rates among children and other respiratory diseases.

Passive Solar Energy: Use of the sun to help meet a building's energy needs by means of architectural design or material choices. Unlike solar photovoltaics, no direct electricity is produced. Rather, passive solar can be viewed as a form of energy efficiency, substituting other fuels for heating. Common applications include lighting and water heating.

Peak Load: The highest electrical demand placed on any system during a particular point in time. In warm weather climates such as California, electricity peaks occur on weekdays during the late afternoon or early evenings. Annual peaks occur on hot summer days as a result of air-conditioning needs. Back east and in the Midwest, it is more common to have annual peaks occur in the winter as a result of high heating demands.

Peaking Unit: A power plant used to produce electricity during peak load periods of time. Common peaking units are gas-fired combustion turbines or solar photovoltaics.

Petroleum: A generic name for hydrocarbons obtained from the Earth, including crude oil, natural gas liquids, natural gas, and other products.

Pipeline: A continuous conduit featuring valves, compressors, meters, and communication systems to transport natural gas or petroleum from one point to another.

Platform: An offshore structure that is permanently fixed to the ocean floor.

Possible Reserves: Those petroleum reserves that cannot yet be described as "probable." While potentially significant, these reserves have less than a 50 percent chance of being technically and economically feasible.

Probable Reserves: Unproven petroleum reserves that have a greater than 50 percent chance of being technically and economically feasible.

PTC: Production Tax Credit, a subsidy for generating wind power established at the federal government level, and recently amounting to 1.9 cents per kilowatt-hour. The PTC has a major impact on the development of wind power in California because it makes wind more attractive, particularly when natural gas prices are at today's current high levels.

PURPA: The Public Utilities Regulatory Policies Act, passed and signed into law by President Carter in 1978, which required utilities to purchase available electricity from independent co-generators and smaller renewable energy facilities, deemed Qualified Facilities (QFs). PURPA has been credited with jump-starting the world's renewable energy industry in California, and it was the first step in moving toward a deregulated electricity marketplace.

PV: Photovoltaics rely on semiconductors to convert energy from light directly into electricity. Although more expensive than other power supply technologies, solar PV offers many benefits that are not reflected in the wholesale price for electricity. Because solar PV is most often installed as an on-site distributed generation resource, it might be more helpful to compare its costs to retail prices charged for electricity.

QF: Qualified Facility, a co-generator or small independent power-generating facility that has the right to sell power to an electric utility under PURPA.

Real-Time Pricing: The instantaneous pricing of energy based on the cost of generating the electricity at the exact moment in time that the customer wishes to consume the energy.

Recoverable Reserves: The portion of an oil or natural gas reserve that can be extracted using current commercial techniques.

Renewable Energy: Resources that constantly renew themselves or that are regarded as practically inexhaustible. These include solar, wind, geothermal, hydro, and biomass. All of these resources have been developed in California. New forms of renewable energy include tidal power, sea currents, and ocean thermal gradients.

REC: Renewable Energy Certificate, also known as a "green tag," representing the green attributes of renewable energy supply. RECs are now considered a distinct commodity after disaggregation from commodity electricity sales. RECs are a critical implementation feature of the Renewable Portfolio Standard, and the values of RECs rise and fall according to market demand.

Reserve Margin: The extra generating capacity that an electric utility needs above and beyond the highest demand level it is required to supply to meet its aggregate customer needs. Reserve margins are typically in the range of 15–20 percent of peak demand.

Retail Wheeling: The transmission of power from competing suppliers over a utility's power lines directly to retail customers. From the customer's point-of-view, this process is also known as "direct access" to alternative power suppliers.

RPS: The Renewable Portfolio Standard, a policy established in California by the passage of AB 1078 in 2002 that sets a target of obtaining 20 percent of the state's total electricity supply from unspecified renewable energy resources by 2017.

SO_2: Sulfur dioxide, a heavy, colorless, and suffocating gas primarily produced by burning of coal. SO_2 is a prime ingredient in acid rain. Because California burns so little coal, SO_2 is not a major pollution threat here. However, the more California imports electricity from coal facilities in other western states, the more Californians export our pollution to regions of the country containing some of the West's most stunning vistas.

Substation: A facility that steps up or steps down the voltage in utility power lines. Voltage is stepped up when power is sent through long-distance transmission lines. It is stepped down when the power enters local distribution lines.

Tariff: A document approved by the appropriate regulatory agency that lists the terms and conditions, including a schedule of prices, for the delivery of electricity service.

Tidal Power: Renewable energy obtained by using the motion of the tides (caused by the gravity of the moon) to run water turbines that then drive electric generators.

Time-of-Use Rates: Electricity prices that vary depending on the time periods in which the energy is consumed. Higher prices are charged during utility peak load times. Such rates provide price signals to consumers about the real costs of electricity and are often promoted as a way to curb power use during peak times.

Transmission: The transporting of bulk electricity over long-distance transmission lines. Transmission is the only part of the electricity business dominated by federal regulators and is increasingly managed on a regional basis by quasi-governmental bodies such as the California Independent System Operator.

Unbundling: Disaggregating electric utility service into basic components and offering these components separately for sale. For example, generation, transmission, and distribution can be offered up as discrete businesses, each with its own costs and obligations.

Uranium: The most important material for nuclear power. A heavy, silvery radioactive metal, uranium comprises several isotopes. Uranium-235 undergoes fission when struck by a neutron, producing energy. The most common isotope, uranium-238, does not undergo fission but can be transformed into fissionable plutonium-239 in a nuclear reactor, a process called breeding.

Volt: A metric measurement of electric potential (the amount of energy per unit of electric charge), named after Alessandro Volta. A drop through a potential difference of one volt imparts one joule of energy to one coulomb of charge.

Watt: A practical unit of power, equal to one joule of work done per second. One watt of power is developed in an electrical circuit by a current of one ampere flowing through a potential difference of one volt. This term was named after James Watt, an eighteenth-century Scottish inventor.

Wellhead Price: Literally, the price of a fossil fuel such as crude oil or natural gas at the mouth of the well, including charges assessed for liquids derived from a gas, fees for gathering and compressing gas, and taxes and other fees imposed by state or federal governments.

Wholesale Competition: A system in which a distributor of electricity has the option to buy bulk power from a variety of power producers, and the power producers are able to compete to sell electricity to a variety of distribution utilities.

Wildcat Well: Also known as an "exploration well," an attempted oil well drilled in an unproven region. This term was originally used in Texas in the 1920s.

Wind Power: Power derived from the horizontal motion of air near the surface of the Earth caused by uneven heating of the planet's surface by the sun.

REFERENCES

American Coal Foundation. 2005a. How coal is formed. www.ket
.org/Trips/Coal/AGSMM/agsmmhow.html (accessed July 10,
2007).

———. 2005b. How coal is produced. www.ket.org/Trips/Coal/
AGSMM/agsmmproduced.html (accessed July 10, 2007).

———. 2005c. Types of coal. www.ket.org/Trips/Coal/AGSMM/
agsmmtypes.html (accessed July 10, 2007).

———. 2005d. www.ket.org/Trips/Coal/AGSMM/agsmmusing.html
(accessed July 10, 2007).

———. 2005e. What is coal's future? ket.org/Trips/Coal/AGSMM/
agsmmfuture.html (accessed July 10, 2007).

Andrews, E., and M. Wald. 2007. Energy bill aids the expansion
plans of atomic power plants. *New York Times,* August 31.

Answers.com. 2007. Sempra Energy. www.answers.com/topic/
sempra-energy?cat=biz-fin (accessed on June 19, 2007).

Asmus, P. 1997. Empowering California. *The Amicus Journal* 19 (1):
14–16.

———. 2001. *Reaping the wind: How mechanical wizards, visionaries
and profiteers helped shape our energy future.* Washington, DC:
Island Press.

———. 2002. *Gone with the wind.* San Francisco: Energy Foundation.

———. 2005. Loving nuclear power. www.AlterNet.org/story/29596/
(accessed October 13, 2008).

———. 2006a. Texas blows by California in wind energy. www
.AlterNet.org/story/39477/ (accessed October 13, 2008).

———. 2006b. Go green and make green: California may profit
from climate law. *San Francisco Chronicle,* October 15.

———. 2007a. Green ventures rake in money, but power can rise
and fall. *San Francisco Chronicle,* May 13.

———. 2007b. Can California save the planet from climate change? *San Francisco Chronicle*, September 17.

Asmus, P., and B. Piasecki. 1989. State energy policies and global warming.In *California Policy Choices*, ed. J. Kirlin and D. Winkler, 53–79. Sacramento: University of Southern California School of Public Administration.

Baker, D. 2006. Prop. 87 shines light on state's oil history: For 140 years, independent operators have pumped crude into the California economy. *San Francisco Chronicle*, October 29.

Barnes, P. 2001. *Who owns the sky? Our common assets and the future of capitalism*. Washington, DC: Island Press.

Bedard, R., M. Previsic, G. Hagerman, B. Polagye, W. Musial, J. Klure, A. von Jouanne, U. Mathur, C. Collar, C. Hopper, and S. Amsden. 2007. *North American Ocean Energy Status—March 2007*. Palo Alto: Electric Power Research Institute.

Berst, J. 2005. Center for Smart Energy. Phone interview conducted by author October 25.

Bodanis, D. 2005. *Electric universe: How electricity switched on the modern world*. New York: Three Rivers Press.

Broehl, J. 2004. National security to lead to renewable energy deployment.www.renewableenergyaccess.com/rea/news/story?id=19841 (accessed on December 14, 2004).

Cabanatuan, M. 2007. Fueling a revolution: biodiesel moving into the mainstream. *San Francisco Chronicle*, February 22.

California Biomass Energy Alliance. n.d. California's biomass power industry. www.calbiomass.org/history.htm (accessed on August 2, 2007).

California Department of Conservation's Division of Oil, Gas and Geothermal Resources. 2005. *Oil and Gas Production: History in California*. Sacramento: California Department of Conservation's Division of Oil, Gas and Geothermal Resources.

California Energy Commission. 2004. Unpublished data base of historical energy events. Sacramento: California Energy Commission.

———. 2007. *2007 integrated energy policy report*. Sacramento: California Energy Commission.

———. 2007. *Public interest energy research (PIER) 2006 annual report*. Sacramento: California Energy Commission.

———. 2008. *Public interest energy research (PIER) 2007 annual report*. Sacramento: California Energy Commission.

———. 2008. Nuclear energy in California. www.energy.ca.gov/nuclear/california.html (accessed on October 12, 2008).

Canine, C. 2006. California illuminates the world. *One Earth* 1 (1): 23–27.

Chang, A., A. Rosenfeld, and P. McAuliffe. In press. Energy efficiency in California and the United States: Reducing energy costs and greenhouse gas emissions. In *Climate Change Science and Policy,* ed. S. Schneider, A. Rosencranz, and M. Mastrandrea. Washington, DC: Island Press.

Cheney, M. 1983. *Man out of time.* New York: Dell.

Clean Edge News. 2007a. PG&E to study wave power in Humboldt and Mendocino. *Clean Edge News,* March 14.

———. 2007b. Solar cell production jumps 50 percent in 2007. *Clean Edge News,* December 27.

Collier, M. 1999. *A land in motion: California's San Andreas fault.* Berkeley: University of California Press.

Collier, R. 2007. California says no to coal, but world disagrees. *San Francisco Chronicle,* May 28.

Coleman, C. 1952. *P. G. & E of California: The centennial story of Pacific Gas and Electric Company, 1852–1952.* New York: McGraw-Hill Book Company, Inc.

Cooper, A. 2007. Footprint Recycling. Phone interview conducted by author, September 7.

Economic and Technology Advancement Advisory Committee. 2008. *Technologies and policies to consider for reducing greenhouse gas emissions in California.* Sacramento: California Air Resources Board.

Electric Power Research Institute. 2007a. *Assessment of waterpower potential and development needs.* March 2007. Palo Alto, CA: Electric Power Research Institute.

———. 2007b. *Primer: power from ocean waves and tides.* Palo Alto, CA: Electric Power Research Institute.

Environment News Service. 2007. Global wind power generated record year in 2006. *Environment News Service,* February 12.

Fineextra.com. 2008. Leading Wall Street banks establish carbon lending principles. www.finextra.com/fullpr.asp?id=19702 (accessed on February 11, 2008).

Ferguson, R. 2007. Center for Energy Efficiency and Renewable Technologies. In-person interview, August 20.

———. n.d. *A matter of time* (unpublished book manuscript).

Finn, B. S. 2002. Powering the past: A look back. http://americanhistory.si.edu/powering/past/prehist.htm (accessed October 12, 2008).

Geothermal Energy Association. 2008. All about geothermal energy—current use. www.geo-energy.org/aboutGE/currentUse.asp (accessed on October 13, 2008).

————. n.d. All about geothermal energy—mythbusters. www
.geo-energy.org/aboutGE/mythbusters.asp (accessed July 24,
2007).

Government Accounting Office. 2007. *Crude oil—uncertainty about
future oil supply makes it important to develop a strategy for
addressing a peak and decline in oil production.* Washington, DC:
Government Accounting Office: GAO-07-283.

Galloway, J. 2006. Natural oil and gas seepage in the coastal areas
of California. www.mms.gov/omm/pacific/enviro/seeps1.htm
(accessed May 9, 2007).

Gelbspan, R. 1998. *The heat is on.* New York: Basic Books.

Goodell, J. 2006. *Big coal: The dirty secret behind America's energy
future.* Boston: Houghton Mifflin.

Gordon, R. 2001. S.F. voters turn off public power bid. *San Francisco
Chronicle,* November 10.

GreenBiz.com. 2007. BofA banks $20 billion to grow green economy.
www.greenbiz.com/news/printer.cfm?NewsID=34688 (accessed
March 14, 2007).

Gunter, P. 2001. The pebble bed modular reactor (PBMR) fact sheet.
Washington, DC: Nuclear Information and Resources Ser-
vice. www.nirs.org/print/factsheets/pbmrfactsheet.htm (accessed
October13, 2008).

Hamrin, J. 2007. Center for Resource Solutions. In-person interview
by author, July 20.

Harden, D. 1998. *California geology.* Upper Saddle River, NJ: Prentice
Hall, Inc.

Heinberg, R. 2003. *The party's over: Oil, war and the fate of industrial
societies.* Gabriola, Canada: New Society Publishers.

Herig, C. 2000. *Assessing rooftop solar-electric distributed energy
resources for the California Local Government Commission.*
Golden, CO: National Renewable Energy Laboratory.

Hydropower Reform Coalition. 2006. An opportunity for river restoration. http://hydroreform.org/aboutreform/an-opportunity-
for-river-restoration (accessed July 27, 2007).

————. 2006. Hydropower's dirty secret. http://hydroreform.org/
aboutreform/hydropowers-dirty-secret (accessed July 27, 2007).

————. 2006. Modernizing hydropower. http://hydroreform.org/
aboutreform/modernizing-hydropower (accessed on July 27,
2007).

Infoplease.com. 2007. California history. http://infoplease.com/ce6/
us/A0857128.html (accessed on May 17, 2007).

International Energy Agency. 2007. *Medium-term oil market report.* Paris: International Energy Agency.

Johnson, A. D. 1997. The Nevada "Rome" powerhouse and the birth of PG&E. www.ncgold.com/Museums_Parks/syrp/hydrohis .html (accessed April 4, 2007).

———. 2007. In-person interview by author, May 10.

Johnson, K. 2007. Alternative energy hurt by a windmill shortage. *Wall Street Journal,* July 9.

Johnston, D. 2006. Flaws seen in markets for utilities. *New York Times,* November 21.

Kammen, D. 2006. Why Sept. 27, 2006, will be a day to remember. *San Francisco Chronicle.* September 26.

———. 2007a. Transportation's next big thing is already here. www .greenbiz.com/news_third.cfm?/NewsID=35321 (accessed July 11, 2007).

———. 2007b. Berkeley Institute of the Environment. In-person interview by author, July 29.

Knox, J. (with A. Foley Scheuring). 1991. *Global climate change and California: Potential impacts and responses.* Berkeley: University of California Press.

Krebs, M. 2006–2007. Public Interest Energy Research Program, California Energy Commission. In-person interviews by author, December 15, 2006, February 4, 2007, and March 3, 2007.

Lawrence Berkeley National Laboratory. 1998. *China Energy Group: Sustainable growth through energy efficiency.* Washington, DC: U.S. Department of Energy.

Lawrence, N. 1996. Do high-voltage power lines cause cancer? *Midwest Today,* April/May. www.bloclemf.com/catalog/article_info .php?articles_id=2 (accessed February 14, 2008).

Leahy, S. 2007. Biofuels boom spurring deforestation. *Inter Press Service,* March 22.

Margonelli, L. 2007. Cutting risk of tanker accidents starts with conservation habits. *San Francisco Chronicle,* May 6.

Marshall, B. 2007. Plumas–Sierra Rural Cooperative. Phone interview by author, August 29.

McNeil, J. 2001. The history of energy since 10,000 B.C. www .theglobalist.com/DBWeb/printStoryId.aspx?StoryId=2018 (accessed November 11, 2006).

Murray, M. 2007. Sempra Energy. Phone interview conducted by author, September 13.

Nelder, Chris. 2007. Hydrogen hype. www.renewableenergyworld.com/rea/news/reinsider/story?id=49540 (accessed August 8, 2007).

Nuclear Information and Resources Service. 2007. 150 organizations slam NRC finding that no terrorist threat exists at Diablo Canyon nuclear site. Press release, July 5. Washington, DC: Nuclear Information and Resources Service.

Office of Nuclear Energy, Science and Technology. 1998. *The history of nuclear energy*. Washington, DC: U.S. Department of Energy, Department of Nuclear Engineering. DOE/NE-0088.

Office of the Governor. 2006. Gov. Schwarzenegger signs landmark legislation to reduce greenhouse gas emissions. Press release, September 27. http://gov.ca.gov/index.php?/press-release/4111/ (accessed October 13, 2008).

Pacific Gas & Electric. 2007a. Pacific Gas & Electric Company energizes Silicon Valley with vehicle-to-grid technology. Press release, April 9.

———. 2007b. PG&E teams with Google to demonstrate vehicle-to-grid technology at the company's Mountain View campus. Press release, June 19.

Page Museum, La Brea Tar Pits. n.d. Frequently asked questions. www.tarpits.org/info/faq/faqfossil.html (accessed July 6, 2007).

Paul, D. 2007. Chevron. In-person interview by author, July 17.

Pasternak, M. 2007. Devil's Gulch Ranch. In-person interview by author, February 19.

Perlin, J. 1999. *From space to earth: The story of solar electricity*. Cambridge, MA: Harvard University Press.

Perlin, J., and K. Butti. 1980. *A golden thread: 2500 years of solar architecture and technology*. Fort Bragg, NC: Cheshire Books.

Pernick, R., and C. Wilder. 2007. *The clean tech revolution: The next big growth and investment opportunity*. New York: Harper Collins.

Pew Center on Global Climate Change. n.d. Coal and climate change facts. www.pewclimate.org/global-warming-basics/coalfacts.cfm (accessed July 10, 2007).

Powerscorecard.org. 2000. Electricity from hydro. http://powerscorecard.org/tech_detail.cfm?resource_id=4 (accessed July 27, 2007).

Powers, M. 2007. World wide web of electricity key to fighting climate change. http://sustainablebusiness.com/features/feature_printable.cfm?ID=1431 (accessed on March 22, 2007).

Reese, P. 2007. California Biomass Energy Alliance. Personal communication by email to author, August 3.

RenewableEnergyAccess.com. 2007. Global wind energy markets: 2006 another record year. http://www.renewableenergyworld .com/rea/news/story?id=47361 (accessed October 13, 2008).

Reuters. 2007. California lawmaker seeks vote on nuclear power. *Reuters*, July 11.

Rifkin, J. 2002. *The hydrogen economy: the creation of the worldwide energy web and the redistribution of power on earth.* New York: Penguin.

Roe, D. 1984. *Dynamos and virgins.* New York: Random House.

Rosenfeld, A. 1999. The art of energy efficiency: protecting the environment with better technology. *Annual Review of Energy and the Environment.* 24: 33–82.

———. 2006. In-person interview by author and Phyllis Faber, August 8.

Ruedisili, L., and M. Firebaugh. 1978. *Perspectives on energy.* New York: Oxford University Press.

Sabin, P. 2005. *Crude politics: the California oil market, 1900–1940.* Berkeley: University of California Press.

Sampson, A. 1991. *The seven sisters: The great oil companies and the world they made.* New York: Bantam Books.

Schmid, R. 2007. NOAA confirms human cause behind warming. *Associated Press*, published in *San Francisco Chronicle*, August 29.

Senge, P., A. Kleiner, C. Roberts, R. Ross, G. Roth, and B. Smith. 1999. *The dance of change: The challenges of sustaining momentum in learning organizations.* New York: Doubleday.

Silverstein, Ken. 2007a. Squeezing hydropower. www.energycentral .com/centers/energybiz/ebi_detail.cfm?id=335 (accessed June 8, 2007).

———. 2007b. Feeding nuclear power. www.energycentral.com/ centers/energybiz/ebi_detail.cfm?id=334 (accessed July 5, 2007).

———. 2007c. Japan's nuclear blunder. www.energycentral.com/ centers/energybiz/ebi_detail.cfm?id=358 (accessed July 24, 2007).

———. 2007d. Scrutinizing coal. www.energycentral.com/centers/ energybiz/ebi_detail.cfm?id=378 (accessed September 5, 2007).

Smeloff, E., and P. Asmus. 1997. *Reinventing electric utilities: Competition, citizen action and clean power.* Washington, DC: Island Press.

Southern California Gas Company. 1998–2008. Company profile. www.socalgas.com/aboutus/profile.html (accessed October 13, 2008).

State of Colorado. 2008. Glossary of oil and gas terms. http://oil-gas .state.co.us/COGIS_Help/glossary.htm (accessed February 2, 2008).

Stern, B. 2007. Southern California Edison. Phone interview conducted by author, September 16.

Stubbs, M., and T. Stubbs. 2007. Stubbs Winery. In-person interview by author, March 4.

Tang, A. 2007. Pacific Gas & Electric. Phone interview conducted by author, October 1, 2007.

Tiangco, V., P. Sethi, and Z. Zhang. 2005. *Biomass strategic value analysis.* Sacramento: California Energy Commission.

Torous, J. 2006. *Clarence Cory and a history of early electrical engineering at U.C. Berkeley.* Paper submitted to UC Department of History. Berkeley: University of California.

Union of Concerned Scientists. 2008. How hydrokinetic energy works. http://www.ucsusa.org/clean_energy/technology_and _impacts/energy_technologies/how-hydrokinetic-energy-works .html (accessed October 13, 2008).

Uranium Information Center. 2007. Nuclear power in the world today. http://www.uic.com.au/nip07.htm (accessed August 4, 2007).

U.S. Department of Energy, Solar Energy Technologies program. 2008. Learning about PV: the myths of solar electricity. http:// www1.eere.energy.gov/solar/printable_versions/myths.html (accessed October 21, 2008).

Warren, C. 2007. Retired California State Legislator. In-person interview by author, July 26.

Wasserman, H. 2007. Nuclear under fire. www.greenpeace .org/international/news/nuclear-under-fire-050707# (accessed September 20, 2007).

Weiss, M. 2008. Drought could force nuke-plant shutdowns. *The Associated Press*, January 28.

Wildermuth, J. 2007. State air board pledges quick start on greenhouse gas rules. *San Francisco Chronicle*, September 7.

Williams, J. 1997. *Energy and the making of modern California.* Akron, OH: University of Akron Press.

Williams, R. 2007. Pacific Gas & Electric. Phone interview conducted by author, September 18.

Willits Economic Localization. 2007. WELL overview. http:// willitseconomiclocalization.org/WELLOverview (accessed September 24, 2007).

Wilson, J., and E. Douglass. 2007. Renewable energy gains still far off, reports show. *Los Angeles Times*, January 20.

ACKNOWLEDGMENTS

The author acknowledges that much of the material appearing in the first four sections of "Progress: Seven Ongoing Experiments: Recent Success Stories" is derived from the California Energy Commission's 2006 Public Interest Energy Research (PIER) Annual Report, which was written by the author as an independent consultant. It is reproduced here, in modified form, with permission from the California Energy Commission. The discussion of CAISO and windmills under Challenge 5 in "Challenges: The Risks of the Status Quo and Systems Overhaul" was derived from a PIER report titled *Strategic Value Analysis* (also edited by the author), and this material is reprinted (in modified form), also with permission from the California Energy Commission.

The discussions of AB 32 and of CCAs in "Innovation: The Search for Solutions" and of lower-carbon transportation fuels and smart land use planning in "Progress: Seven Ongoing Experiments: Recent Success Stories" were derived from the Economic and Technology Advancement Advisory Committee report to the California Air Resources Board. The author served as technical editor of this document, and these materials are also reprinted, in modified form, with permission by the California Air Resources Board.

Materials on wind power appearing in "Alternatives: The Growth of Renewable Energy" (up through "Wind Power Today") are culled from the author's Island Press book *Reaping The Wind: How Mechanical Wizards, Visionaries and Profiteers Helped Shape Our Energy Future.*

Materials on development of hydrogen in California and on hydrogen today in "Alternatives: The Growth of Renewable Energy" were modified from the author's article "The Governor's Energy Plan Boasts of 'Hydrogen Highways' by 2010," which originally appeared in the *San Francisco Chronicle* on January 4, 2004. Materials on global climate change in "Innovation: The Search for Solutions" are modified from the author's article "Go Green and Make Green," published in the *San Francisco Chronicle* on October 15, 2006; materials on the same topic in the "Conclusion" are modified from the author's article "Is California the World's Last Best Hope against Climate Change?" published in the *San Francisco Chronicle* on September 16, 2007.

The author would like to offer a special thank you to Bob Aldrich, webmaster for the California Energy Commission, for his research assistance. Thanks also to Art Program assistants Stephanie Rubin and Tim Sloane.

A Note About Estimates of Electricity Prices

Throughout this book, price estimates are used to compare the relative costs of various energy alternatives. These estimates rely upon a methodology known as "levelized costs," which means the up-front capital investments are amortized over the life of the project. Relying upon this methodology enables a more accurate depiction of how each electricity resource compares to the others and will be used throughout this book, particularly when comparing renewable energy options. Since the majority of power plants being developed today are by merchant developers, the default cost projections used throughout this book will reflect this form of development. Development of a municipal utility or other governmental entity would be cheaper because of tax-exempt financing. Development by a private electric utility is also now often cheaper because of the lingering fallout over the 2000–2001 energy crisis, which increased financing costs for private merchant developers.

PHOTO CREDITS

ARGONNE NATIONAL LABORATORY, plate 90

G. DONALD BAIN, University of California, Berkeley, plate 3

BANCROFT LIBRARY, University of California, Berkeley, plate 6

BERKELEY, CITY OF, plate 97

CALIFORNIA ENERGY COMMISSION, plates 72, 105, 106, 107

CALIFORNIA HISTORICAL SOCIETY, plate 19

CALIFORNIA HISTORY ROOM, California State Library, Sacramento, plate 17

CENTER FOR LIQUEFIED NATURAL GAS, plate 73

CHEVRON CORPORATION, reproduced with permission of, plates 14, 15, 16, 41, 43, 91

DAVID CLITES, © David Clites, plates 4, 29, 31, 32, 33, 34, 37, 45, 53, 57, 60, 75, 82, 87, 88, 93, 102, 111, 112

LISA DANIELS, Windustry, plate 80

BOB DUNCAN, nacnud34@cox.net, plate 25

FEDERAL EMERGENCY MANAGEMENT AGENCY, plate 77

FINAVERA RENEWABLES, plate 61, fig. 18

GEOTHERMAL EDUCATION OFFICE, plate 47

PHILIP GREENSPUN, copyright 1995, philg@mit.edu, plate 36

JOE GUASTI, photo courtesy of, plate 54

GUTENBERG.ORG, plate 52

ELLEN HALE, U.S. Environmental Protection Agency Region 10, plate 64

JAN HAMRIN, plates 67, 68

GEORGE W. HARTWELL, plate 85

STEVE HUBBARD, plate 58

DANIEL M. KAMMEN, plate 89

KENT KESSINGER, South Wings (flight provided by South Wings), plate 74

KEYSTONE-MAST COLLECTION, California Museum of Photography, University of California, Riverside, plate 46

WARREN K. LEFFLER, copyright of, Library of Congress, plate 27

LIBRARY OF CONGRESS, plate 20

JERRY LUNSFORD, plate 98

MORGUEFILE.COM, plate 92

NATIONAL AERONAUTICS AND SPACE ADMINISTRATION, plates 48, 70

OAK RIDGE NATIONAL LABORATORY, plate 101

PACIFIC GAS AND ELECTRIC COMPANY, plates 7, 8, 9, 10, 11, 12, 59

PDPHOTO.ORG, plate 71

JOHN PRINZ, plate 66

TED RAMELLI, plate 24

SEAN RAMSAY, photos by; copyright 2008 by *The Energy Overseer* (Arthur O'Donnell), plates 1, 13, 22, 23, 28, 30, 35, 39, 42, 44, 49, 62, 76, 78, 103, 113, 114

SACRAMENTO ARCHIVES AND MUSEUM COLLECTION CENTER, plate 5

SACRAMENTO MUNICIPAL UTILITY DISTRICT, plate 56

SATTERLEE PHOTODESIGN, plate 83

T. R. SLOANE, courtesy of, plate 94

SOUTHERN CALIFORNIA EDISON, photos courtesy of, plates 21, 26, 79

STIRLING ENERGY SYSTEMS, plate 51

STOCK.XCHANG, plate 69

SUNPOWER CORPORATION, plates 50, 81, 84

TESLA WARDENCLYFFE PROJECT ARCHIVES, plate 8

U.S. DEPARTMENT OF ENERGY, plate 63

U.S. GEOLOGICAL SURVEY, plate 2

U.S. OFFICE OF MANAGEMENT AND BUDGET, plate 86

WIKIMEDIA.ORG, plate 96

YOLO COUNTY, plate 104

INDEX

ABOUT THE AUTHORS

Peter Asmus has been covering energy issues for over 20 years. Previous books include *Reaping the Wind* and *Reinventing Electric Utilities*, both published by Island Press. His articles on energy have been published in leading newspapers such as the *Washington Post*, *Los Angeles Times*, and *San Francisco Chronicle*, as well as a host of magazines, journals, and Web-based communications. He has served as a consultant to the California Energy Commission, California Air Resources Board, and Local Government Commission, as well as to Marin County. He is also a poet and musician, writing songs about our energy challenges and performing with his activist band throughout Northern California at festivals, fairs, and other events advancing the concept of sustainability and energy policy reforms.

Arthur O'Donnell, after more than 25 years as an independent energy journalist, has recently become the executive director of the Center for Resource Solutions, a San Francisco–based nonprofit organization with a global impact on energy policy and renewable power markets. He is author of several books, including *Soul of the Grid: A Cultural Biography of the California Independent System Operator* and *The Guilty Environmentalist*. He can be reached via www.energyoverseer.com.

Arthur Rosenfeld is a highly acclaimed energy physicist and a pioneering champion of energy conservation. Recipient of the presidential Enrico Fermi Award in 2006 in honor of his scientific achievements, Rosenfeld currently serves as a commissioner to the California Energy Commission. He began teaching at the University of California in 1955 and worked as a researcher at Lawrence Berkeley National Laboratory, where he created the Center for Building Science in 1975, a center that still leads the world in developing solutions that reduce energy consumption in buildings. He also worked for the Department of Energy and President Clinton's National Science and Technology Council in the 1990s. Rosenfeld is perhaps best known for his exuberant curiosity about new ways to save energy, and his ability to enlist others in working toward this laudable goal.

Series Design:	Barbara Jellow
Design Enhancements:	Beth Hansen
Design Development:	Jane Tenenbaum
Composition:	Publication Services, Inc.
Text:	9.5/12 Minion
Display:	Franklin Gothic typefaces
Printer and binder:	Golden Cup Printing Company Limited

Introduction to California Mountain Wildflowers, Revised Edition, by Philip A. Munz, edited by Dianne Lake and Phyllis M. Faber

Introduction to California Spring Wildflowers of the Foothills, Valleys, and Coast, Revised Edition, by Philip A. Munz, edited by Dianne Lake and Phyllis M. Faber

Introduction to Shore Wildflowers of California, Oregon, and Washington, Revised Edition, by Philip A. Munz, edited by Dianne Lake and Phyllis Faber

Introduction to California Desert Wildflowers, Revised Edition, by Philip A. Munz, edited by Diane L. Renshaw and Phyllis M. Faber

Introduction to California Plant Life, Revised Edition, by Robert Ornduff, Phyllis M. Faber, and Todd Keeler-Wolf

Introduction to California Chaparral, by Ronald D. Quinn and Sterling C. Keeley, with line drawings by Marianne Wallace

Introduction to the Plant Life of Southern California: Coast to Foothills, by Philip W. Rundel and Robert Gustafson

Introduction to Horned Lizards of North America, by Wade C. Sherbrooke

Introduction to the California Condor, by Noel F. R. Snyder and Helen A. Snyder

Regional Guides

Natural History of the Point Reyes Peninsula, by Jules Evens

Sierra Nevada Natural History, Revised Edition, by Tracy I. Storer, Robert L. Usinger, and David Lukas